90

SELECTED LIST OF OTHER TITLES BY CASS R. SUNSTEIN

AUTHOR

Simpler: The Future of Government

After the Rights Revolution: Reconceiving the Regulatory State

Democracy and the Problem of Free Speech

Free Markets and Social Justice

Going to Extremes: How Like Minds Unite and Divide

Infotopia: How Many Minds Produce Knowledge

Legal Reasoning and Political Conflict

On Rumors: How Falsehoods Spread, Why We Believe Them, What Can Be Done

Republic.com 2.0

The Second Bill of Rights: FDR's Unfinished Revolution and Why We Need It More Than Ever

Why Societies Need Dissent

COAUTHOR

Nudge: Improving Decisions About Health, Wealth, and Happiness

CONSPIRACY THEORIES & OTHER DANGEROUS IDEAS

Cass R. Sunstein

SIMON & SCHUSTER
NEW YORK LONDON TORONTO SYDNEY NEW DELHI

Simon & Schuster
1230 Avenue of the Americas
New York, NY 10020

First Simon & Schuster hardcover edition March 2014

Designed by Claudia Martinez
Jacket design by Jason Heuer
Jacket illustrations by Mark Stutzman

Manufactured in the United States of America

10 9 8 7 6 5 4 3 2 1

Library of Congress Cataloging-in-Publication Data

Sunstein, Cass R.
Conspiracy theories and other dangerous ideas / Cass R. Sunstein.
pages cm
1. Conspiracy theories. I. Title.
HV6275.S86 2014
001.9—dc232013012476

ISBN 978-1-4767-2662-5
ISBN 978-1-4767-2664-9 (ebook)

CONTENTS

PREFACE

Why do intelligent people believe conspiracy theories, even when they are utterly baseless? Why does false information spread and sometimes incite violence? What rights do human beings have? Do we have a right to education or health care? What makes people happy? Do animals have rights? Is there a right to marriage? If so, who gets to marry? Does the United States owe poor nations compensation for climate change? Amidst the most fundamental disagreements—not least on these questions—how can we proceed? And just who are minimalists and trimmers, anyway?

Of the hundreds of academic articles I have written, the most controversial appear in these pages. Academic articles do not usually get a lot of attention, but many of the chapters here escaped anonymity. Some of them even achieved a modest degree of public notoriety. One reason is that on dozens of occasions, Glenn Beck, the television and radio personality, described me on national television as "the most dangerous man in America"—apparently because of the essays here, especially those involving Franklin Delano Roosevelt, conspiracy theories, and the rights of animals. I don't know how many people actually read those papers, but I do know that they helped produce a lot of hate mail (and a few death threats).

The unexpected notoriety was a product of the fact that from 2009 to 2012, I was privileged to serve as the administrator of the White House Office of Information and Regulatory Affairs (OIRA). The OIRA administrator is often called the nation's "regulatory czar," and while the United States has no czars, the administrator does have a good deal of authority. To get that particular job, you have to be nominated by the president and confirmed by the Senate. At least in the current period, the writings of Senate-confirmed presidential appointees are subject to intense scrutiny. And if someone with a lot of writing is fortunate enough to be confirmed, the scrutiny is likely to continue, certainly while he serves, and perhaps even after. I didn't quite anticipate this. I certainly didn't anticipate the degree of animosity that would be generated by some of the articles in this book.

In many nations, rational people end up believing crazy things, including (false) conspiracy theories. Those crazy thoughts can lead to violence, including terrorism. Many terrorist acts have been fueled by false conspiracy theories, and there is a good argument that some such acts would not have occurred in the absence of such theories. The key point—and, in a way, the most puzzling and disturbing one—is that the crazy thoughts are often held by people who are not crazy at all.

The essay on conspiracy theories was written in the aftermath of the attacks of 9/11, but the lessons are far more general. It was originally coauthored with Harvard law professor Adrian Vermeule, but it has been significantly revised and updated for this book. The focus is on threats—especially terrorist threats—that arise when people in other nations believe false conspiracy theories about the United States. Its central goal is to explore how information tends to spread, even to go viral, among like-minded people. And while some people think that the topic of conspiracy theories is narrow and specialized, the discussion bears on the spread of false information of many different kinds, not least in the internet era.

A primary focus of the essay is "the crippled epistemology of extremism," a brilliant phrase that I borrow from political scientist Russell Hardin. In my view, the idea of crippled epistemology is full of implications. All of us have, at least to some degree, a crippled epistemology, in the sense that there is a lot that we don't know, and we have to rely on people we trust. We lack direct or personal evidence for most of what we think, especially about politics and government. We are often confident in what we believe, but we don't have reason to be. Much of what we know can turn out to be badly wrong. Chapter 1 explores the mechanisms that account for this troubling fact, which is of great importance throughout the world. And while the central concern is how conspiracy theories spread—not what to do about them—there is a brief discussion of a possible approach, which is to counteract crippled epistemologies through "cognition infiltration," an admittedly provocative (and, I confess, probably unfortunate) term that is meant to refer to how truth tellers can dispel falsehoods.

Somehow the argument of this essay, or some version of it, has gone viral, at least in certain circles. The irony is that the essay itself has been subject to the very mechanisms it explores about the spread of false information. Indeed, those mechanisms worked so directly and so precisely that many people contended, and apparently continue to believe, that while in government, I attempted to "implement" some of its alleged prescriptions. (I had no involvement with any such issues during my time in the Obama administration.)

Here are some examples. The website Salon featured a lengthy essay entitled "Obama Confidant's Spine-Chilling Proposal," which said that I want to "'cognitively infiltrate' antigovernment groups." One blog post about the essay was called "Got Fascism?" In fact, an entire book was written about the essay, *Cognitive Infiltration: An Obama Appointee's Plan to Undermine the 9/11 Conspiracy Theory*. (As of this writing, the book has forty-one reviews on Amazon.com—all of them with perfect five-star ratings.) The essay has been seen as dangerous partly because it was read to suggest that I had a "plan" to infiltrate not only foreign organizations that believe the United States was responsible for the 9/11 attacks, and that seek to threaten our security, but also conservative organizations as a whole. (Of course, nothing could be further from my mind.)

In 1944 President Franklin Delano Roosevelt proposed a Second Bill of Rights, including the rights to education, health care, Social Security, and a job (chapter 2). In my view, Roosevelt's widely overlooked speech ranks among the very greatest of the twentieth century—and it has informed thinking about rights throughout the world. The enactment of the Affordable Care Act in 2010 might well be seen to reflect a significant part of Roosevelt's vision. To be sure, politicians tend to be pragmatists, not philosophers, and they tend to see "rights" as pragmatic instruments for protecting important human interests. Roosevelt was not engaging with natural rights theories or Jeremy Bentham or Immanuel Kant. He was contending that government should respect, and try to foster, the rights to decent opportunity and to minimal security. In many respects, the United States has come to agree with him.

But a lot of people hate the idea of a Second Bill of Rights. They think that it is inconsistent with American traditions and part and parcel of socialism, or worse. And it is true that many sensible questions can be raised about Roosevelt's Second Bill. But the public reaction has not been limited to those questions. (A representative remark from Glenn Beck: "Why would they need a Second Bill of Rights . . . If government provides everyone jobs, pay, a home, and medical care, how would that work? Simple: communism.")

Cost-benefit analysis is now a deeply engrained part of American regulatory practice. In fact, it can be seen as part of the informal, unwritten constitution of the American regulatory state. Its central goal is to insure that before government acts, it has an understanding of the human consequences of its options—and that it selects the approaches most likely to benefit people. Cost-benefit analysis is an effort to discipline that endeavor.

Nonetheless, cost-benefit analysis remains highly controversial, especially on the left. Behavioral economics—which attempts to study the behavior of real people, as opposed to the rational actors of economics textbooks—is also controversial, perhaps because it is taken to license certain forms of paternalism. Chapter 3 enlists behavioral economics on behalf of cost-benefit analysis. It is not easy to know the actual effects of regulatory policies, and many of our intuitions turn out to be wrong. Cost-benefit analysis can supply a crucial corrective.

Some of the most exciting recent work in social science explores the nature of happiness, or subjective well-being. In Washington and elsewhere, this research is ridiculed. It shouldn't be. We are learning a great deal, and what we are learning is important. We know, for example, that some apparently terrible losses are not as bad as we expect. If you lose the use of a finger, or even an ear or a limb, you'll probably suffer a lot less than you anticipate (at least if you are not in pain). Human beings are able to adapt to many adverse events (and also to many good ones)—and we don't anticipate our adaptation. By contrast, mental illness, physical pain, and unemployment create a great deal of suffering, and it is essential to try to reduce that suffering. Chapter 4 explores the implications of what we are learning for some issues in law and policy.

Do animals have rights? In my view, almost everyone thinks so, at least in the limited sense that people agree that cruelty to animals is unacceptable and that animal suffering is not a matter of indifference. Civilized nations have anticruelty laws. To be sure, people argue intensely about the question whether, and in what sense, animals really ought to be thought to have "rights." But extraordinarily large numbers of animals are treated cruelly, and made to suffer, in ways that are not easy to justify in moral terms. Reducing that cruelty and that suffering should be an important social goal. At least, that is the central claim of chapter 5.

My work on the rights of animals struck an especially raw nerve—and actually endangered my chances at Senate confirmation. As I learned, the negative attention was partly a product of the desire of many people to attack anyone associated with the Obama administration. But many people have strong economic reasons to disparage and ridicule anyone who takes animal welfare seriously. At the same time, it must be acknowledged that the moral issues are difficult and that reasonable people disagree. One goal of chapter 5 is to disentangle the underlying concerns—to show where people differ and where they do not.

The debate over same-sex marriage has raised an international debate over the nature of marriage as an institution. The whole idea of a "right to marry" raises many puzzles. Can three people, or four, or five, get married? Can people marry their aunts or their dogs? Why not? Chapter 6 explores these questions. In the process, it entertains the genuinely radical view that marriage should be privatized. Under this approach, states would not use the word *marriage* as such. Of course, private institutions could perform and recognize marriages, but governments would speak only of civil unions and contracts. Ultimately I reject the argument for privatizing marriage. But at the same time, I emphasize that, as long as marriage is a legal category, there is no good argument against allowing same-sex marriage.

Chapter 7, coauthored with University of Chicago law professor Eric Posner, treats climate change as a serious threat, and it strongly urges the United States to do something about it. But the chapter is largely a sustained *objection* to the view that on grounds of justice, America should enter into a climate change agreement that is not in its best interest. In this respect, the chapter takes a hard line against an argument much favored by many people in poor nations—and also by many people who are greatly concerned about climate change. Nonetheless, the chapter does contend that it is a very good idea for wealthy countries to provide economic assistance to poor countries, not least because poor people can benefit a lot more from a few extra dollars than can wealthy people.

In many religious institutions, sex discrimination is pervasive; it is part of the very fabric of some religious practices. If religious institutions are immunized from laws that forbid discrimination, there will be a lot of discrimination—a particular problem in view of the fact that religious institutions help to develop preferences and beliefs, and thus can inculcate discriminatory norms at an early stage. At the same time, religious liberty lies at the heart of free societies. Chapter 8 explores the question of how we should handle this difficult conflict.

Throughout much of the twentieth century, political debates sharply divided those who believed in markets and those who believed in planning. Chapter 9 outlines problems in both approaches. It attempts to sketch an alternative—a New Progressivism—that is not only alert to the inadequacies of laissez-faire but also acutely aware of the many problems in government planning. It explores a number of routes (ranging from nudges to economic incentives to public-private partnerships) that might meet some of the distinctive challenges of the twenty-first century.

The concluding chapters—for which I confess a particular fondness—are not about controversial questions. They address a basic problem that cuts across all such questions. The problem is this: How might human beings be able to talk, live, work, and govern together in the face of deep and apparently irreconcilable disagreements? One answer is provided by *minimalists*, who try to resolve the particular matter at hand without resolving other issues and without coming to terms with big theoretical disagreements (chapter 10). In a catchphrase, *minimalists want to make it possible for people to settle questions where settlement is necessary, without making it necessary for people to settle questions where settlement is impossible*.

I can attest to the fact that in government, minimalism is extremely useful. It is sometimes both possible and desirable to bracket the largest questions and leave them for another day. Indeed, theoretical disputes are often not relevant within government itself, and so it is unnecessary to resolve them in order to move forward.

If anything, the practice of *trimming* is even more useful in government, and I believe that it can be an important and productive practice in multiple domains (chapter 11). Unlike minimalists, trimmers do not want to leave questions undecided. On the contrary, they seek and even crave settlement and closure. But they want to resolve questions in a way that attends to, and preserves, the legitimate concerns of all sides. They do not want anyone to be excluded, ignored, or hurt. Trimmers might well seek to compromise, but if so, they typically seek solutions that incorporate the best arguments of those involved. In government, trimming is indispensable. Time and again, public officials disagree with one another. Most of them are both reasonable and informed. Of course, it is true that some of them are wrong. But even those who are wrong tend to have a legitimate concern, and the ultimate outcome ought to be designed in a way that addresses that concern.

If I were writing the essays from scratch, they would not, of course, turn out the same. With respect to conspiracy theories, for example, I would now work a lot harder to clarify the prescription, so as to avoid the false impression that the idea of cognitive infiltration is meant to support efforts to spy on Americans who distrust their government. Civil liberties are a foundation of free societies, and while the essay was meant to take that point as an obvious background fact, it should have put the point firmly in the foreground. The focus of the essay is on serious terrorist threats abroad.

With respect to animals, I would now write more cautiously—not so much to retreat from the basic suggestions as to indicate a clearer awareness of the trade-offs involved. And indeed, I have revised the original discussions for this volume, and in some cases softened or clarified them significantly, so as to correct possible misconceptions and to insure that they are not so far from what I now think. Nonetheless, I have not recast them in fundamental ways. If some of them are less cautious and qualified than the author would now be, well, it is not always clear that caution and qualification are improvements.

But I do want to say something about the differences between the academic and public spheres. Those differences cannot be overstated. In government, officials tend to be extremely careful in their public remarks, whether oral or in writing. They are part of a team. As such, they should not and cannot speak freely. On the contrary, they must work with others, including those in communications, to make sure that their remarks are appropriate. It would not be acceptable for a high-level official to give a speech or to publish an article without going through a formal clearance process, to insure that what he says is consistent with administration policy. Many ideas that are legitimately part of public discussion are not legitimately ventured by administration officials, just because of their particular role.

This was a great puzzle, and a source of frustration, to my friends in academic life and perhaps even more to my friends in journalism. While in government, I was invited to give academic workshops on various topics, including some of those explored in these pages. I had to decline. In fact, whether to decline may have been the easiest question I had to answer in government. A public official working in the Executive Office of the President cannot possibly give speculative speeches on conspiracy theories, Roosevelt's Second Bill of Rights, or animal rights. Nor can such officials give some kind of academic workshop reflecting their current thinking. Such an enterprise would be a diversion from their job, which is to serve the public, and it could also be a distraction and positively harmful for others who are trying to do exactly that.

Reporters frequently tried to ask me about some of the views expressed here; of course, I had to decline. It is extremely important for any administration to speak with one voice, especially because its members are working for the president. The need for caution is heightened by the fact that many people are both eager and able to characterize official remarks in the most provocative or uncharitable ways—or to use isolated sentences in order to suggest that some part of the government is moving in directions that are dangerous or daft. Unfriendly headlines can be produced in that way, thus producing an unwelcome distraction for government officials.

There is a closely related point. In government, the term *common sense* is used a lot, and it is always a term of praise. Whatever their party, a lot of elected officials say, "I support common sense solutions." No elected official proclaims, "I'm abandoning common sense on this one." Unfortunately, common sense may turn out to be wrong or unhelpful. In deciding how to deal with air pollution from particulate matter, or whether to require refrigerators to be more fuel efficient, common sense may not exactly be irrelevant, but it won't tell us a whole lot.

Nonetheless, it is true that some combination of common sense and feasibility constrains what can be done in government. Public servants need to have humility; they need to know that they are, in the deepest sense, servants. A policy that plainly departs from commonsense will not easily get off the ground. (Any White House needs a communications team in part to help explain the relationship between its policies and common sense.) An idea that is not feasible—for economic or political reasons—is not worth a lot of discussion.

In academic life, of course, common sense is not a constraint. If an academic article simply asserts common sense, or what most people already think, it probably shouldn't be published. Who would learn anything from it? Today's common sense is yesterday's wild academic speculation. Of course, it might be useful for academics to defend common sense, or explain what lies behind it, or recount its history—but none of these should or will say something obvious. A goal of academic writing is to say something novel or illuminating, even or perhaps especially if it defies common sense. Whether or not anyone should act on the resulting ideas is another matter. In a well-functioning democracy, that question gets to be decided by a large number of officials. Some of them are minimalists, while others are trimmers, and all of them are chosen and checked by the public.

CONSPIRACY THEORIES
&
OTHER DANGEROUS IDEAS

CHAPTER 1

CONSPIRACY THEORIES

Conspiracy theories are all around us. In August 2004, a poll by Zogby International found that 49 percent of New York City residents believed that officials of the US government "knew in advance that attacks were planned on or around September 11, 2001, and that they consciously failed to act."[1] In a Scripps-Howard poll in 2006, some 36 percent of respondents agreed that "federal officials either participated in the attacks on the World Trade Center or took no action to stop them."[2] Another 16 percent said that it was either very likely or somewhat likely that "the collapse of the twin towers in New York was aided by explosives secretly planted in the two buildings."[3]

Among normally sober-minded Canadians, a September 2006 poll found that 22 percent believed that "the attacks on the United States on September 11, 2001, had nothing to do with Osama bin Laden and were actually a plot by influential Americans."[4] In a poll conducted in seven Muslim countries, 78 percent of the respondents did not believe that the 9/11 attacks were carried out by Arabs.[5] The most popular account in these countries was that 9/11 was the work of the US or Israeli government.[6]

In 2013, a poll in the United States found that 37 percent of Americans believe that climate change is a hoax and that 21 percent believe that the US government is hiding evidence of the existence of aliens.[7] In China, a bestseller attributed various events (the rise of Adolf Hitler, the Asian financial crisis of 1997–98, and environmental destruction in the developing world) to the Rothschild banking dynasty. The analysis was apparently read and debated at high levels of business and government.[8] In the aftermath of the explosions at the Boston Marathon in 2013, it was rumored that one of the bombers was an FBI informant and that the organizers of the marathon knew about the attacks in advance. Throughout American history, race-related violence has often been spurred by false rumors, generally pointing to alleged conspiracies by one group against another.[9] And with the help of the internet, conspiracy theories can be made available to the world in an instant. There is even a *Conspiracy Theories & Secret Societies for Dummies*.

What causes such theories to arise and spread? Are they important and even threatening, or merely trivial and even amusing? What, if anything, can and should government do about them? The principal goal of this chapter is to sketch some psychological and social mechanisms that produce, sustain, and spread conspiracy theories. An understanding of those processes helps to identify the circumstances in which such theories should be taken seriously and may warrant some kind of official response.

The main (though far from exclusive) focus involves conspiracy theories relating to (and helping to inspire) terrorism, including theories that are connected with or postdate the 9/11 attacks. These theories exist within the United States and, even more virulently, in foreign countries, especially Muslim nations. The existence of both domestic and foreign conspiracy theories is no trivial matter; they can help give rise to serious risks, including risks of violence. While terrorism-related theories are hardly the only ones of interest, they provide a crucial testing ground.

While most people do not accept false conspiracy theories, they can nonetheless hear the voice of their inner conspiracy theorist, at least on occasion. As we shall see, conspiracy theorizing is, in a sense, built into the human condition. As we shall also see, an understanding of conspiracy theories has broad implications for the spread of information and beliefs. Many erroneous judgments, including those that play an important and damaging role in the political arena, are products of the same forces that produce conspiracy theories.

If we are able to see how conspiracy theories arise, we will understand the dynamics behind the dissemination of false rumors and false beliefs of many different kinds. And if we are able to understand how to counteract such theories, we will have some clues about how to correct widespread falsehoods more generally—and about why some efforts at correction fail while others succeed.

DEFINITIONS AND MECHANISMS

There has been much discussion of what, exactly, counts as a conspiracy theory, and about what, if anything, is wrong with those who believe one. Let us bracket the most difficult questions here and suggest more pragmatically that a conspiracy theory can be counted as such if it is *an effort to explain some event or practice by referring to the secret machinations of powerful people who have also managed to conceal their role*.

Consider, for example, the following beliefs, which have found varying degrees of acceptance in different communities:

- the US Central Intelligence Agency (CIA) was responsible for the 1963 assassination of President John F. Kennedy;
- doctors deliberately manufactured the AIDS virus;
- the 1996 explosion and crash of TWA Flight 800 off the coast of Long Island was caused by a US military missile;
- the theory of climate change is a deliberate fraud;
- civil rights leader Dr. Martin Luther King Jr. was killed by federal agents in 1968;

- the 2002 plane crash that killed Paul Wellstone, the liberal Democratic senator from Minnesota, was engineered by Republican politicians;
- the *Apollo 11* moon landing was staged and never actually occurred;
- the Rothschilds and other Jewish bankers have been responsible for the deaths of presidents and for economic distress in Asian nations;
- the Great Depression was a result of a plot by wealthy people to reduce workers' wages.

Some conspiracy theories have, of course, turned out to be true. The Watergate hotel room used by the Democratic National Committee was, in fact, bugged by Republican officials in 1972, operating at the behest of the White House. In the 1950s and 1960s, the CIA did, in fact, administer drugs such as LSD under Project MKULTRA in an effort to investigate the possibility of "mind control." Also during the Cold War, Operation Northwoods, a rumored plan by the US Department of Defense to simulate acts of terrorism and blame them on Cuba, really was proposed by high-level officials (though the plan never went into effect). In 1947, space aliens did, in fact, land in Roswell, New Mexico, and the government covered it all up. (Well, maybe not.)

An important clarification: the focus throughout this chapter is on demonstrably false conspiracy theories, such as the various 9/11 conspiracy theories, not ones that are or may be true. The ultimate goal is to explore how public officials might undermine false theories, and true accounts should not be undermined.

Within the set of false conspiracy theories, it is also important to limit the scope to potentially harmful theories. Not all false conspiracy theories are harmful. Consider the false conspiracy theory, held by many younger members of our society, that a secret group of elves, working in a remote location under the leadership of the mysterious "Santa Claus," makes and distributes presents on Christmas Eve. This theory turns out to be false but is itself instilled through a widespread conspiracy of the powerful—parents—who conceal their roles in the whole affair. (Consider, too, the Easter Bunny and the Tooth Fairy.) Unfortunately, not all conspiracy theories are equally benign.

Conspiracy theories generally attribute to certain agents extraordinary powers: to plan, to control others, to maintain secrets, and so forth. Those who believe that those agents possess such powers are especially unlikely to give respectful attention to debunkers, who, in their eyes, may, after all, be agents or dupes of those responsible for the conspiracy in the first place. Because debunkers are untrustworthy, the simplest governmental technique for dispelling false (and also harmful) beliefs—providing credible information—may fail to work for conspiracy theories. This extra resistance to correction through simple techniques is part of what makes conspiracy theories distinctively worrisome.

A broader point is that conspiracy theorists typically overestimate the competence and discretion of officials and bureaucracies, which are assumed to be capable of devising and carrying out sophisticated secret plans—despite abundant evidence that in open societies, government action does not usually remain secret for very long. Consider all the work that must be done to hide and cover up the government's role in orchestrating a terrorist attack on its own territory or in arranging to kill political opponents. In a closed society, secrets are far easier to keep, and distrust of official accounts makes a great deal of sense. In such societies, conspiracy theories are both more likely to be true and harder to disprove in light of available information. But when the press is free, and when checks and balances are in force, government cannot easily hide its conspiracies for long.

These points do not mean that it is impossible, even in free societies, for conspiracy theories to be true; we have seen some counterexamples. But it does mean that institutional checks make it unlikely, in such societies, that powerful groups can keep dark secrets for extended periods, at least if those secrets involve important events.

A further question about conspiracy theories—whether true or false, harmful or benign—is whether they are justified. Justification and truth are different issues; a true belief may be unjustified, and a justified belief may be untrue. I may believe, correctly, that there are fires within the earth's core, but if I believe it because the god Vulcan revealed it to me in a dream, my belief is unjustified. Conversely, the false belief in Santa Claus is justified, because children generally have good reason to believe what their parents tell them and follow a sensible heuristic ("If my parents say it, it is probably true"); when children realize that Santa is the product of a widespread conspiracy among parents, they have a justified and true belief that a conspiracy has been at work.

Are conspiracy theories generally unjustified? Under what conditions? Here there are competing accounts and many controversies in epistemology and analytic philosophy. It is unnecessary to take a final stand on the most difficult questions here, in part because the relevant accounts need not be seen as mutually exclusive; each accounts for part of the terrain. A brief review of the possible accounts will be useful for later discussion.

The philosopher Karl Popper famously argued that conspiracy theories overlook the pervasive unintended consequences of political and social action; they assume that all consequences must have been intended by someone.[10] The basic idea is that many social outcomes, including large movements in the economy, occur as a result of the acts and omissions of many people, none of whom intended to cause those effects. The Great Depression of the 1930s was not self-consciously engineered by anyone; increases in the unemployment or inflation rate, or in the price of real estate or gasoline, may reflect market pressures rather than intentional action. Nonetheless, there is a pervasive human tendency to think that effects are caused by intentional action, especially by those who stand to benefit (the maxim "Cui bono?"), and for this reason, conspiracy theories have considerable but unwarranted appeal. On one reading of Popper's account, those who accept conspiracy theories are following a sensible heuristic, to the effect that consequences are intended; that heuristic often works well, but it also produces systematic errors, especially in the context of outcomes that are products of social interactions among numerous people.

Popper captures an important feature of some conspiracy theories. They have appeal in light of the attribution of otherwise inexplicable events to intentional action, and of some people's unwillingness to accept the possibility that significant bad consequences may be a product of invisible-hand mechanisms (such as market forces or evolutionary pressures) or of simple chance rather than of anyone's plans. A conspiracy theory posits that a social outcome reflects an underlying intentional order, overlooking the possibility that the outcome arises from either spontaneous order or random forces.

Popper is picking up on a still more general fact about human psychology, which is that most people do not like to believe that significant events were caused by bad (or good) luck, and much prefer nonarbitrary causal stories. Note, however, that the domain of Popper's explanation is quite limited. Many conspiracy theories, including those involving political assassinations and the attacks of 9/11, point to events that are indeed the result of intentional action. The conspiracy theorists go wrong not by positing intentional actors but by misidentifying them.

A broader point is that part of what makes (unjustified) conspiracy theories unjustified is that those who believe them must also have a kind of spreading distrust of all knowledge-producing institutions, in a way that makes it difficult for them to believe anything at all.[11] To believe, for example, that the US government destroyed the World Trade Center and then covered its tracks requires an ever-widening conspiracy theory in which the 9/11 Commission, congressional leaders, the Federal Bureau of Investigation (FBI), and the media were either participants in or dupes of the conspiracy. But anyone who believed that would undercut the grounds for many of his other beliefs, which are warranted only by trust in the knowledge-producing institutions created by government and society. How many other things must not be believed, if we are not to believe something accepted by so many diverse actors?

There may not be a logical contradiction here, but conspiracy theorists might well have to question a number of propositions that they seem willing to take for granted. Why reject so many of the claims and judgments supplied by knowledge-producing institutions while accepting the rest? As Robert Anton Wilson notes of the conspiracy theories advanced by Holocaust deniers, "a conspiracy that can deceive us about 6,000,000 deaths can deceive us about anything, and [then] it takes a great leap of faith for Holocaust Revisionists to believe World War II happened at all, or that Franklin Roosevelt did serve as President from 1933 to 1945, or that Marilyn Monroe was more 'real' than King Kong or Donald Duck."[12] Consider in this light the words of Oliver Stone, director of the conspiracy-focused film *JFK*: "I've come to have severe doubts about Columbus, about Washington, about the Civil War being fought over slavery, about World War I, about World War II and the supposed fight against Nazism and Japanese control of resources . . . I don't even know if I was born or who my parents were."[13]

This is not a claim that conspiracy theories are always wrong or unwarranted. We have seen that some such theories are true. But if knowledge-producing institutions are generally trustworthy, in part because they are embedded in an open society with a well-functioning marketplace of ideas and a free flow of information, then conspiracy theories will usually be unjustified. On the other hand, citizens of societies with systematically censored, malfunctioning, biased, or skewed institutions of knowledge—say, people who live in an authoritarian regime lacking a free press—may have good reason to distrust all or most of the official denials they hear. For these individuals, conspiracy theories will more often be justified, whether they are true or not. (And because of the absence of democratic safeguards, they will more often be true as well.)

Likewise, people living in isolated groups or networks who are exposed only to skewed information will more often hold conspiracy theories that are false but nonetheless justified given their limited information. Most of us have direct or personal knowledge of very few of the facts that we firmly believe. We do not know, from direct personal knowledge, that the Earth is round; or that Mars exists; or that William Shakespeare, Christopher Columbus, and Babe Ruth really lived; or that matter is composed partly of electrons. Most of what we know comes from other people's statements, beliefs, and actions. When those in isolated groups or social networks accept conspiracy theories, they may be accepting—simply and not unreasonably—everyone else's beliefs. Even Holocaust deniers might be considered in this light. When isolated groups operate within a society that is both wider and more open, their theories may be unjustified from the standpoint of the wider society but justified from the standpoint of the group (so long as it maintains its isolation). In these situations, the problem for the wider society is to breach the informational isolation of the small group or network.

These points help to explain a central feature of conspiracy theories, which is that they tend to be extremely resistant to correction, certainly through direct denials or counterspeech by government officials. Conspiracy theorists believe that the agents of the conspiracy have unusual powers, so that apparently contrary evidence can be seen as a product of the conspiracy itself. The self-sealing quality of conspiracy theories creates severe practical problems for those who seek to dispel them, including government. Direct attempts to dispel the theory are often folded into the theory as just one more ploy by powerful machinators to cover their tracks. On this count, the creativity and inventiveness of conspiracy theorists should not be underestimated.[14]

A denial might even be taken as a confirmation, and the evidence mustered on behalf of the denial might be seen as corroborative rather than contradictory. A few years ago, for example, both liberals and conservatives were provided with apparently credible information showing that the administration of President George W. Bush was wrong to conclude that Iraq had an active unconventional weapons program. Yet after receiving the accurate information, conservatives became even *more* likely to believe that Iraq possessed such weapons and was seeking to develop more.[15] (Liberals are no less subject to this general effect.)

When someone denies one of your strongest commitments, you might respond by holding it more fiercely. One reason involves your motivations. If you believe something deeply, you might well have a strong emotional commitment to it and hold on to it even more intensely if it is attacked. Another reason is that if you think that you have strong reasons for a belief, a denial might seem corroborative. If you are highly suspicious, the very effort to deny the commitment suggests that it is likely to be true. Why else would people bother to deny it?

HOW CONSPIRACY THEORIES ARISE AND SPREAD

Conspiracist Propensities and Crippled Epistemologies. Why do people accept conspiracy theories that turn out to be false and for which the evidence is weak or even nonexistent? It is tempting to answer in terms of individual pathology. Perhaps conspiracy theories are a product of mental illness, such as paranoia or narcissism. And indeed, there can be no doubt that some people who accept conspiracy theories are mentally ill and subject to delusions. But we have seen that in many communities, and even in nations, such theories are widely held. It is not plausible to suggest that all or most members of those communities are afflicted by mental illness. The most important conspiracy theories are hardly limited to those who suffer from any kind of psychological pathology.

Putting pathology to one side, evidence does suggest the existence of stable differences in people's propensity to accept conspiracy theories.[16] The best predictor of whether people will accept a conspiracy theory appears to be whether they accept other conspiracy theories. Those who accept one such theory (for example, that the FBI killed Martin Luther King Jr.) are especially likely to accept others (for example, that climate change is a hoax). Most striking, researchers have found that "this tendency even extends to beliefs in mutually contradictory conspiracy theories, and to beliefs in fully fictitious conspiracy theories. Thus, those who believe that Princess

Diana faked her own death are also more likely to believe that she was murdered; those who believe in 'real-world conspiracy theories' (i.e., that John F. Kennedy fell victim to an organized conspiracy) are more likely to believe that there was a conspiracy behind the success of the Red Bull energy drink—a conspiracy theory that was purposely developed for a social psychology study."[17]

Some people do show an unusually strong inclination to accept conspiracy theories. Peculiar as it is, the willingness to accept contradictory conspiracy theories is especially suggestive of this inclination, as reflected in the remarkable finding that those people who believe that Osama bin Laden was already dead at the time when US special forces raided his compound in Pakistan are also more likely to believe he is still alive.[18] Some people appear to hold a broad view of the world according to which the authorities are engaged in conspiracies; accounts that fit with that view of the world are appealing even if they contradict each other. On this account, "conspiracism [is] a coherent ideology, rather than as a cluster of beliefs in individual theories."[19] In other words, a willingness to believe in conspiracy theories is the master concept, organizing particular beliefs. (As we will shortly see, however, conspiracists are made, not born.)

In fact, there is evidence that those who believe that a particular scientific finding is made up, and actually a product of a conspiracy, are more likely to have the same view about other scientific findings.[20] Suppose that certain people believe that the moon landings never happened and were faked by NASA. Those people are especially likely to believe that climate change is a hoax as well. Indeed, conspiracist thinking in areas that have nothing to do with science (reflected, for example, in the view that the FBI was involved in the killing of Martin Luther King Jr.) predicts the rejection of scientific findings as a product of conspiracies. Intriguingly, those who believe in conspiracy theories have been found to be more willing to conspire themselves.[21]

Is it possible to say more about the characteristics that lead people to accept such theories? We do not have full answers, but research suggests that conspiracist thinking is especially likely to appeal to people who are cynical about politics, who have lower self-esteem, and who are generally defiant of authority.[22] Causation works both ways. Those who believe in conspiracy theories become less likely to engage in politics.[23]

For present purposes, however, the most useful way to understand the pervasiveness of conspiracy theories is to examine how people come to acquire their beliefs. In some domains, people suffer from what Professor Russell Hardin has called a *crippled epistemology*, in the sense that they know relatively few things, and what they know is wrong.[24] Many extremists fall in this category. Their extremism stems not from irrationality but from the fact that they have little relevant information, and their extremist views are supported by what little they know. Conspiracy theorizing often has the same feature. For instance, those who believe that Israel was responsible for the 9/11 attacks, or that the CIA killed President Kennedy, may well be responding quite rationally to the informational signals that they receive.

Consider here the suggestive claim that terrorism is more likely to arise in societies that lack civil rights and civil liberties.[25] If this is so, it might be because terrorism is not abstract violence but an extreme form of political protest. When people lack the usual outlets for registering their protest, they resort to violence. A contributing factor is that when civil rights and civil liberties are restricted, little information is available, and the information that comes from government cannot be trusted. In those circumstances, conspiracy theories are more likely to spread, and terrorism is more likely to arise.

Rumors and Speculation. Some conspiracy theories seem to bubble up spontaneously, appearing roughly simultaneously in some or many different social networks. In such cases, they may be a response to specific disturbing events, to general or localized economic or social distress, or to real or apparent injustice. Others are initiated and spread quite intentionally by *conspiracy entrepreneurs*, who may play a large role in the spread of conspiracy theories, and who profit directly or indirectly from propagating their preferred theories.

One example in the latter category is the author of the Chinese bestseller mentioned earlier. Another is the French author Thierry Meyssan, whose book *9/11: The Big Lie* became a bestseller and a sensation for its claim that the destruction at the Pentagon on 9/11 was caused by a missile fired as the opening salvo of a coup d'état by the military-industrial complex rather than by American Airlines Flight 77. (In the context of the 9/11 attacks, there are many other examples.)

Some conspiracy entrepreneurs are entirely sincere; others are interested in money or fame, or in achieving some general social goal. In the context of the AIDS virus, a diverse set of people have initiated rumors, many involving conspiracies, and, in view of the confusion and fear surrounding that virus, several of those rumors spread widely.[26] Even for conspiracy theories ventured by conspiracy entrepreneurs, the key question is why some theories take hold, while many more vanish into obscurity. There are plausible answers to that question, but a great deal may depend on random and unpredictable factors, including who says what to whom, and exactly when.[27] The success or failure of conspiracy theories, like that of rumors in general, is far from preordained.

Whenever a crisis or tragedy occurs, rumors and speculation are inevitable. Most people are not able to know, on the basis of personal or direct knowledge, why an airplane crashed, or why a leader was assassinated, or why a terrorist attack succeeded, or why an economy suddenly ran into terrible trouble. In the aftermath of such an event, numerous speculations will be offered, and some of them will likely point to some kind of conspiracy. To some people, those speculations will seem plausible, perhaps because they provide a suitable outlet for outrage and blame, or because the speculation is in some sense gratifying or fits well with other deeply rooted beliefs, or because the absence of an explanation is disturbing. Terrible events produce outrage, and when people are outraged, they are all the more likely to seek causes that justify their emotional states, and also to attribute those events to intentional action.

It is important to see that preexisting inclinations and beliefs are key to the success or failure of conspiracy theories. To the extent that some people show a propensity to believe such theories, they will be drawn to them even on the basis of highly speculative accounts. Some people would find it impossibly jarring to think that the FBI was behind the assassination of Martin Luther King; that thought would unsettle too many of their other judgments. Others would find those other judgments supported strongly, even confirmed, by the suggestion that the FBI was responsible. For most Americans, a claim that the US government attacked its own citizens, and thus was responsible for a terrorist attack, would make it impossible to hold on to a wide range of other judgments. Clearly, this point does not hold for many people in Islamic nations, for whom it is far from jarring to believe that responsibility lies with the United States (or Israel).

Here, as elsewhere, people attempt to find some kind of equilibrium among their many beliefs, and accepting or rejecting a conspiracy theory will often depend on which of the two brings equilibrium. Some beliefs are also *motivated*, in the sense that people are pleased to hold them or displeased to reject them. Acceptance (or, for that matter, rejection) of a conspiracy theory is frequently motivated in that sense. Reactions to a claim of conspiracy to assassinate a political leader, or to commit or to allow some atrocity either domestically or abroad, are often determined by the motivations as well as the antecedent knowledge of those who hear the claim.

These are points about individual judgments, bracketing social influences. But after some devastating event has occurred, those influences are crucial. How many people know, directly or on the basis of personal investigation, whether Al Qaeda was responsible for the 9/11 attacks, or whether Lee Harvey Oswald assassinated President Kennedy on his own, or how the AIDS crisis began, or whether a tragic death in an apparent airplane accident was truly accidental, or what caused the economic collapse of 2008, or the precise background of the explosions at the Boston Marathon in 2013? Inevitably, people must rely on the beliefs of others. Some of us will require a great deal of evidence in order to accept a conspiracy theory, while others will require much less. People will therefore have different thresholds for accepting or rejecting such a theory. One way to meet a relevant threshold is to supply direct or indirect evidence. Another is simply to show that some, many, or most (trusted) people accept or reject the theory. These are the appropriate circumstances for social cascades, both informational and reputational.

Conspiracy Cascades, 1: The Role of Information. To see how informational cascades work,[28] imagine that a group is trying to assign responsibility for some loss of life. Assume that the group's members are announcing their views in sequence. Each member attends, reasonably enough, to the judgments of others. Andrews is the first to speak. He suggests that the event was caused by a conspiracy of powerful people. Barnes now knows Andrews's judgment; she should certainly go along with Andrews's account if she agrees independently with him. But if she does not have a lot of private information, and really does not know what happened, she might well be swayed by his judgment and agree that the event was a product of a conspiracy.

Now turn to a third person, Charleton. Suppose that both Andrews and Barnes have embraced the conspiracy theory, but that Charleton's view, based on limited information, is that they are probably wrong. Because his own information is limited, Charleton might well ignore what he knows and follow Andrews and Barnes. It is likely, after all, that both Andrews and Barnes have evidence for their conclusions, and unless Charleton thinks that his own information is better than theirs, he should follow their lead. If he does, Charleton is in a cascade. Of course, Charleton will resist if he has sufficient grounds to believe that Andrews and Barnes are being foolish. But if he lacks those grounds, he will go along with them.

Now suppose that Charleton is speaking in response to what Andrews and Barnes said, not on the basis of his own information, and also that subsequent group members David and Esther know what Andrews, Barnes, and Charleton said. On reasonable assumptions, they will reach the same conclusion regardless of their private information (which, we are supposing, is not decisive). David and Esther might ask, "How could Andrews, Barnes, and Charleton all be wrong?" This will happen even if Andrews initially speculated in a way that does not fit the facts—especially if people discount, as they tend to,[29] the possibility that the shared belief is, for Barnes and Charleton, based not on independent information but merely on a reaction to Andrews's speculation. In such cases, the initial speculation starts a process by which a lot of people are led to participate in a cascade, accepting a conspiracy theory built upon a most fragile foundation.

Of course, the example is stylized and unrealistic. Conspiracy cascades arise through more complex processes in which people's diverse thresholds are important. In the standard pattern, the conspiracy theory is initially accepted by people with low thresholds for its acceptance; as we have seen, some people do have such thresholds. Perhaps the theory will be limited to such people. But sometimes the informational pressure, based on the shared judgments of those people, builds to the point where many other people, with somewhat higher thresholds, begin to accept the theory too. As those with higher thresholds accept the theory, the pressure continues to build, to the point where a large number of people end up accepting it. As we shall see, this outcome is especially likely in close-knit or isolated social networks.

Conspiracy Cascades, 2: The Role of Reputation. Conspiracy theories do not take hold only because of information. Sometimes people profess belief in a conspiracy theory, or at least suppress their doubts, because they seek to curry favor or to avoid disfavor. Reputational pressures help account for conspiracy theories, and they feed conspiracy cascades.

In a reputational cascade, people think that they know what is right, but they go along with the crowd in order to maintain the approval of others. Suppose that Albert suggests that the United States was responsible for some terrible event in the world. Barbara concurs with Albert, not because she actually thinks that Albert is right (she might even think that he is a bit nuts) but because she does not want him to view her as some kind of fool or dupe. And if Albert and Barbara blame the United States for that terrible event, Cynthia might not contradict them publicly and might even appear to share their judgment—not because she believes that they are correct but because she does not want to face their hostility or lose their good opinion of her.

It should be easy to see how this process might generate a cascade. Once Albert, Barbara, and Cynthia offer a united front on the issue, their friend David might be reluctant to contradict them even if he thinks that they are wrong. The apparently shared view of Albert, Barbara, and Cynthia carries information; that view might be right. But even if David has reason to disagree, he might not want to take them on publicly. His silence will help build the informational and reputational pressure on those who follow.

It seems clear that reputational pressures play a large role in the adoption and dissemination of conspiracy theories, certainly among small, close-knit groups and social networks but also more generally. If everyone in your religious community believes that certain people are engaged in a conspiracy against the community, you might silence any private doubts that you might have. In some times and places, doubting a conspiracy theory, or even failing to endorse it, can be literally dangerous, in the sense that doubters are ostracized or worse. Some conspiracy theories are able to persist only because people silence themselves. Dissent is an indispensable corrective, but it does not occur.

Conspiracy Cascades, 3: The Role of Availability. Informational and reputational cascades can occur without any particular triggering event. But a distinctive kind of cascade arises when such an event is highly salient or cognitively "available," in the sense that it comes readily to mind. In the context of many risks, such as those associated with terrorism, crime, economic catastrophe, and environmental disasters, a particular event initiates a cascade. It works as a trigger, an icon, or a symbol justifying public concern, whether or not that concern is warranted. Availability cascades occur through the interaction between a salient event and social influences, both informational and reputational. Often political actors, both self-interested and altruistic, work hard to produce such cascades, making people fearful of risks even if there is no objective basis for the fear.

Conspiracy theories can spread through the same mechanisms. A terrible event becomes "available," in the sense that everyone knows about it, and conspiracy theories are invoked both to explain it and to use it as a symbol for broader social forces. Within certain nations and groups, the claim that the United States or Israel was responsible for the attacks of 9/11 fits well within a general narrative about who is the aggressor, and the liar, in a series of disputes—and the view that Al Qaeda was responsible raises questions about that same narrative. Conspiracy theories are frequently a product of availability cascades.

Conspiracy Cascades, 4: The Role of Emotions. Thus far, the account has been largely emotion-free and cognitive; conspiracy theories circulate in the same way that other beliefs circulate, as people give weight to the views of others and attend to their own reputations. But it is clear that emotions, and not merely information, play a large role in the circulation of rumors of all kinds. Many rumors persist and spread because they serve to justify or rationalize an antecedent emotional state produced by some landmark event, such as a disaster or a war. When people are especially angry or fearful, they may be more likely to focus on particular sorts of rumors and spread them to others. And when rumors trigger intense feelings, they are far more likely to be circulated.

Experimental evidence strongly supports this speculation in the analogous context of so-called urban legends,[30] involving, for example, a decapitated motorcycle rider, a rat in a soda bottle, or a can of cat food mislabeled as tuna. When urban legends trigger strong emotions (such as disgust), people are more likely to pass them along. On the internet, emotionally gripping tall tales are especially likely to proliferate. In the marketplace of ideas, a form of "emotional selection" plays a significant role, and it helps to explain such diverse phenomena as moral panics about deviant behavior and media attention to relatively rare sources of risk such as road rage and the flesh-eating bacterial infection known as necrotizing fasciitis. A particular problem involves "emotional snowballing": runaway selection for emotional content rather than for information.

The implications for conspiracy theories should not be obscure. When an awful event has occurred, acceptance of such theories may justify or rationalize the emotional state produced by that event; consider conspiracy theories in response to political assassinations or terrorist attacks. Such theories typically involve accounts, or rumors, that create intense emotions such as indignation—thus promoting a kind of emotional selection that will spread beliefs from one person to another. Of course, evidence matters, and so long as there is some kind of process for meeting falsehoods with truth, mistaken beliefs can be corrected in principle. But sometimes the conditions for corrections are not present; or, even if they are present, people are strongly motivated to disregard them.

Group Polarization. There are clear links between cascades and the well-established phenomenon of group polarization, by which members of a deliberating group typically end up taking a more extreme position in the same direction as their inclinations before deliberation began.[31] Group polarization has been found in hundreds of studies involving over a dozen countries. Belief in conspiracy theories is often fueled by group polarization.

Here is an example of how group polarization works. A few years ago, I participated in some studies designed to shed light on how people's political beliefs are formed.[32] My coauthors and I assembled a number of people in Colorado into two sets of groups. Half of them consisted only of liberals; the other half consisted only of conservatives. We asked the participants to discuss three issues: climate change, affirmative action, and civil unions for same-sex couples. We also asked them to state their opinions on each topic at three stages. The first occurred before they started to talk, when we recorded their views privately and anonymously. In the second stage, we asked them to discuss the issues with one another and then to reach a kind of group verdict. In the final stage, we asked people to record their views after discussion, privately and anonymously.

Our findings were simple. On all three issues, both liberals and conservatives became more unified and more extreme after talking only to one another—not merely in their public verdicts but also in their private, anonymous views. Group discussions made conservatives more skeptical of climate change and more hostile to affirmative action and same-sex unions, while liberals showed the opposite pattern. Before discussion, both groups showed far more diversity than they did afterward, and the individuals in the liberal groups were not so very far apart from those in the conservative groups. After discussion, the two sets of groups became much more divided. This is group polarization in action.

Another study finds that that those who disapprove of the United States and are suspicious of its intentions will increase their disapproval and suspicion if they talk to one another. After speaking together about America and its foreign aid policy, citizens of France came to distrust the United States significantly more.[33] It should be easy to see how similar effects could occur for conspiracy theories. Those who tend to think that Israel was responsible for the attacks of 9/11, and who speak only or mostly with one another, will end up with a greater commitment to that belief.

A striking result of group polarization is that, as in our Colorado study, different groups may end up with radically different attitudes toward conspiracy theories in general and in particular. Speaking with like-minded others, some people may come to find such a theory irresistible. Others may come to find it preposterous.

Group polarization occurs for reasons that closely parallel those that explain cascades. Information plays a large role. In any group having some initial inclination, the arguments offered by most people will inevitably be skewed in favor of that very inclination. If, for example, most people in the group start out believing that Wall Street conspired to create an economic collapse, then everyone in the group will hear a lot of arguments in support of that position, and not so many to the contrary. As a result of hearing the various arguments, people will be hardened in their original belief and are likely to be led toward a more extreme view in line with what group members initially thought. Reputation matters too. People usually want to be perceived favorably by other group members. Once they hear what others believe, some will adjust their positions in the direction of the dominant position.

For purposes of understanding how conspiracy theories spread, it is especially important to see that group polarization is particularly likely, and particularly pronounced, when people have a shared sense of identity and are connected by bonds of solidarity. Social networks matter greatly, and tightly connected networks are more likely to subscribe to conspiracy theories. These are circumstances in which arguments by outsiders, unconnected with the group, will lack much credibility and fail to have much effect in reducing polarization. In such circumstances, direct government rebuttals of the reigning conspiracy theory are especially likely to prove ineffective.

Selection Effects. A crippled epistemology can arise not only from informational and reputational dynamics but also from self-selection of members into and out of groups with extreme views. Once cascades arise or polarization occurs, and the group's view begins to move in a certain direction, skeptics and partial believers will tend to depart, while intense believers remain. The overall size of the group may shrink, but the group may also pick up new believers who are even more committed. By self-selection, the remaining members will display more fanaticism.

Group members may segregate themselves in order to protect their beliefs from challenges by outsiders. Group leaders may enforce such segregation in order to insulate the rank and file from information or arguments that would undermine the leaders' hold on the group. Even if contrary information and arguments are in some literal sense heard, they will be ridiculed and made a subject of contempt—and, if at all possible, used as further confirmation of the conspiracy theory. As a result, group polarization will intensify.

Members of isolated groups sometimes display a kind of paranoid cognition and become increasingly suspicious of others or of the larger society, falling into a "sinister attribution error."[34] This error occurs when people mistakenly feel that they are under pervasive scrutiny, attribute personalized motivations, and greatly overestimate the amount of attention they actually receive. (The last is an aggravated version of a general human tendency known as the spotlight effect.)[35] Benign actions that happen to disadvantage the group are taken as purposeful plots intended to harm. Although these conditions resemble individual-level pathologies, they need not be. On the contrary, they arise from the social and informational structure of the group, and in the circumstances of interest here, are not usefully understood as a form of mental illness.

GOVERNMENTAL RESPONSES

What can government do about conspiracy theories? And among the things it can do, what *should* it do? Simply in order to understand the options (without endorsing any of them), imagine a series of possible responses.

1. Government might ban conspiracy theories.
2. Government might impose some kind of tax, financial or otherwise, on those who disseminate such theories.
3. Government might itself engage in counterspeech, marshaling arguments to discredit conspiracy theories.
4. Government might hire or work with credible agents in the private sector to engage in counterspeech.

Each instrument has a distinctive set of potential effects, or costs and benefits, and each will have a place under imaginable conditions. Under current free-speech law, of course, responses 1 and 2 are likely to be unconstitutional, and in a free society, censorship of any kind should be used, if at all, only under the most extraordinarily unusual conditions (for example, to prevent imminent violence).

It is also quite possible that government should stand to one side. Private organizations can and do work hard to respond to false conspiracy theories. An example is the internet site Snopes.com, which researches rumors and conspiracy theories and reports on their truth or falsity. For those concerned about the proliferation of conspiracy theorizing on the internet, this site provides a reliable and helpful reality check. It would be easy to find numerous similar ventures, small and large, in this vein, for the internet provides not only a mechanism by which to spread conspiracy theories but also a range of corrective tools. The more general point is that in free societies, false conspiracy theories are generally debunked by private citizens and institutions far more than by public officials.

Because the cost of spreading information is low, it is easy for private monitors to rebut false conspiracy theories. In just a few seconds, people can find a credible rebuttal of a conspiracy theory or produce a rebuttal themselves. At the same time, that very reduction in information costs makes it easier for conspiracy theorists to generate and spread their theories in the first place. The overall effect of new technology is unclear, as is the ability of private monitors to correct conspiracy theories. In part because this is so, an official response may be important or even essential, at least in some cases.

The first-line response to conspiracy theories is to maintain a free and open society. In such a society, those who might be tempted to believe such theories are exposed to evidence and corrections, and they are unlikely to distrust all knowledge-creating institutions. But we have seen that even in open societies, conspiracy theories can have some traction. Far more important, open societies may have a strong interest in debunking such theories when they arise, and threaten to cause harm, in closed societies. In the most serious cases, those who spread conspiracy theories, and those who receive them, are more likely to cause violence as a result.

DO CONSPIRACY THEORIES MATTER?

One line of thinking denies that conspiracy theories matter. There are several possible reasons to think that they may not, and for the vast majority of conspiracy theories, these reasons seem convincing. First, conspiracy theories may be held by only a tiny fraction of the population. Perhaps only a handful of kooks believe that US government officials had any kind of role in the events of 9/11. Second, even if a particular conspiracy theory is widespread, in the sense that many people will confess to it when polled, conspiracy theories may typically be held as "quasi beliefs": beliefs that are not costly and possibly even fun to hold, such as a belief in space aliens or UFOs, and that do not form a premise for action. Perhaps those who seem to accept conspiracy theories have "soft" beliefs, in a way that generally leads them to keep quiet and rarely act on what they tend to think.

At the same time, there is ample evidence that some conspiracy theories are not at all confined to small segments of the population, and that, at least when they are widely held, they may not be innocuous. According to a 2002 Gallup Poll conducted in nine Islamic countries, 61 percent of those surveyed thought that Muslims had nothing to do with the attacks of September 11, 2001. An anonymous State Department official stated that "a great deal of harm can result 'when people believe these lies and then act on the basis of their mistaken beliefs.'" For example, Al Qaeda members "were 'encouraged to "join the jihad" at least in part because of disinformation.'"[36] At various points in history, many members of some racial and religious groups have believed, falsely, that other groups were plotting against them, and those beliefs have not always been harmless.

Even if only a small fraction of adherents to a particular conspiracy theory act on the basis of their beliefs, that small fraction may be enough to cause serious harm, as in the 1995 truck bombing of the Alfred P. Murrah Federal Building in Oklahoma City. Convicted perpetrators Timothy McVeigh, Terry Nichols, and Michael Fortier shared a set of conspiratorial beliefs about the federal government.

Many others who shared their beliefs did not act on them, but those three people did, with terrifying consequences: 168 people were killed and 500 injured, making this the deadliest terrorist attack on US soil until September 11, 2001.

In cases of this sort, the conspiracy theory itself supports violent action on the part of its believers; conspiracy theorizing leads to an actual conspiracy. (Recall that people who are prone to conspiring are especially likely to accept conspiracy theories.) Within a network of members who believe that the federal government is a hostile and morally repellent organization that is taking over the country, akin to a foreign invader, armed resistance might seem a sensible course, at least to some.

DILEMMAS AND RESPONSES

Imagine a situation in which a particular conspiracy theory is becoming widespread. The government faces two recurring dilemmas. First, should it ignore or rebut the theory? Second, should it (1) address the supply side of conspiracy theorizing by attempting to convince its purveyors that they are wrong, (2) address the demand side by attempting to immunize audiences from the theory's effects, or (3) do both (if resource constraints permit)?

IGNORE OR REBUT?

The first dilemma is that either ignoring or rebutting a conspiracy theory has its own risks and costs. On the one hand, disregarding the theory allows its proponents to draw ominous inferences from the government's silence. On the other hand, if the theory stands unrebutted, people may pay less attention to it. The government's silence might suggest that the theory is too ludicrous to warrant a rebuttal—and has the advantage of not encouraging people to focus on it. These points counsel in favor of silence for the vast majority of conspiracy theories, which are roundly and rightly ignored and fall from their own weight. But another possibility is that the government is silent because it cannot offer convincing evidence to the contrary. Conspiracy theorists will, of course, contend that "no comment" is a concession of some kind.

At the same time, the very effort to rebut the theory may legitimate it. People may infer from the government's rebuttal that it considers the conspiracy theory to be plausible and fears that many people will be persuaded. The very act of rebuttal also focuses the audience on the theory in a way that may increase its salience. Those who might reject the theory, or not give it much thought, may take the rebuttal as a reason to think about it and perhaps consider it seriously.

Some members of the audience may also infer that many other members of the audience must believe the conspiracy theory, or the government would not be taking the trouble to rebut it. Consider circumstances of "pluralistic ignorance," in which citizens are unsure what other citizens believe. If the government's rebuttal is a signal that other citizens accept the conspiracy theory, it may make the theory more plausible. The perverse result of the rebuttal may then be to increase the number of believers. We have also seen that corrections can backfire. People may be motivated to intensify their commitment to their convictions once that commitment is placed under strain.

How should government cope with this dilemma? There is no general or obvious answer. Reasonable officials may adopt a wait-and-see strategy: ignore the conspiracy theory unless it reaches some ill-defined threshold of widespread popularity and then rebut. But waiting too long can also be harmful, at least if there is a significant chance that the theory will gain sufficient traction to cause harm. Conspiracy theories sometimes spread by rumor, and empirical study of rumor psychology shows that "[t]o curb rumors, one must act quickly . . . [A]s a rumor circulates, it tends to evolve into a more believable version and therefore becomes harder to contain. [Also], the more times people hear the rumor, the more likely they are to believe it."[37] In particular, some studies show that when officials or firms are asked about rumors, a response of "no comment" is affirmatively harmful; audiences tend to suspect a cover-up. When asked explicitly, officials should deny the rumor by pointing to specifics. Counterintuitively, a blanket denial may be inferior to one that incorporates, and thus mentions, the rumor itself.[38]

WHICH AUDIENCE?

Should the governmental response be addressed to the suppliers of conspiracy theories, with the goal of persuading them, or should it be addressed to the mass audience, with the goal of inoculating people against pernicious theories?

Perhaps the best approach is to straddle the two audiences with a single response or simply to provide multiple responses. If there are resource constraints, government may face a choice about where to place its emphasis. Apart from resource constraints, there may be trade-offs across these strategies. The very arguments that are most convincing to the mass audience may be least convincing to the conspiracy theorists, and vice versa.

We have seen that those who embrace a conspiracy theory are especially resistant to contrary evidence offered by the government, because the government's rebuttal might be folded into the conspiracy theory itself. After 9/11, one set of conspiracy theories involved American Airlines Flight 77, which hijackers crashed into the Pentagon. Some theorists claimed that no plane had hit the Pentagon. Even after the Department of Defense released video frames showing Flight 77 approaching the building and a subsequent explosion cloud, theorists pointed out that the actual moment of impact was absent from the video, in order to keep alive their claim that the plane had never hit the building. (In reality, the moment of impact was not captured because the video had a low number of frames per second.)[39] Moreover, even those conspiracists who were persuaded that the Flight 77 conspiracy theories were wrong folded that view into a larger conspiracy theory. The problem with the theory that no plane hit the Pentagon, they said, is that the theory was too transparently false, disproved by multiple witnesses and much physical evidence. Thus, the theory must have been a straw man initially planted by the government in order to discredit other conspiracy theories and theorists by association.[40]

Because of these difficulties, direct responses to the suppliers of conspiracy theories might be dismissed as exercises in futility. Those with strong commitments often engage in "biased assimilation" of evidence,[41] and conspiracy theorists are likely to be especially biased assimilators. In the context of the assassination of President Kennedy, for example, biased assimilation has been explicitly observed, with balanced information leading believers to be more, not less, committed to their conspiracy theory.[42]

Sometimes officials choose to frame their responses to the mass audience, hoping to stem the spread of conspiracy theories by dampening the demand rather than by reducing the supply. Philip Zelikow, the executive director of the 9/11 Commission, says that "[t]he hardcore conspiracy theorists are totally committed. They'd have to repudiate much of their life identity in order not to accept some of that stuff. That's not our worry. Our worry is when things become infectious . . . [t]hen this stuff can be deeply corrosive to public understanding. You can get where the bacteria can sicken the larger body."[43] Likewise, when public officials issued a fact sheet to disprove the theory that the World Trade Center was brought down by a controlled demolition, one official stated, "We realize this fact sheet won't convince those who hold to the alternative theories that our findings are sound. In fact, the fact sheet was never intended for them. It is for the masses who have seen or heard the alternative theory claims and want balance."[44]

COGNITIVE INFILTRATION AND PERSUASION

Rather than taking the continued existence of the hard core as a constraint, and addressing itself solely to the mass audience, government might take steps to break up the tight cognitive clusters of conspiracist theories, arguments, and rhetoric that are produced by the hard core and that reinforce it in turn. A potential approach (growing directly out of the account here of how such theories spread) is cognitive infiltration of extremist groups. As used here, this admittedly provocative term does not mean 1960s-style infiltration with a view to surveillance and collecting information, possibly for use in future prosecutions. Rather, it means that government efforts might succeed in weakening or even breaking up the ideological and epistemological complexes that constitute these networks and groups. Of course, any such efforts should be consistent with domestic law, including constitutional protections of free speech and personal privacy. The focus of the discussion is on situations involving serious security risks, above all risks of terrorism, that arise from conspiracy theories in foreign countries.

How might this tactic work? Recall that extremist networks and groups, including those that purvey conspiracy theories, typically suffer from a kind of crippled epistemology. Hearing only conspiratorial accounts of government behavior, their members become ever more prone to believe and generate such accounts. Perhaps the generation of ever-more-extreme views within these groups can be dampened or reversed by the introduction of cognitive diversity. Government might introduce such diversity—needless to say, only under circumstances in which there is a compelling and legitimate need to respond to the conspiracy theory, as, for example, to reduce a threat of violence from potential terrorists in another nation. Under this approach, government agents and their allies might enter foreign chat rooms, online social networks, or even real-space groups and attempt to undermine percolating conspiracy theories by raising doubts about their factual premises, causal logic, or implications for action, political or otherwise. Because conspiracy theories are self-sealing, government agents face serious challenges. But there are several possible routes.

In one variant, government agents would openly proclaim—or at least make no effort to conceal—their institutional affiliations.

A 2007 newspaper story reported that Arabic-speaking Muslim officials from the State Department had participated in dialogues in radical Islamist chat rooms and on websites in order to calm the situation by offering arguments not usually heard among the groups that post messages on those sites, with some success.[45] In another variant, government officials would participate anonymously or even with false identities. Each approach has distinct costs and benefits; the second raises ethical concerns and is riskier, but it might bring higher returns. Where government officials participate openly, hard-core members of the relevant networks, communities, and conspiracy-minded organizations may entirely discount what the officials say, right from the beginning. Because conspiracy theorists are likely to approach evidence and arguments in a biased way, they are not likely to respond well to the claims of public officials. Those claims might be received as self-refuting; conspiracists who hear them might well respond with the dismissive phrase "consider the source."

The advantage of anonymous participation, and of working with agents, is that such dismissals are less likely. A great deal of work suggests the potential credibility of "surprising validators": people who are not expected to take a particular position and are persuasive for that reason.[46] If, for example, a prominent conservative, known to be a skeptic about environmentalism, says that climate change is real and needs to be addressed, some people might well be moved. So, too, with conspiracy theories. If a person who is credible in the relevant community—say, someone who is known not to be friendly to the United States—says plainly that a conspiracy theory about America is false, people may listen, and waters might be calmed.

The problems with anonymous participation and hidden agents involve both ethics and disclosure. Outside of unusual circumstances (above all, genuine national security threats), public officials should not conceal their identity. And if the tactic becomes known, the theory may become further entrenched, and any real member of the relevant groups who raises doubts may be suspected of having government connections. The two forms of cognitive infiltration offer evidently different risk-reward mixes.

There is a similar trade-off along another dimension: whether the efforts should occur in the real world or strictly in cyberspace. The latter is safer but potentially less productive. The former will sometimes be indispensable, where the groups that purvey conspiracy theories (and perhaps themselves plan conspiracies) formulate their views through real-space informational networks rather than virtual networks. Infiltration of any kind poses risks, but they are generally greater for real-world infiltration, where the agent is exposed to more serious harms.

There are also hard questions about how, exactly, to introduce cognitive diversity into a group of people strongly committed to a conspiracy theory. Even if the infiltrators are generally credible, they are unlikely to be effective if they simply proclaim that the theory "is wrong" or even if they introduce evidence suggesting that the widely held view is mistaken. A growing body of research indicates that if the goal is to dislodge a particular belief of an individual or group, the best approach is to begin by affirming other beliefs—or at least the competence and character—of that individual or group.[47] For example, those who have strong views about capital punishment or abortion are far more likely to listen to counterarguments if those who make such counterarguments take significant steps to affirm those with whom they are engaging. The general conclusion is that cognitive diversity, as such, is hardly enough; it is necessary also to insure a degree of receptivity toward those with divergent views.

CONSPIRACIES AND THE FORMATION OF BELIEFS

Some people have a propensity to accept conspiracy theories, as reflected in the finding that people who tend to believe one are likely to believe another, even if the two are in direct contradiction. Many people who accept conspiracy theories suffer from a crippled epistemology. Their beliefs are a function of what they hear. For that reason, isolated social networks can be a breeding ground for conspiracy theories.

In some cases, those theories help to fuel violence. To reduce that risk, it is indispensable to understand how those theories arise and how rational people can come to hold them even if they are palpably false. Conspiracy theories are, of course, an extreme case, but an understanding of the mechanisms that lie behind them helps to shed light on the formation of political beliefs in general and on why some of those beliefs go wrong.

CHAPTER 2

THE SECOND BILL OF RIGHTS

THE SPEECH OF THE CENTURY?

On January 11, 1944, America's war against fascism was going well. Most informed observers believed that ultimate victory was not in serious doubt. A looming question was what would happen after the war. At noon, America's optimistic, aging, self-assured, wheelchair-bound president, Franklin Delano Roosevelt, delivered the text of his State of the Union address to Congress. Because he was ill with a cold, Roosevelt did not make the customary trip to Capitol Hill to appear in person. Instead, he spoke to the nation via radio—the first and only time a State of the Union address was also a fireside chat. Millions of Americans assembled by their radios that night to hear what Roosevelt had to say.

His speech wasn't elegant. It was messy, sprawling, unruly, a bit of a pastiche, and not at all literary. It was the opposite of Abraham Lincoln's tight, poetic Gettysburg Address. But because of what it said, this largely forgotten address, proposing a Second Bill of Rights, has a strong claim to being the greatest speech of the twentieth century.

Roosevelt began by emphasizing that the war against fascism was a shared endeavor in which the United States was simply one participant: "This Nation in the past two years has become an active partner in the world's greatest war against human slavery." As a result of that partnership, the war was in the process of being won. "But I do not think that any of us Americans can be content with mere survival." Hence, "the one supreme objective for the future"—the objective for all nations—was captured "in one word: security." Roosevelt argued that the term "means not only physical security which provides safety from attacks by aggressors," but includes as well "economic security, social security, moral security." Roosevelt insisted that "essential to peace is a decent standard of living for all individual men and women and children in all nations. Freedom from fear is eternally linked with freedom from want."

Moving directly to domestic affairs, Roosevelt emphasized the need to bring security of all kinds to America's citizens. He argued for a "realistic tax law—which will tax all unreasonable profits, both individual and corporate, and reduce the ultimate cost of the war to our sons and daughters." He stressed that the nation "cannot be content, no matter how high that general standard of living may be, if some fraction of our people—whether it be one-third or one-fifth or one-tenth—is ill-fed, ill-clothed, ill-housed, and insecure."

At this point, the speech became much more ambitious. Roosevelt looked back to the framing of the Constitution. At its inception, the nation had grown "under the protection of certain inalienable political rights—among them the right of free speech, free press, free worship, trial by jury, freedom from unreasonable searches and seizures." Over time, these rights had proved inadequate. Unlike the Constitution's framers, "we have come to a clear realization of the fact that true individual freedom cannot exist without economic security and independence . . . In our day, these economic truths have become accepted as self-evident. We have accepted, so to speak, a second Bill of Rights under which a new basis of security and prosperity can be established for all—regardless of station, race, or creed."

Then he listed the relevant rights:

> The right to a useful and remunerative job in the industries or shops or farms or mines of the Nation;
>
> The right to earn enough to provide adequate food and clothing and recreation;
>
> The right of every farmer to raise and sell his products at a return which will give him and his family a decent living;
>
> The right of every businessman, large and small, to trade in an atmosphere of freedom from unfair competition and domination by monopolies at home or abroad;
>
> The right of every family to a decent home;
>
> The right to adequate medical care and the opportunity to achieve and enjoy good health;
>
> The right to adequate protection from the economic fears of old age, sickness, accident, and unemployment;
>
> The right to a good education.

Having catalogued these eight rights, Roosevelt immediately recalled the "one word" that captured the overriding objective for the future. He argued that these "rights spell security"—and hence that the recognition of the Second Bill was continuous with the war effort. "After this war is won," he said, "we must be prepared to move forward, in the implementation of these rights." There was a close connection between this implementation and the coming international order: "America's own rightful place in the world depends in large part upon how fully these and similar rights have been carried into practice for our citizens. For unless there is security here at home, there cannot be lasting peace in the world." Roosevelt concluded that government should promote security instead of paying heed "to the whining demands of selfish pressure groups who seek to feather their nests while young Americans are dying."

GOVERNMENT INTERVENTION

What made it possible for the president of the Greatest Generation to propose the Second Bill of Rights? Part of the answer lies in a simple idea, one now largely lost but pervasive in American culture in Roosevelt's time: *no one really opposes government intervention as such*. Of course, private initiative is crucial, but markets and wealth depend on government. Without a government that is ready to establish and protect property rights, property itself cannot exist, at least not in recognizable form.[1] Those who denounce government interference most loudly depend on it every day. Their own rights do not come from minimizing government but are a product of government. Political scientist Lester Ward vividly captured the point in 1885: "[T]hose who denounce state intervention are the ones who most frequently and successfully invoke it. The cry of laissez-faire mainly goes up from the ones who, if really 'let alone,' would instantly lose their wealth-absorbing power."

Think, for example, of the owner of a radio station, or a house in the suburbs, or an expensive automobile, or a large bank account. Every such owner is likely to depend on the protection given by a coercive and well-funded state, equipped with a police force, judges, prosecutors, and an extensive body of criminal and civil law. As Friedrich Hayek, perhaps the greatest critic of socialism and excessive state authority, wrote, "In no system that could be rationally defended could the state just do nothing. An effective competitive system needs an intelligently designed and continually adjusted legal framework as much as any other."[2]

From the beginning, Roosevelt's White House understood all this quite well. In accepting the Democratic nomination in 1932,

Roosevelt insisted, "We must lay hold of the fact that economic laws are not made by nature. They are made by human beings." Or consider an important address he gave the same year, in which he emphasized, "[E]ven Jefferson realized that the exercise of the property rights might so interfere with the rights of the individual that the government, without whose assistance the property rights could not exist, must intervene, not to destroy individualism but to protect it." The key point here is that without government's active assistance, property rights could not exist at all, certainly not in their current form. As Walter Lippmann wrote in his 1937 book *The Good Society*, "While the theorists were talking about laissez-faire, men were buying and selling legal titles to property, were chartering corporations, were making and enforcing contracts, were suing for damages. In these transactions, by means of which the work of society was carried on, the state was implicated at every vital point."

In this light, it seemed implausible to contend that government should simply let people fend for themselves. Against the backdrop of the Great Depression and the threat from fascism, Roosevelt was entirely prepared to insist that government should "protect individualism" not only by protecting property rights but also by promoting decent opportunities and some minimum of security for all. The ultimate result was his proposal for the Second Bill of Rights.

The basic idea first emerged in a meeting in August 1939. With the New Deal on hold and the fascist threat looming, Frederic Delano, Roosevelt's uncle and head of his National Resources Planning Board (NRPB), suggested the idea of expanding the Bill of Rights from the political to the social arena, to include educational opportunity, health and medical care, decent shelter, the right to work, and economic security. Delano elaborated on that idea in a memorandum written for the president in the summer of 1940. On June 29, 1941, an Economic Bill of Rights was specifically proposed to Roosevelt by NRPB advisors working at his Springwood estate, also known as the Summer White House, in Hyde Park, New York. Roosevelt approved of the idea and asked for a revision. Their list, released to Congress in March 1943, took the following form:

1. The right to work, usefully and creatively through the productive years;
2. The right to fair play, adequate to command the necessities and amenities of life in exchange for work, ideas, thrift, and other socially valuable service;
3. The right to adequate food, clothing, shelter, and medical care;
4. The right to security, with freedom from fear of old age, want, dependency, sickness, unemployment, and accident;
5. The right to live in a system of free enterprise, free from compulsory labor, irresponsible state power, arbitrary public authority, and unregulated monopolies;
6. The right to come and go, to speak or to be silent, free from the spyings of secret political police;
7. The right to equality before the law, with equal access to justice in fact;
8. The right to education, for work, for citizenship, and for personal growth and happiness; and
9. The right to rest, recreation, and adventure, the opportunity to enjoy life and take part in advancing civilization.

The NRPB proposed a number of steps to protect these rights, including a national health and education program, a broadened system of Social Security, strengthened protections against monopoly, and a permanent policy for large-scale public works.

The governing ideas played a role in later correspondence in 1943. Chester Bowles, director of the Office of Price Administration, sent the White House a memorandum discussing a Second Bill of Rights and urging that Roosevelt "reannounce his liberal program and his determination to push it as soon as the exigencies of war permitted." During discussions of the annual message for 1943, White House officials showed the Bowles memorandum and Delano's catalogue of rights to Roosevelt, who insisted that the topic should be covered in his message. The Second Bill of Rights speech was born.

AN AMERICAN EXPORT

Roosevelt, dead fifteen months after delivering his speech, was unable to take serious steps toward putting his Bill of Rights into effect. But his proposal, not widely known within the United States, has had an extraordinary influence internationally. It played a major role in the writing of the Universal Declaration of Human Rights, finalized in 1948 under the leadership of former first lady Eleanor Roosevelt and publicly endorsed by American officials at the time. The declaration proclaims that everyone has a "right to a standard of living adequate for the health and well-being of himself and his family, including food, clothing, housing and medical care and necessary social services, and the right to security in the event of unemployment, sickness, disability, widowhood, old age, or other lack of livelihood in circumstances beyond his control." The declaration also provides a right to education and Social Security. It proclaims that everyone "has a right to work, to free choice of employment, to just and favorable conditions of work and to protection against unemployment."

By virtue of its effect on the Universal Declaration, the Second Bill of Rights has influenced dozens of constitutions throughout the world. In one or another form, it can be found in countless political and legal documents. The constitution of Finland guarantees everyone "the right to basic subsistence in the event of unemployment, illness, and disability and during old age as well as at the birth of a child or the loss of a provider." The constitution of Spain announces, "To citizens in old age, the public authorities shall guarantee economic sufficiency through adequate and periodically updated pensions." Similarly, the constitutions of the Ukraine, Romania, Bulgaria, Hungary, Russia, and Peru recognize some or all of the social and economic rights catalogued by Franklin Roosevelt.

Without overexaggeration, we might even call the Second Bill of Rights a leading American export. In fact, the United States itself continues to live, at least some of the time, under Roosevelt's constitutional vision. There is considerable support for the rights he listed—most obviously, the right to education, the right to Social Security, and the right to be free from monopoly. With the enactment of the Affordable Care Act in 2010, the United States is now committed to something like a right to health care. It would not be difficult to connect each of the rights on the Second Bill to laws, policies, and social commitments that are now well entrenched in American culture.

RIGHTS? REALLY?

Of course, there are many complexities, both conceptual and empirical, in the idea that people have rights of these kinds. Roosevelt was no socialist, and he believed that the Second Bill was entirely consistent with the system of free enterprise. But did he mean to suggest a system of entitlements? Of what kind? It is reasonable to wonder whether entitlements of this sort might sap morale, undermine individual initiative, and cause a host of economic problems, potentially leading to violations, not protections, of rights. The Republican presidential candidate in 2012, former Massachusetts governor Mitt Romney, said with apparent contempt, "There are forty-seven percent . . . who believe that government has a responsibility to care for them, who believe that they are entitled to health care, to food, to housing, to you name it. That that's an entitlement." It is not clear whether Governor Romney knew that the alleged belief of the 47 percent could be connected to an important speech by one of America's greatest presidents. The contempt was unfortunate, but it is entirely legitimate, even important, to ask hard questions about the content of these rights—about who is entitled to make demands on government, and when, and how much.

Nothing in Roosevelt's speech answers these questions. Certainly he was not engaging with abstract theories of any kind. His focus was on two things: decent opportunities for all and minimal security. With respect to opportunity, the right to a good education is the most obvious example. But other rights have the same focus. Consider, for example, an item that is perhaps the easiest to overlook but should be understood as central: "The right of every businessman, large and small, to trade in an atmosphere of freedom from unfair competition and domination by monopolies at home or abroad." What Roosevelt was emphasizing here is that for real opportunity to exist, governments must take steps to insure against private or public monopolies. Because monopolies squelch competition, they deprive people of a fair chance at wealth. Genuinely free markets are indispensable to opportunity. In a free society, those who seek to start businesses are permitted to do so. They should not be hampered by anticompetitive practices. And there is another point: if entrepreneurs are free to trade in an atmosphere of open competition, workers and consumers are large beneficiaries as well.

What about the right to a "useful and remunerative job"? This right certainly can be connected with security. But does it have anything to do with opportunity? It is important to understand what Roosevelt did and did not mean by this. Against the backdrop of the Great Depression, Roosevelt was referring, first and foremost, to government's efforts to promote economic growth so as to increase the likelihood that people will be able to find work. The best way to protect the right to a "useful and remunerative job" is not through publicly guaranteed employment or through government jobs. It is instead through a flourishing economy that is promoting growth and thus creating more opportunities. As the Depression demonstrated—and as many subsequent periods in American history, including the economic crisis of 2008 and beyond, have made clear—a system of free enterprise, without sensible safeguards in place, can lead to devastatingly high levels of unemployment.

Roosevelt sought a set of initiatives that would increase the availability of decent positions for people who wanted work. He did not mean that the unemployment rate must be zero or close to it.

But he did mean that government must make substantial efforts to promote an economy that can produce employment for people who want it.

Opportunity is the best way to provide economic security. But some aspects of the Second Bill cannot be understood as guaranteeing opportunity. They aim at security directly, by creating a floor below which human lives are not supposed to fall. As Roosevelt said in 1938, "Government has a final responsibility for the well-being of its citizenship. If private cooperative endeavor fails to provide work for willing hands and relief for the unfortunate, those suffering hardship from no fault of their own have a right to call upon the Government for aid; and a government worthy of its name must make fitting response."[3] Certain aspects of the Second Bill protect *freedom from desperate conditions*, which should be seen as a form of liberty, not equality. Roosevelt's goal was not to produce equality of outcomes but to create that form of freedom that comes from having minimal security against life's worst misfortunes.[4]

CONSTITUTIONAL RIGHTS?

In the 1950s and 1960s, the US Supreme Court started to go much further than Roosevelt did, embarking on a process of granting constitutional recognition to some of the rights that Roosevelt had listed. (There is a general lesson here. In the United States, constitutional debates are often a direct result of political debates from the previous decade.) Remarkably, the Court suggested that there might be some kind of right to an education. It ruled that people could not be deprived of welfare benefits without a hearing. It said that citizens from one state could not be subject to "waiting periods" that deprive them of financial and medical help in another state. In its 1970 decision in *Goldberg v. Kelly*, the Court proclaimed: "Welfare, by meeting the basic demands of subsistence, can help bring within the reach of the poor the same opportunities that are available to others to participate meaningfully in the life of the community."

Public assistance, the Court added, "is not mere charity but a means to 'promote the general Welfare, and secure the Blessings of Liberty to ourselves and our Posterity.'"

By the late 1960s, respected constitutional thinkers could conclude that the Supreme Court was on the verge of recognizing a right to be free from desperate conditions—a right that would capture a significant part of what Roosevelt had championed. But all that was undone by the election of Richard Nixon in 1968. Over the next few years, Nixon appointed four justices—Warren Burger, William Rehnquist, Lewis Powell, and Harry Blackmun—who showed no interest in the Second Bill of Rights. In a series of decisions, the new justices, joined by one or two others, rejected the claim that the existing Constitution protects the kind of rights that Roosevelt had named.

Roosevelt himself did not argue for constitutional change. He wanted the Second Bill of Rights to be part of the nation's deepest commitments—to be recognized and vindicated by the public, not by federal judges. He trusted democratic processes, not judicial ones. He thought that the Second Bill of Rights should be seen in the same way as the Declaration of Independence—as a statement of the fundamental aspirations of the United States. In fact, the "Second Bill of Rights" speech unambiguously echoed Thomas Jefferson's Declaration: "We have come to a clear realization of the fact that true individual freedom cannot exist without economic security and independence . . . In our day, these economic truths have become accepted as self-evident."

Roosevelt's hopes have not been fully realized. Some of the time, political leaders in the United States seem to embrace a confused and pernicious form of individualism, one that has no real foundations in our history. As Roosevelt well knew, no one is really against government intervention. The wealthy, at least as much as the poor, receive help from government and from the benefits that it bestows. Recall his statement that the exercise of "property rights might so interfere with the rights of the individual that the government, without whose assistance the property rights could not exist, must intervene, not to destroy individualism but to protect it." Those of us who are doing well, and who have plenty of money and opportunities, owe a great deal to an active government that is willing and able to protect what we have. The same people who object to "government intervention" depend on it.

Remarkably, the confusions that Roosevelt identified have had a rebirth since the early 1980s. Time and again, influential politicians have argued that they oppose government intervention as such, even though property rights themselves cannot exist without such intervention. Time and again, American culture is said to be antagonistic to "positive rights," even though property rights themselves require "positive" action. In recent decades, we have seen a false and ahistorical picture of American culture and history—a picture that is occasionally prominent in Europe and America itself.

Unfortunately, that picture is far from innocuous. America's self-image—our sense of ourselves—has a significant impact on what we actually do. We should not look at ourselves through a distorted mirror.

Roosevelt was right to insist that there is an inextricable link between freedom from fear and freedom from want. Both liberty and citizenship are rooted in security. The Second Bill of Rights should be reclaimed in its nation of origin.

CHAPTER 3

IF "MISFEARING" IS THE PROBLEM, IS COST-BENEFIT ANALYSIS THE SOLUTION?

Many people have argued for cost-benefit analysis on economic grounds. In their view, a primary goal of regulation is to promote economic efficiency, and cost-benefit analysis is admirably well suited to that goal. Societies should not waste resources, and cost-benefit analysis reduces the risk of waste. Arguments of this kind have been met with sharp criticism from those who are not so enthusiastic about economic efficiency or who believe that in practice, cost-benefit analysis is likely to produce a kind of regulatory paralysis ("paralysis by analysis") or to represent a victory for business interests.

In this chapter, I offer support for cost-benefit analysis not from the standpoint of conventional economics but on grounds associated with cognitive psychology and behavioral economics. My basic suggestion is that cost-benefit analysis is best defended as a means of responding to the general problem of "misfearing." That problem arises when people are afraid of trivial risks and neglectful of serious ones.

For purposes of law and policy, the central points are twofold. First, misfearing is part of the human condition, and both ordinary people and public officials are subject to it. Second, misfearing plays a role in public policy, in part because of how human beings think, in part because of the power of self-interested private groups, and in part because of the ordinary political dynamics. Misfearing can produce unfortunate misallocations of public resources when nations devote a lot of money to small problems and much less to big ones. Because cost-benefit analysis draws attention to the actual consequences of the various options, it reduces that risk. So understood, cost-benefit analysis is a way to insure better priority setting and to overcome predictable obstacles to desirable regulation.

Of course, much of the controversy over cost-benefit analysis stems from the difficulty of specifying what that form of analysis entails. An understanding of misfearing cannot support any particular understanding of cost-benefit analysis. This is not the place to offer any such understanding. My goal is to provide a general defense of cost-benefit analysis, rooted in behavioral economics, that should be able to attract support from people who have diverse theoretical commitments or who are uncertain about the appropriate theoretical commitments. (See the discussion of minimalism in chapter 10.)

MISFEARING AND THE PUBLIC DEMAND FOR REGULATION

Why, exactly, do people fall prey to misfearing? I shall offer several answers, but it will be helpful to orient them under a simple framework. A great deal of recent work in psychology has explored two families of cognitive operations in the human mind, sometimes described as System 1 and System 2, through which people evaluate many things, including risky activities and processes.[1]

System 1 is fast, associative, and intuitive. System 1 tends to be frightened by loud noises and big animals, and it does not care much about the abstract idea of air pollution. (When it objects to something someone has done, System 1 tends to say, "I hate you!") By contrast, System 2 is deliberative, calculative, slow, and analytic. (When it objects to something someone has done, System 2 offers a constructive suggestion.) System 2 engages in some kind of assessment of whether loud noises or big animals pose a genuine threat. Though aspects of the two systems may well have different locations in the human brain, the distinction is useful whether or not identifiable brain sectors are involved; it should be understood as an effort to capture, in simple form, the difference between effortless, automatic processing and effortful, slower processing.

Because of the operation of System 1, people have immediate and often visceral reactions to persons, activities, and processes, and their immediate reactions operate as mental shortcuts for a more deliberative or analytic assessment of the underlying issues. Sometimes the shortcut can be overridden or corrected by System 2. For example, System 1 might lead people to be terrified of flying in airplanes, but System 2 might create a deliberative check, leading people to recognize that the risks are minimal.

Misfearing is often a product of System 1, and cost-benefit analysis can operate as a kind of System 2 corrective, giving people a better sense of what is actually at stake. People might think that some activity creates serious risks, but cost-benefit analysis can establish that the risks are quite low. To be sure, System 2 itself can go badly wrong, and the analysis of costs and benefits may be erroneous. Perhaps the underlying scientific judgments are incorrect; perhaps the scientists are unduly optimistic. In addition, the translation of risks into monetary equivalents creates many challenges.[2] It would be foolish to contend that System 2 is infallible, even if it is competent and working extremely hard. The only claims are that System 1 is prone to making systematic errors, that those errors produce misfearing, and that an effort to assess the costs and benefits of risk reduction, if done properly, will operate as a helpful constraint. If, for example, Jones is afraid of flying and Smith is unafraid of smoking cigarettes, some kind of cost-benefit analysis—formal or informal—might help them both.

These points work most naturally for individual judgments. Remarkable as the human brain is, it evolved for particular purposes, and it can blunder, especially in unfamiliar contexts. But the political process is also influenced by System 1, certainly in the most responsive democracies. Of course, it is also true that when the public demand for law threatens to produce excessive reactions to minor risks, there are constraints. Any such reactions must overcome a series of barriers to ill-considered public action. And when a legislature or administrative agency is moved to act, a number of factors are responsible, perhaps including the activities of self-interested private groups with strong incentives to move government in their preferred directions.

Nonetheless, it is clear that public misfearing helps to produce significant misallocations of public resources. Misfearing can be a result of social interactions, as fear or complacency spreads rapidly from one person to another, and also of political influences, as sophisticated political actors try to stir people up or calm them down. To the extent that misallocations are a product of these and related factors, the argument for cost-benefit analysis is strengthened rather than weakened.

These claims raise an immediate question: What, exactly, is cost-benefit analysis? For present purposes, let us understand that approach to require regulator to identify—and to make relevant for purposes of decision—the positive effects and the negative effects of regulation, and to quantify these as much as possible in terms of monetary equivalents, capturing everything that matters, including lives saved, hospital admissions prevented, workdays gained, and so forth. For purposes of illustration, here is a representative effort at valuation, from the Environmental Protection Agency in 2013 (with blank spaces for unavailable estimates):

Unit Values for Economic Valuation of Health Endpoints[3]

	CENTRAL ESTIMATE OF VALUE PER STATISTICAL LIFE	
HEALTH ENDPOINT	1990 INCOME LEVEL	2020 INCOME LEVEL
Premature Mortality (Value of a Statistical Life)	$8,000,000	$9,600,000
Nonfatal Myocardial Infarction (heart attack)		
3 percent discount rate		
Age 0–24	$87,000	$87,000
Age 25–44	$110,000	$110,000
Age 45–54	$120,000	$120,000
Age 55–64	$200,000	$200,000
Age 65 and over	$98,000	$98,000
7 percent discount rate		
Age 0–24	$97,000	$97,000
Age 25–44	$110,000	$110,000
Age 45–54	$110,000	$110,000
Age 55–64	$190,000	$190,000
Age 65 and over	$97,000	$97,000

HOSPITAL ADMISSIONS	2000 INCOME LEVEL	2020 INCOME LEVEL
Chronic Lung Disease (18–64)	$21,000	$21,000
Asthma Admissions (0–64)	$21,000	$21,000
All Cardiovascular		
Age 18–64	$42,000	$42,000
Age 65–99	$41,000	$41,000
All Respiratory (Age 65 and over)	$36,000	$36,000
Emergency Department Visits for Asthma	$430	$430

RESPIRATORY AILMENTS NOT REQUIRING HOSPITALIZATION	2000 INCOME LEVEL	2020 INCOME LEVEL
Upper Respiratory Symptoms	$31	$33
Lower Respiratory Symptoms	$20	$21
Asthma Exacerbations	$54	$58

Let us assume that government uses figures of this sort and that those figures have adequate technical foundations. Let us also assume that cost-benefit analysis can accommodate, or be supplemented by, factors that are not easy to monetize, giving special weight to human dignity or to adverse effects on disadvantaged social groups.[4] How might cost-benefit analysis help to correct the problem of misfearing?

THE AVAILABILITY HEURISTIC

It is well known that people use mental shortcuts, or heuristics, in thinking about risks. The first problem is purely cognitive: the availability heuristic.[5] People tend to think that an event is more probable if they can recall an incident in which it came to fruition.[6] Ease of recall greatly affects our judgments about probability. In a famous paper, Amos Tversky and Daniel Kahneman found that people think that, on any given page, more words will end with the letters *ing* than will have *n* as the second-to-last letter (though a moment's reflection shows that this is not possible).[7] With respect to risks, judgments are typically affected by the availability heuristic, so that people overestimate the number of deaths from highly publicized events (motor vehicle accidents, tornados, floods, botulism) but underestimate the number from less publicized sources (stroke, heart disease, stomach cancer).[8] It is in part for this reason that direct personal experience can play a large role in perceptions of risk.[9]

Consider in this regard a 2004 study of perceptions of risk associated with terrorism and severe acute respiratory syndrome (SARS).[10] The study involved Americans and Canadians. In the aftermath of the 9/11 attacks, Americans perceived terrorism to be a far greater threat to themselves and to others than SARS—whereas in the aftermath of an outbreak of SARS, Canadians perceived SARS to be a greater threat to themselves and to others than terrorism. Americans estimated their chance of serious harm from terrorism as 8.27 percent, about four times higher than their estimate of their chance of serious harm from SARS (2.18 percent). Canadians estimated their chance of serious harm from SARS as 7.43 percent, significantly higher than their estimate for terrorism (6.04 percent). The estimated figures for SARS were unrealistically high, especially for Canadians; the best estimate of the risk of contracting SARS, based on Canadian figures, was just .0008 percent (and the chance of dying as a result, less than .0002 percent). For obvious reasons, the objective risks from terrorism are much harder to calculate, but if it is estimated that the United States will suffer at least one terrorist attack each year with the same number of deaths as on September 11, 2001, the risk of death from terrorism is about .001 percent—a highly speculative number under the circumstances, but suggestive that Americans were exaggerating the risk.

What accounts for such large differences between two neighboring nations? The availability heuristic provides a large part of the answer. In the United States, risks of terrorism have (to say the least) received a great deal of attention, producing a continuing sense of threat, especially in the years immediately following 9/11. But in the United States, there have been no incidents of SARS, and the media coverage has been limited to events elsewhere—producing a modest degree of salience but far lower than that associated with terrorism. In Canada, the opposite was the case in the relevant period. The high degree of public discussion of SARS cases, accompanied by readily available instances, produced an inflated sense of the numbers—sufficiently inflated to exceed the same numbers from terrorism (certainly a salient risk in Canada, as in most nations following 9/11).

To the extent that people lack information or base their judgments on mental shortcuts that produce errors, there is a risk that a highly responsive government will blunder. Indeed, private groups often exploit the availability heuristic, emphasizing a particular incident that is supposed to be taken as representative of a much larger problem. Cost-benefit analysis is a natural corrective, above all because it focuses attention on the actual effects of regulation, including, in some cases, the existence of surprisingly small benefits from regulatory controls. When cost-benefit analysis is working well, it can counteract both "availability bias," in the form of an inflated sense of risk, and "unavailability bias" (excessive complacency), stemming from an absence of available incidents.

To this extent, cost-benefit analysis should not be taken as undemocratic. On the contrary, it should be seen as a means of fortifying democratic goals by insuring that government decisions are responsive not to temporary fears but to well-informed public judgments.

AGGRAVATING SOCIAL INFLUENCES: INFORMATIONAL AND REPUTATIONAL CASCADES

The availability heuristic does not, of course, operate in a social vacuum. It interacts with emphatically social processes.[11] The first of those processes involves the spread of information within social networks and societies in general. The second process involves the role of reputation, and, in particular, people's desire to protect their own.

Especially in the modern era, risk perceptions can go viral. One reason is that when individuals do not have information of their own, initial signals by a few people may initiate an informational cascade, with significant consequences for private and public behavior, and potentially with distorting effects on regulatory policy. When the public is fearful, it may be because of cascade effects, leading people to rely on what other people think, and thus lending their voices to an increasingly loud chorus—even if there is little or no reason for fear.

In chapter 1, we saw that cascade effects play a role in the spread of conspiracy theories. Now turn to environmental risks and imagine that Anita says that abandoned hazardous waste sites are dangerous, or that she initiates protest activity because such a site is located nearby. Benjamin, otherwise skeptical or unsure, may go along with Anita. Charles, otherwise unsure, may be convinced that if Anita and Benjamin share the same belief, the belief must be true; and it will take a confident Declan to resist the shared judgments of Anita, Benjamin, and Charles. The result of this set of influences can be informational cascades, as hundreds, thousands, or millions of people come to accept a certain belief simply because of what they think other people think.[12]

There is nothing fanciful in the idea. Cascade effects help account for widespread public concern about abandoned hazardous waste dumps (a problem to be sure, but not the most serious environmental hazard), and they spurred excessive public fears of the pesticide Alar in the late 1980s. Such effects helped produce massive declines in beef production in Europe in connection with bovine spongiform encephalopathy, sometimes known as mad cow disease; they have also spurred fear of genetically engineered food in Europe.

Now turn to the reputational side. If many people are alarmed about some risk, you might not voice your doubts about whether the alarm is justified, simply in order not to seem obtuse, cruel, or indifferent. You might be especially likely to silence yourself if the alarm is felt by people who are your friends or in your social network. And if many people believe that a certain risk is trivial, you might not disagree through words or deeds, lest you appear cowardly or confused. The result of these forces can also be cascade effects, and those effects can produce a public demand for regulation even if the risks are small. At the same time, there may be little or no demand for regulation of risks that are, in fact, quite large. Self-interested private groups can exploit these forces. For instance, European companies have tried to play up fears of genetically engineered food as a way of fending off American competition.

As we saw in chapter 1, there are interactions between the availability heuristic and cascade effects. A particular incident may spread rapidly from some people to others, giving rise to *availability cascades*.[13] If such an incident is the source of the spread of information or the reputational effects, an availability cascade may be at work, perhaps leading people to think that a rare or isolated event is reflective of some terrible social risk.

Cost-benefit analysis has a natural role here. If agencies are disciplined by that form of analysis, they will have a degree of insulation from cascade effects produced by informational and reputational forces, even when the availability heuristic is at work. The effect of cost-benefit analysis is to subject misfearing to a kind of technocratic scrutiny—to insure that the public demand for regulation is not rooted in myth and to insure as well that government is regulating real risks even when the public demand is low. And here, too, there is no democratic problem with the inquiry into consequences. If people's concern is fueled by the information spread by others, and if such information is unreliable, a technocratic constraint on "hot" popular reactions is hardly inconsistent with democratic ideals. Similarly, there is nothing undemocratic about a governmental effort to shift resources to serious, life-threatening problems that have not gotten public attention as a result of cascade effects.

EMOTIONS AND PROBABILITY NEGLECT

Because of the availability heuristic, people can have an inaccurate assessment of probability. But sometimes people focus on bad outcomes and not much on the question of probability, especially when strong emotions are involved. What affects thought and behavior is the worst case, not the likelihood that it will occur. Here is another source of misfearing.

The phenomenon of *probability neglect* received its clearest empirical confirmation in a striking study of when people pay attention to outcomes, and when they focus on probability as well.[14] In the relatively emotion-free setting, participants were told that the experiment entailed some chance of a $20 penalty. Some of the subjects were told that there was only a 1 percent chance of receiving the bad outcome (the $20 loss), while others were told that the chance was 99 percent. Not surprisingly, the difference in probability mattered greatly. The difference between the median willingness to pay for a 1 percent chance and the median payment for a 99 percent chance was large: $1 to avoid a 1 percent chance, and $18 to avoid a 99 percent chance.

In the strong-emotion setting, subjects were asked to imagine that they were taking part in an experiment involving some chance of a "short, painful, but not dangerous electric shock." Here again, some of the subjects were told that there was only a 1 percent chance of receiving the bad outcome (the electric shock), while others were told that the chance was 99 percent. In this setting, probability mattered a lot less. The median willingness to pay was $7 to avoid a 1 percent chance of an electric shock—and $10 to avoid a 99 percent chance! The general implication is clear: when people's emotions are especially strong—when System 1 is activated—people might well focus on bad outcomes and not pay much attention to the likelihood that they will occur.

There is much evidence in the same vein. Consider these findings:

1. When people discuss a low-probability risk, their concern rises even if the discussion consists mostly of apparently trustworthy assurances that the probability of harm is small.[15]
2. If people are asked how much they will pay for flight insurance for losses resulting from "terrorism," they will pay

more than if they are asked how much they will pay for flight insurance for all causes.[16]

3. People show "alarmist bias." When presented with competing accounts of danger, they tend to gravitate toward, and to accept, the more alarming account.[17]
4. In experiments designed to test levels of anxiety in anticipation of a painful electric shock of varying intensity, the probability that people would actually receive the shock had no effect. As the study's authors noted, "Evidently, the mere thought of receiving a shock is enough to arouse individuals, but the precise likelihood of being shocked has little impact on level of arousal."[18]

We need not venture into controversial territory in order to observe that some risks seem to produce extremely sharp, largely visceral reactions. The role of cost-benefit analysis is straightforward here. Just as the Senate was designed to have a "cooling effect" on the passions of the House of Representatives, cost-benefit analysis can help insure that policy is driven not by hysteria or alarm but by a full appreciation of the effects of relevant risks and of trying to control them. Nor is cost-benefit analysis, in this setting, only a check on unwarranted regulation. It can and should serve as a spur to regulation as well. If risks do not produce visceral reactions, partly because the underlying activities do not provoke vivid mental images, cost-benefit analysis can show that they warrant regulatory control. The elimination of lead in gasoline, driven by cost-benefit analysis, is a case in point.

SYSTEMIC EFFECTS AND "HEALTH-HEALTH TRADE-OFFS"

Often regulation has complex systemic effects. A decision to ban asbestos may cause manufacturers to use less safe substitutes. In compliance with the Montreal Protocol, the 1987 treaty that called for phasing out ozone-depleting chemicals, the US government has prohibited certain asthma medications on the grounds that they emit such chemicals. The problem is that such a prohibition could put asthma patients at risk by increasing the price of their medicines and perhaps by making their preferred medicines unavailable. Aggressive regulation of certain forms of air pollution can increase electricity prices, and such regulation may harm poor people.[19] Higher prices for energy are especially hard on people who do not have a lot of money.

These are a few examples of the many situations in which a government agency is inevitably making "health-health trade-offs" in light of the systemic effects of one-shot interventions. Any regulation that imposes high costs may, by virtue of that fact, produce some risks to life and health, since richer people are likely to be safer as well.[20] An advantage of cost-benefit analysis is that it tends to overcome people's tendency to focus on parts of problems, by requiring them to look globally at the consequences of apparently isolated actions.

DANGERS ON-SCREEN, BENEFITS OFF-SCREEN

Why do some people believe that minimal risks from pesticides should be regulated, even if they do not much worry about other minimal risks, such as those from X-rays? Why are people so concerned about the risks of genetically modified food when many experts believe that those risks are quite low—lower, in fact, than the risks from high levels of sugar consumption, which may not much trouble people?

Consider this finding: when people think that a product or activity is dangerous, they tend to think that it has low benefits too.[21] And when people think that a product or activity is highly beneficial, they tend to think that it is not dangerous. In people's minds, danger and benefit tend to be bundled, even though it is certainly possible that some activities are harmful in some ways and beneficial in others (consider coal-fired power plants, which emit high levels of pollution, but also produce cheap energy).

The obvious conclusion is that sometimes people favor regulation of some risks because the underlying activities are not seen to have compensating benefits.[22] The problem is that in such cases, people do not see that difficult trade-offs are involved. Dangers are effectively on-screen, but benefits are off-screen.

An important factor here is *loss aversion*, which leads people to see a loss from the status quo as more undesirable than a gain is seen as desirable.[23] To appreciate the power of loss aversion, consider an ingenious study of teacher incentives.[24] Many people have been interested in encouraging teachers to do a better job of improving their students' achievements. The results of providing economic incentives are decidedly mixed; unfortunately, many of these efforts have failed.[25] But the relevant study enlisted loss aversion by giving teachers money in advance and telling them that if students did not show real improvements, *the teachers would have to give back the money*. The result was a significant increase in math scores—indeed, an increase equivalent to a substantial improvement in teacher quality. The underlying idea here is that losses from the status quo are especially unwelcome, and people will work hard to avoid those losses.[26]

In the context of risk regulation, the consequence of loss aversion is that any newly introduced risk, or any aggravation of existing risks, might well be seen as a serious problem, even if the accompanying benefits are both real and large. When a new risk adds danger, people may focus on the danger itself and not on the benefits that accompany the danger. In these circumstances, the role of cost-benefit analysis should not be obscure. It can be a necessary corrective, by placing all of the various effects on-screen.

FEAR ITSELF

The behavioral argument for cost-benefit analysis is now in place. It is true but obvious to say that a lack of information can lead to an inadequate or excessive demand for regulation, or a form of "paranoia and neglect." What is less obvious is that predictable features of cognition may lead to a public demand for regulation that is not based on the facts. Self-interested private groups and political actors can exploit those features of cognition, attempting to enlist availability and probability neglect so as to propagate misfearing. In many cases, cost-benefit analysis demonstrates that regulatory controls are desirable; consider the problem of ozone-depleting chemicals, where the Reagan administration favored aggressive regulation, in part because cost-benefit analysis demonstrated that it was justified.[27] When intuitions and anecdotes are unreliable, when poor priority setting is a problem, or when interest groups press public officials in their preferred directions, cost-benefit analysis serves as an indispensable safeguard.

CHAPTER 4

THE LAWS OF HAPPINESS

FIVE CLAIMS

In this chapter, I attempt to defend five claims.

1. In advance, people greatly overestimate the harmful effects of many bad events on their happiness, largely because they do not anticipate the remarkable human capacity to adapt. This capacity stems in part from a distinctive feature of *attention*: after a short period, people who have suffered many losses do not focus, constantly or much, on those losses. Some losses turn out to be illusory or at least exaggerated, in the sense that they inflict far less damage than people anticipate.
2. It is important for the legal system to distinguish between harms that impose enduring losses, such as chronic pain and mental illness, and harms that do not, such as losses

of fingers and toes. The distinction between enduring and illusory losses—for which ringing in the ears and loss of toes are illustrative cases, respectively—has many implications for economic and regulatory policy.

3. Both juries and judges are likely to make mistaken judgments, in a way that produces both inflated and insufficient damage awards. One reason for these errors is that in evaluating losses, observers neglect the capacity to adapt. Another reason is that the legal system asks juries and judges to focus on, and thus to attend to, losses to which plaintiffs might well devote little attention in their ordinary lives. In short, the legal system almost certainly produces *focusing illusions* in tort cases.
4. Without acknowledging that it is doing so, the legal system appears to be awarding "capability damages" under the rubric of damages for "pain and suffering." Juries award damages for the loss of capabilities, even in contexts in which people are not suffering a loss in the enjoyment of their lives.
5. An understanding of our capacity to err, in thinking about what causes happiness and unhappiness, raises the serious possibility that many policies, both fiscal and regulatory, are poorly directed. Governments might be expending resources in the false hope that the expenditures will improve well-being.

Now for the details.

DOLLARS AND WELFARE

Suppose that Jones has lost the use of two toes, or that Smith has become blind, or that Wilson has been paralyzed from the waist down, or that Holmes has developed post-traumatic anxiety, or that Johnson has been subjected to racial harassment, or that Benson has suffered a loss of cognitive capacity, or that Dickerson has become impotent. The legal system allows people to recover for "pain and suffering." The adverse effects captured in the idea of pain and suffering are undoubtedly real, and the legal system should attempt to deter them and to provide compensation. Loss of well-being is often the most serious harm that people face—far more serious than strictly economic losses. But the resulting damage awards are notoriously variable, and it is not clear that they are in any sense rational or coherent. An initial problem is the extreme difficulty of translating pain and suffering into monetary equivalents.

In many states, people are also permitted to recover "hedonic damages," designed to capture people's loss of enjoyment of their lives. The line between pain and suffering on the one hand and hedonic damages on the other can be obscure; events that cause suffering also impose hedonic losses. The basic distinction is that hedonic damages cover neither affirmative distress nor suffering but forgone gains, as when people are unable to engage in valued activities such as sports. People might seek hedonic damages for the loss of a dog; for the inability to have sexual relations; for the loss of a limb; for the loss of use of an elbow; for depression and self-consciousness as a result of amputation of an arm; or for becoming bedridden and thus requiring constant care. Here, too, it is extremely difficult to translate the relevant losses into monetary equivalents.

Even before the translation occurs, juries and judges investigating hedonic damages and pain and suffering are asked, in a sense, to serve as "hedometers," assessing the adverse welfare effects associated with one loss or another. For purposes of analysis, I shall refer to pain and suffering and also to hedonic damages as "hedonic losses," while recognizing that the principles behind them are distinct. The idea of hedonic losses is meant to capture the utility losses or (subjective) welfare losses produced by some bad event. I use the word *hedonic* to underline the connection with the emerging research that attempts to measure how people are enjoying their lives; the word *utility*, understood in the standard way, would work equally well.

As the law now stands, the central goal is one of appropriate compensation or "making whole"—with the understanding that the compensatory award is supposed to restore plaintiffs to the hedonic state, or the level of well-being, that they would have enjoyed had the injury not occurred. Under appropriate assumptions, the award of compensation, properly calculated, will also create the right deterrent signal, so that accurate awards will promote social welfare as well. If those who are harmed seek and receive damages, the goal of compensation and the goal of deterrence should march hand in hand. As we shall see, however, the two goals may diverge—for example, as when a monetary award for serious pain does little or nothing to make the plaintiff "whole" but does deter the kinds of acts that create serious pain or chronic headaches. In such cases, an award that is hard to defend in compensatory terms might nonetheless be justified as a means of promoting the right level of deterrence.

BAD EVENTS AND WELL-BEING

Human beings are unexpectedly resilient. As a result, many apparently significant injuries do not inflict substantial long-term hedonic harms.[1] Perhaps above all, it is important to distinguish between those conditions that impose large and persistent losses and those that, because of human resilience, bring about only transitional, short-term, or modest losses.

For purposes of law and policy, a key point is that people are often unable to anticipate the effects of bad events on how much they enjoy their lives, and their inability on this count produces forecasting errors. A central problem here is *adaptation neglect*: people neglect the extent to which they will be able to adapt to adverse changes and conditions. When we adapt, it is usually not because of conscious efforts to do so; we are speaking of a general feature of human beings, not of successful efforts to embrace some form of Stoicism. Because of our power to adapt, we are not nearly as badly off, in terms of how we feel from day to day, as we expect.

It is reasonable to ask how enjoyment, or hedonic effect, is measured. In most of the relevant research, people use a scale of, say, 0 to 8 to answer questions about how happy they are or how satisfied they are with their lives. Skeptics might wonder whether answers to such questions tell us anything at all. As a matter of fact, people's answers do turn out to be associated with independent tests of hedonic state, including frequent smiling, smiling with the eyes, quality of sleep, happiness ratings by friends, self-reported health, frequent expressions of positive emotions, and being sociable and outgoing.[2] To date, no empirical work has falsified or even seriously undermined the suggestion that people's reports of global happiness reflect their actual happiness, understood as subjective mental states.

Skeptics might persist at this point, suggesting that what matters is not what people say about their global life satisfaction but, instead, how people are actually feeling from day to day or from moment to moment. And, in fact, efforts have been made to assess people's subjective well-being in this way.[3] We should not be surprised to find that in some areas, people's answers to global questions will be different from aggregations of moments. Asked about how their lives are going, divorced or unmarried people might give less than positive answers, focusing on the fact that they are unmarried; but perhaps unmarried people experience more, and not less, moment-by-moment happiness. I will return to this possibility below.

It would also be sensible for skeptics to worry that whatever the measure, people who suffer from adverse conditions might be engaging in "scale recalibration" to reflect those conditions. It is possible that colostomy patients would rank themselves high, on a bounded scale, on the grounds that they are pretty happy, *considering their condition*; but perhaps they would rank themselves much lower if they were comparing themselves with healthy people. If so, the surprisingly high rankings of those with adverse conditions suggest not high levels of subjective well-being but a sense that things are going well enough, all things considered. We do not yet know for sure, but this reasonable conjecture appears to be wrong. A number of efforts have been made to test for scale recalibration, and, thus far, the verdict is clear: there is no strong evidence of recalibration, and considerable evidence to the contrary.[4] I shall be speaking here mainly of findings about global life satisfaction, because these are the most numerous, but on occasion I will refer to moment-by-moment measures as well.

PEOPLE'S UNEXPECTED POWER TO ADAPT

Let us begin with the limited hedonic effects of many *positive* changes. Lottery winners are not happier a year later than other people are.[5] Marriage is often thought to be associated with increased happiness, but after a few years, married people are no happier than they were before.[6] Apparently marriage produces a significant hedonic boost, but it is short lived, and people return fairly quickly to their premarriage state. Increases in salary have a similar feature; a 20 percent increase is highly welcome, but after a short period, people do not show a significant long-term change in self-reported happiness or life satisfaction.

With respect to many negative changes, including those that concern the legal system, the hedonic effects are often surprisingly small. It is remarkable but true that paraplegics are only modestly less happy than other people.[7] Young people who have lost a limb as a result of cancer show no less happiness than similarly situated young people who have not had cancer.[8] Moderately disabled people typically recover to their predisability level of happiness after two years.[9] Kidney dialysis patients do not show lower levels of happiness than healthy people.[10] Colostomy patients report levels of happiness that are about the same as those of people who have not undergone a colostomy.[11] Intriguingly, men and women with a colostomy greatly exaggerate their actual level of happiness before they had the procedure, while those with reversed colostomies—enabling them to have normal bowel movements again—report that before the reversal, they were far less happy than they actually were.[12] I will return to these findings below.

From this evidence, it is fair to conclude that healthy people systematically overestimate the adverse effects of many physical problems on their subjective well-being. Those who face such problems experience unexpectedly little in the way of hedonic loss.[13] As I have noted, it is possible to question the relevant findings; social scientists do not yet have hedometers. But from the existing research, the basic conclusions follow whether we rely on global measures of happiness or life satisfaction, or on moment-by-moment measures of mood and happiness, which might seem to be even more reliable.[14]

In a less dramatic vein, assistant professors greatly overstate the effect on their subjective happiness of not being granted tenure.[15] They expect that this failure to gain job security will affect their happiness for many years—and, in part for that reason, they greatly want to be tenured. But after a few years, those who were denied tenure say they are no less happy than their tenured colleagues.

Many voters believe that the outcome of an election will greatly affect their happiness a month after the election is held. Surely they will be less happy, and maybe even miserable, if their preferred candidate loses. But in that month, supporters of losing and winning candidates are as happy as they were before they went to the polls.[16] People have been found to overestimate the welfare effects of personal insults, the outcomes of sports events, and romantic breakups. In all of these circumstances, the adverse effects, while real and for a time severe, are surprisingly modest and short term.[17]

ENDURING VERSUS LLLUSORY LOSSES (OR LOUD, UNPLEASANT NOISES VERSUS FEWER TOES)

None of these points is meant to deny the fact that some positive events and conditions create large and enduring gains, while some negative events and conditions give rise to serious and persistent losses. Various drugs, such as the medication Prozac, apparently create long-term boosts in subjective well-being. It is easy to imagine changes in the allocation of time—from, say, commuting and work to socializing, vacations, and leisure—that would produce enduring benefits. It is wrong to say that people's resilience, and their capacity for adaptation, insure that social changes and interventions are powerless to affect happiness or life satisfaction.

On the negative side, consider the instructive (and, in a sense, defining) example of loud, unpleasant noises, which people dislike intensely, and which they do not dislike less as time passes.[18] With respect to highway noise, people show approximately the same level of irritation over a period of more than a year. As time passes, they become more pessimistic, not less so, about their ability to adjust to the noise.[19] Nor do the physiological effects of noise diminish in children over a significant period of time,[20] while a study of college students found *greater* levels of annoyance at dormitory noise at the end of the academic year than at the beginning.[21] We should conclude that a loud ringing in the ears will impose very serious and quite long-term hedonic losses.

Many adverse conditions belong in the same category as noise. Just as people overestimate the hedonic harm of many physical losses, such as kidney failure (leading to dialysis) and colostomy, so do they underestimate the effects of depression and chronic pain.[22] Leading sources of unhappiness include mental illness, such as anxiety and obsessive-compulsive disorder; subjectively reported poor health (above all persistent pain); unemployment, which can have truly terrible adverse effects;[23] and separation from a spouse.[24] Some research suggests that while the process of divorce is distressing, it is not as bad as separation. Notably, once the marriage has ended legally, most people adjust fairly quickly and return to their predivorce state of contentment.[25]

More speculatively, we might suggest that some medical conditions produce significant and enduring losses to the extent that people have to keep anticipating medical results and must consider, with some frequency, whether they are getting better or worse. Certain cancers, in which significant periods of time are spent expecting and receiving results, might well fall in the same category as loud noise. Similarly, the process of adaptation might be slowed, and focusing on painful thoughts might increase, if people are worrying about whether a serious medical condition can be improved or reversed. Severe facial disfigurement might produce enduring hedonic losses because of the social consequences of having a disfigured face.

It is therefore important to distinguish among four phenomena: (1) gains that are significant and enduring, such as those brought about by pain relief; (2) gains that are largely illusory, such as those produced by an increase in salary; (3) losses that are significant and enduring, such as those caused by pain, depression, and anxiety; and (4) losses that turn out to be low or even illusory (at least in the long term), such as those produced by losing a limb or by a colostomy. For purposes of the legal questions on which I am focusing here, the latter two phenomena are the most important.

FAILURES OF FORECASTING

From these findings, we can draw two general conclusions. The first is that many apparently serious losses inflict relatively little in the way of long-term hedonic harm. The second is that people do not anticipate this fact; they expect far more harm than they actually experience. A key reason is that people underestimate the power of psychological mechanisms that immunize them from the degree of hedonic loss that they expect to face in the event that things go wrong. It is important to try to understand the sources of the resulting errors.

In many cases, people are subject to "immune neglect": they do not see the power of their internal psychological immune system, which greatly diminishes the detrimental effects of apparently significant changes. A related problem is that people demonstrate a kind of "impact bias,"[26] in the form of a tendency to exaggerate the effect of potential future events on their emotional states. The exaggerations are sometimes described as a consequence of "durability bias,"[27] understood as a propensity to overestimate how long an undesirable effect will leave an emotional imprint. According to one overview: "The conclusion from this body of research is that people are systematically wrong in their expectations about the life circumstances that will increase or decrease their happiness, which in turn implies that life choices that people make in their pursuit of happiness are also likely to be wrong."[28]

The implication for the legal system is clear. If people misjudge the effects of adverse events in their own lives, there is every reason to assume that juries (and judges) will make similar mistakes in assessing the effects of those events on plaintiffs—especially, but not only, when they are projecting future losses. As we shall see, the same point applies to policy makers, including regulators.

ADAPTATION, ATTENTION, AND FOCUSING ILLUSIONS

Why do bad events often have relatively little effect on people's subjective well-being? The first mechanism is adaptation, stemming from people's diminished sensitivity to changes over time. What once seemed like a large hedonic boost or a serious hedonic loss often becomes part of life's furniture. People do not anticipate this fact—hence, adaptation neglect.

A second mechanism involves *attention*. When apparently major losses inflict surprisingly little hedonic harm, it is often because people do not focus much on those losses after a period of transition. There is some evidence that adaptation is the dominant explanation for people's mistaken forecasts with respect to the effects of health conditions. In particular, alerting people to the possibility of adaptation reduces hedonic forecasting errors, whereas efforts that involve attention have no such effect.[29]

The term *hedonic adaptation* refers to the diminishing intensity of people's emotional reactions to adverse events, which leads them to lose less than they had expected.[30] As I have suggested, those who have been denied tenure, or have lost the use of a limb, or have had a colonoscopy, will react intensely at first, but after a year, their affective response will diminish greatly. When moderately disabled people exhibit little or no hedonic loss, adaptation, thus understood, is the key reason.

But attention is also important.[31] When people lose the use of an arm, they do not think, most of the time, about the fact that one of their arms does not work. Instead, they focus on the central features of their everyday lives: jobs, meals, their relationships, the book they are reading, or the television show they are watching. To the extent that significant losses do not cause hedonic damages, it is frequently because people's attention is not usually focused on those losses. Daniel Kahneman describes the problem with a wonderful maxim: "Nothing in life matters quite as much as you think it does while you are thinking about it."[32] A failure to focus on what has been lost helps to explain the absence of substantial hedonic effects from apparently great losses.

Focusing illusions help to account for people's surprise at the absence of such effects. Suppose that you are asked how much your happiness would be affected if you lost the use of a finger or if a leg injury prevented you from running. You might well say that the effect would be horrible—even though it probably would not be. The reason it probably would not be is that most of the time, few people are much affected by whether all of their fingers work or whether they can run. People are surprised by this because they focus specifically on the loss and thus conclude that it would have substantial effects, neglecting to see that those who have experienced the loss do not, most of the time, focus on it.

For hedonic forecasting, the general point is that when asked to focus on a particular aspect of life or a particular element of well-being, people are likely to make serious blunders, simply because in life, we usually do not focus on any particular aspect or any particular ingredient.

Here is a simple demonstration of a focusing illusion. Many Americans appear to believe that they would be happier if they lived in California.[33] This belief is shared both by people who live there and by people who do not. But, in fact, those who live in California are not happier than those who live elsewhere. Focusing on California weather in particular, both Californians and Ohioans believe that those in California are happier even though weather is not an important determinant of most people's happiness. When "primed" to think about weather, or any other factor that is a small ingredient in most people's subjective well-being, focusing illusions lead people to give excessive attention to that factor.

These points, and an understanding of attention in particular, help to explain why some conditions do produce serious or enduring losses. Noise is the exemplar here. Loud and irritating noises create such losses because it is hard to disregard them. Similarly, conditions that impose enduring losses command attention; people necessarily focus on them. It is hard, for example, not to attend to chronic pain. When people are initially separated from their spouses, they are focused, much of the time, on that fact. A few years afterward, divorce becomes a background fact, not a source of constant attention. Parents whose children are suffering or needing constant attention will experience serious hedonic losses. It is hard not to attend to the needs or distress of one's children, and such distress can serve, for parents, as exceedingly loud noise (with remarkable amplifiers).

Other puzzles in the hedonic literature can be similarly understood. Marriage produces a short-term burst in life satisfaction because those who are recently married are thinking, much of the time, about their recent nuptials. But after a few years, marriage ceases to create such a hedonic boost—even if the union is entirely happy.

We are now in a position to understand one of the most counterintuitive findings in the hedonic literature. The life satisfaction of many disabled people is not substantially lower than that of able-bodied people, and for some forms of disabilities, life satisfaction is essentially the same. Yet many disabled people believe that they were significantly happier before they were disabled, and there is clear evidence that they would pay a great deal to return to their predisability state. If the analysis here is correct, disabled people may themselves be subject to, or made subject to, a focusing illusion, when they are asked how their lives were (would be) different when they were (if they were) not disabled, or how much they would pay not to be disabled in terms of money or remaining years of life.

We do not have enough evidence to know if this claim is correct. But if it seems preposterous, consider the following question: Would you be happier if the weather where you live were automatically converted to the weather of San Diego? You might well say yes. But you would probably be wrong.

JURIES, ADAPTATION, AND ATTENTION

For the legal system, there is a concrete implication. Juries and judges are likely to make hedonic judgment errors, often exaggerating the hedonic effects of losses. The first problem is adaptation neglect. The second problem is that when asked to award damages for a certain loss, the attention of the jury (and the judge) is fixed specifically on the loss in question. It is as if juries were asked, "Would you be happier in California?" Focused keenly on a particular injury, juries are unlikely to see that, most of the time, the plaintiff may not be much focused on the particular injury. The very circumstances of a trial invite adaptation neglect and create the focusing illusion.[34] In the legal system, juries and judges are required to contemplate the importance of the things that they are thinking about intensely.

Suppose, for example, that a plaintiff has lost two fingers or an arm, and the jury is asked to monetize the loss, including the pain and suffering associated with it. Because of the power of the psychological immune system, it is not implausible to think that the loss is short term and of minimal impact. After a period of adjustment, those who lose two fingers or even an arm may be only modestly worse off, in hedonic terms, than those who suffer no such loss. In fact, they might not be worse off at all; recall that there is no discernible hedonic difference between ordinary people and those who have lost a limb as a result of cancer.[35]

Juries and judges are unlikely to understand or even to accept this point. In all probability, they will fall into adaptation neglect and suffer from a focusing illusion. It is reasonable to expect that in awarding damages, the legal system will be subject to a systematic bias as a result. We might reach a similar conclusion for hedonic damages. Suppose that someone has lost mobility, so that she can no longer ski or play tennis. If the question is how much that person has lost in terms of "enjoyment of life," understood in hedonic terms, the answer may well be little or nothing.

It is both true and important that even if long-term harms are not likely, the short-term harms might be severe. People might experience a level of distress, fear, mourning, and grief for which a significant degree of compensation is justified. Large monetary awards might well be given for short periods of intense suffering or sense of loss. The point is that juries are likely to exaggerate the long-term effects and thus give excessive damage awards.

As a result of hedonic forecasting errors, it is also possible that juries are awarding small sums in cases in which the hedonic loss is likely to be high. Suppose, for example, that a plaintiff is suffering chronic back pain. The pain may be relatively low grade, but it is persistent. It is not difficult to find cases in which juries award low damages in such instances.[36] For example:

- $4,000 for an accident producing headaches three to four times per week and persistent pain in the hands, knees, and shoulders;[37]
- $25,000 to a nineteen-year-old woman whose accident caused a painful hip deformity, as well as headaches, ringing in the ears, permanent arthritis in her hip, and backaches;[38]
- $47,000 for an accident causing a herniated disk in the lower spine, accompanied by permanent radiating pain and restricted movement;[39] and
- $30,000 for permanent pain in the neck from a herniated cervical spinal disk and in the knee from a torn meniscus.[40]

In each case, the award seems far too low, because the injury was likely to be enduring.

In the abstract, low-level back pain, headaches, ringing in the ears, and pain in the neck and knee may not seem especially serious. These are familiar to many of us, unlike the loss of a limb. It is easy to imagine a jury concluding that while headaches are unpleasant, they can be part of daily life, whereas loss of a limb is devastating. But to the extent that headaches, ringing in the ears, and similar conditions are severe—and more to the point, chronic—they are not likely to improve much over time. Those who face these chronic conditions suffer massive hedonic losses, a fact that jurors are unlikely to appreciate.

CAPABILITY DAMAGES

On the basis of the discussion thus far, awards for pain and suffering, and for hedonic damages, are often inflated from the *hedonic* point of view. But does this mean that they are inflated from the *correct* point of view? The very ideas of "pain and suffering" and "hedonic damages" suggest attention to subjective mental states; the law's official theory speaks in explicitly hedonic terms. But it is reasonable to think that subjective mental states are not all that matter and that the legal system is attentive to this fact.

Let us shift gears from a purely Benthamite perspective, focused only on subjective mental states, to an Aristotelian one, focused on what people are able to do and to be. Suppose that Jones loses the use of a leg; suppose, too, that the loss does not affect his self-reported happiness. After a difficult but short period of adjustment, Jones is as happy as he was before the loss. In other words, Jones has experienced no hedonic loss. Should the legal system therefore disregard his injury?

What Jones has lost is a capability.[41] He cannot walk on his leg; he certainly is unable to run. He is unable to engage in many activities that he used to take for granted. Jones may not be in pain, and he may not be suffering hedonic damage. Might the legal system nonetheless award damages anyway? If the answer is yes, it is not justified by a hedonic loss. Instead, what is involved is the loss of a real and significant capability, even if hedonic measures are unable to identify it. Consider the fact that most people would likely be willing to pay significant amounts to avoid losing a capability, even if they could be persuaded that the loss would inflict no hedonic harm.

The claim on behalf of capability losses is based on the objective harm faced by those who lose physical or cognitive abilities. If people must receive kidney dialysis treatments several times a week, they have suffered a significant loss, whatever their hedonic state. As we have seen, people with colostomies do not report less happiness than people without colostomies, but at the same time, they say that they would shorten their lifespan by up to 15 percent if they could live without a colostomy.[42] Similarly, dialysis patients report little adverse hedonic effect, but many of them say that they would willingly subtract over half their remaining years in order to have normal kidney function.[43] These answers seem to suggest a concern for capabilities, not merely for hedonic states.

In invoking this evidence, I do not mean to suggest that people's statements on such points should be taken as authoritative. Begin with the case of healthy people. If such people are horrified at the prospect of having to undergo a colostomy, and if they cannot easily bear the thought of being on a dialysis machine, they might well believe (falsely) that the relevant change would make life barely livable, or so the evidence suggests.[44] Hedonic judgment errors of this kind might well be impervious to debiasing.[45] It is imaginable, for example, that people would demand a great deal to lose a leg, even if they could be given a fully adequate prosthetic (perhaps better than the original) and even if they could be given reliable evidence that they would suffer no hedonic loss after a brief period of transition. People's conclusions about what they would pay to avoid or to eliminate a loss might well reflect a hedonic judgment error. If so, policy should not be based on those conclusions. If a hedonic judgment error is at work, people are not, in fact, showing an appreciation of capability losses.

In short, I am not insisting that when people say that they want to avoid conditions that do not impose hedonic losses, they are necessarily motivated by a recognition of capability losses; a hedonic judgment error may lie behind their statements. My only contention is that when people have lost a capability, they have lost something major, even if they have suffered no hedonic loss.

For those who believe that the legal system should accept this view, two difficult questions remain. First: What kinds of capability losses should the system recognize? Second: How can capabilities be translated into monetary equivalents? At first glance, a notion of normal human functioning would seem to provide the baseline from which to measure capability loss. It would follow that if someone has lost the use of a leg or an arm, or has suffered cognitive or sexual deficits, a capability loss is involved.

Recognition of the importance of capabilities has broader implications for thinking about well-being. A person who is able to run, or who can have sexual relations, is better off than someone who lacks these capabilities, even if the difference cannot be picked up in hedonic terms. The poorly educated have less in the way of capability than the well educated, even if hedonic measures cannot identify a difference between the two groups. It is possible that people with less education do not show more negative affect, or less positive affect, during their days than people with a great deal of education do. But education, taken as such, contributes to a richer life.

In a variety of cases, supposedly hedonic damages are probably best justified as capability damages. For example, courts have awarded hedonic damages to people who have lost the ability to engage in sports.[46] Hedonic damages have been awarded for the loss of the senses of taste and smell.[47] Courts have also awarded significant hedonic damages for the loss of a limb, in a way that may reflect, or be defensible in terms of, a capability loss rather than a hedonic forecasting error.[48] Hedonic damages have been awarded where the tort victim could no longer engage in sexual activities as a result of the injury.[49]

Suppose that Jones has been severely injured and suffers a serious loss in cognitive capacity. Suppose, too, that his pain and suffering have been modest and that he has suffered little or no loss in terms of subjective well-being. Should Jones receive capability damages? Under the official theory of hedonic damages, the question is whether he has suffered a diminution in his enjoyment of life. If that idea is understood in purely hedonic terms, there is a real doubt as to whether damages should be awarded. But Jones is now unable to engage in certain activities and experiences that are available only to those who function at a particular cognitive level. The loss of the capacity for those enjoyments ought to matter.

For some of the cases, John Stuart Mill's distinction between higher and lower pleasures is clearly relevant.[50] As Mill writes: "[I]t is an unquestionable fact that those who are equally acquainted with, and equally capable of appreciating and enjoying, both, do give a most marked preference to the manner of existence which employs their higher faculties . . . [N]o intelligent human being would consent to be a fool, no instructed person would be an ignoramus, no person of feeling and conscience would be selfish and base, even though they should be persuaded that the fool, the dunce, or the rascal is better satisfied with his lot than they are with theirs."[51] When hedonic damages are awarded for the loss of cognitive capacities, judges and juries might well be responding to a logic of this kind.

BROADER LESSONS

These remarks bear on much larger questions. In this section, I offer a few brief notations.

Willingness to Pay and Happiness. Many economists and economically oriented lawyers work with the criterion of willingness to pay (WTP). If people are willing to pay $50 to eliminate a 1/100,000th risk of losing a foot, it is widely believed that government should start with that number in deciding on appropriate policies. Suppose, however, that people's WTP is a product of some kind of mistake, perhaps in the form of a focusing illusion. If so, there is a real problem. And if this is so, there are serious problems with relying on WTP, because it operates as a crude proxy for welfare effects, understood in hedonic terms. In short, hedonic forecasting errors may raise problems for standard ways of conducting cost-benefit analysis.

Suppose that people are asked, "How much would you be willing to pay to avoid a 1/100,000th chance of losing a finger?" The problem is that such questions focus the study's subjects on a certain loss and, for that reason, create a grave risk of a focusing illusion.[52]

Perhaps free markets will reduce the problem. When people pay for goods, they face a budget constraint, and they are aware of the full menu of possible expenditures—far more than in the circumstances of surveys. Perhaps in their daily lives, people will not suffer serious focusing illusions when deciding how much to pay to reduce risks, because they are alert, at the relevant times, to the full range of possible expenditures. When people have experience and obtain prompt feedback, they are far less likely to err. Nonetheless, sellers of products try their hardest to generate focusing illusions in order to get people to buy their goods. A great deal of work remains to be done on this problem, which seems to unsettle many of the standard claims and views in economic analysis of policy and law.

A Note on Meaning. I have mentioned "meaning," a concept that deserves independent analysis. If someone loses cognitive capacities, the loss is not only one of a capability; his life also becomes less meaningful. And if someone is usually in a good mood, perhaps because her life is constantly and only fun, she might think, on reflection, that her activities are superficial or even silly, and that moment-by-moment measures of her moods miss something that is exceedingly important. A global life satisfaction question might pick up this concern, but perhaps people respond to that question in hedonic terms. And even if an absence of meaning is not reflected in people's answers to survey questions, or in subjectively felt experience, it matters nonetheless.

Whether or not this is so, we can now see an additional objection to purely hedonic measures. Those who are always in happy moods may nonetheless be missing an important ingredient of well-being. Happiness, understood in hedonic terms, does matter a great deal, but well-being includes a number of disparate goods, emphatically including meaning.

ILLUSORY LOSSES, REAL HARMS, AND PRIORITY SETTING

If people make serious hedonic judgment errors in their own lives, it is highly likely that juries and judges will make equivalent errors. In particular, the legal system may well overestimate significantly the hedonic losses associated with certain injuries. The exaggerations stem in part from a failure to appreciate people's powers of adaptation (adaptation neglect) and also from the kind of focusing illusion shown when people think about the effects of weather. Apparently significant losses often turn out to be illusory, at least if they are understood in hedonic terms. In addition, those involved in the legal system may well underestimate certain losses, including those that produce chronic pain and depression.

Some injuries fall within the same category as unpleasant noises, to which people do not adapt and on which people cannot help but focus. Other injuries, such as the loss of toes, inflict little hedonic harm. Capability damages deserve independent analysis. Even if little or no hedonic loss is suffered, it is reasonable to conclude that people deserve to be compensated in the event that they lose some or all of their capabilities.

It should be clear that these points, and the emerging research findings, have implications for how policy makers might think about a wide range of important questions. These include the limits of willingness to pay, the value of national income growth, and appropriate priority setting for governments concerned with improving social well-being. Recent work strongly suggests that national income growth does have large and beneficial effects on happiness and well-being,[53] and, indeed, that there is no point of "satiation."[54] It follows that growth should be a high priority for those who are concerned about the well-being of the population. As noted, unemployment produces severe hedonic losses, and for that reason, reductions in unemployment deserve considerable attention. (See chapter 2.) Another implication is that governments should give far higher priority than they do now to relieving chronic pain and mental illness. More generally, it would not be surprising to find that governments make significant errors in fiscal and regulatory policy. If so, efforts to correct the resulting errors would produce major gains in terms of human welfare.

CHAPTER 5

THE RIGHTS OF ANIMALS

There are tens of millions of domestic dogs in the United States, owned by tens of millions of households. Over half of these households give Christmas presents to their dogs. Millions of them celebrate their dogs' birthdays. If a family's dog were somehow forced to live a short and painful life, the family would undoubtedly feel some combination of rage and grief. What can be said about dog owners can also be said about cat owners, who are more numerous still. But as a result of human action, millions, even billions, of animals, not so different from dogs and cats, live short and painful lives. Should people change their behavior? Should the law promote animal welfare? Should animals have legal rights? To answer these questions, we need to step back a bit.

Many people find the very idea of animal rights implausible and perhaps even ridiculous. Immanuel Kant urged that animals are neither rational nor self-aware. He thought of animals as "man's instruments," deserving protection only to help human beings in their relationships with one another. "He who is cruel to animals becomes hard also in his dealings with men," he wrote."[1] But the English utilitarian Jeremy Bentham took a radically different approach, going so far as to suggest that the mistreatment of animals was akin to slavery and racial discrimination:

> The day may come when the rest of the animal creation may acquire those rights which never could have been withholden from them but by the hand of tyranny. The French have already discovered that the blackness of the skin is no reason why a human being should be abandoned without redress to the caprice of a tormentor . . . A full-grown horse or dog is beyond comparison a more rational, as well as a more conversable animal, than an infant of a day, or a week, or even a month, old. But suppose the case were otherwise, what would it avail? The question is not, Can they *reason*? Nor, Can they *talk*? But, Can they *suffer*?[2]

John Stuart Mill concurred, repeating the analogy to slavery.[3] Most people consider that analogy extreme. But the animal rights debate has been gaining traction. In 2002 Germany became the first European nation to guarantee animal rights in its constitution, adding the words "and animals" to a clause that obliges the state to respect and protect the dignity of human beings.[4] The European Union has done a great deal to reduce animal suffering. In the United States, consumer pressures have led to improved conditions for animals used as food.

Notwithstanding its occasional appeal, the idea of animal rights has also been disputed with extraordinary intensity. Many people think that animal rights advocates are fanatical and even bizarre, willing to trample on important human interests for the sake of rats, mice, and salmon. For their part, some advocates believe that their adversaries are selfish, unthinking, cruel, and even morally blind.

In this chapter, I have three goals. The first is to suggest the possibility of reducing the intensity of the debate by demonstrating that almost everyone believes in animal rights, at least to some degree.

The real question is what the idea of "animal rights" actually means. The second is to give a clear survey of the lay of the land—to show the range of possible positions and to explore what issues separate reasonable people. In this way, I attempt to provide a kind of primer for current and coming debates. My third goal is to defend a particular position about animal rights, one that, like Bentham's, emphasizes the issue of animal suffering. This position requires rejection of some of the most radical claims by animal rights advocates, especially those that stress the "autonomy" of animals, or that object to any human control and use of animals.

But my position has strong implications of its own. For example, it suggests that to avoid unjustified suffering, the uses of animals in entertainment, scientific experiments, and agriculture should be regulated. One hundred years from now, some of those uses might well be regarded as forms of unconscionable barbarity. In this respect, Bentham and Mill were not entirely wrong to offer an analogy between the treatment of animals and human slavery.

WHAT ANIMAL RIGHTS MIGHT ENTAIL

THE STATUS QUO

If we understand "rights" to confer legal protection against harm, then many animals already do have rights, and the idea of animal rights is not terribly controversial. And if we take the word to mean a moral claim to such protection, there is general agreement that animals possess certain kinds of rights. Of course, some people, including the French philosopher Descartes, have argued that animals are like robots and lack emotions; according to this view, people should be allowed to treat an animal however they wish. But to most people, including sharp critics of the very idea of animal rights, this position is untenable. Almost everyone agrees that people should not be able to torture animals or engage in acts of cruelty against them. And indeed, state law contains a wide range of protections against cruelty and neglect. We can build upon existing law to identify a simple, minimal position in favor of animal rights: *the law should prevent acts of cruelty to animals.*

In the United States, state anticruelty laws include prohibitions on torturing, beating, injuring, and the like, and they also impose affirmative duties on people with animals in their care. New York's provisions are representative. In that state, criminal penalties are imposed on anyone who transports an animal in a cruel or inhumane manner, or in such a way as to subject it to torture or suffering—conditions that can come about through neglect. People who transport an animal on railroads or in cars are required to allow the animal out for rest, feeding, and water every five hours. Nonowners who have impounded or confined an animal are obliged to provide breathable air, water, shelter, and food. Those who abandon an animal, including a pet, in public places face criminal penalties. A separate provision forbids people to torture, beat, maim, or kill any animal, and also requires them to provide adequate food and drink.

Like most states, New York forbids overworking animals or using them for work when they are not physically fit. Compare in this regard the unusually protective California statute, which imposes criminal liability on negligent as well as intentional overworking, overdriving, or torturing of animals. *Torture* is defined not only in its conventional sense but also to include any act or omission "whereby unnecessary or unjustified physical pain or suffering is caused or permitted."

If taken seriously, provisions of this kind would do a great deal to protect animals from suffering, injury, and premature death. But animal rights, as recognized by state law, are sharply limited, and for two major reasons. First, enforcement can occur only through public prosecution. If horses and cows are being abused at a local farm, or if greyhounds are forced to live in small cages in violation of state law, protection will come only if the prosecutor decides to provide it. Of course, prosecutors have limited budgets, and animal protection is rarely a high priority. The result is that violations of state law occur with some frequency, and there is no way to prevent them. The anticruelty prohibitions contrast sharply, in this respect, with most prohibitions protecting human beings, which can be enforced both publicly and privately. For example, the prohibitions on assault and theft can be enforced through criminal prosecutions, brought by public officials, and also by injured citizens, proceeding directly against those who have violated the law.

Second, the anticruelty provisions of state law contain large exceptions. They do not apply to the use of animals for medical or scientific purposes. To a large degree, they do not apply to the production and use of animals as food. The latter exemption is the most important. Billions of animals are killed for food annually in the United States, with 24 million chickens and some 323,000 pigs slaughtered every day.[5] The cruel and abusive practices sometimes involved in contemporary farming are largely unregulated at the state level. Because the overwhelming majority of animals are raised and used for food, the coverage of anticruelty laws is actually relatively narrow.

ENFORCING EXISTING RIGHTS

If the suffering of animals matters—and most people seem to think that it does—we should be troubled by these limitations. Perhaps the least controversial response would be to narrow the "enforcement gap" by allowing private suits to be brought in cases of unlawful cruelty and neglect. Reforms might be adopted with the limited purpose of stopping misconduct that is already against the law, so that the law actually means in practice what it says on paper. Here, then, we can find a slightly less minimal understanding of animal rights. On this view, representatives of animals (typically their owners) should be able to bring private suits to insure that anticruelty and related laws are actually enforced. If, for example, a farm is treating horses cruelly and in violation of legal requirements, a suit could be brought on behalf of those animals to bring about compliance.

In a sense, this would be a dramatic proposal, because it could even be understood to mean that animals should be allowed to sue in their own name (though the owner would be the more likely plaintiff). Whoever the nominal plaintiff was, there would be no question that the suit was being brought to protect animals, not human beings. The very idea might seem absurd. But it is simpler and more conventional than it appears. Needless to say, any animal would be represented by a human being, just like any other litigant who lacks ordinary (human) competence. For example, the interests of children are protected by prosecutors and also by trustees and guardians in private litigation brought on children's behalf.

Why should anyone oppose an effort to promote greater enforcement of existing law by supplementing the prosecutor's power with private lawsuits that are squarely founded in that law? Perhaps the best answer—and it is a reasonable one—lies in a fear that some or many of those lawsuits would be unjustified, even frivolous. Perhaps animal representatives would bring a flurry of suits, not because of cruelty or neglect or any violation of law, but because of some kind of ideological commitment to improving animal welfare in a way that might go well beyond what the law actually says. If this is a genuine risk, it might make sense to require anyone who brings a frivolous suit to pay the defendant's legal fees (and perhaps additional penalties as well).

Of course, there would be issues in deciding on the identity of representatives and choosing the people who would pick them. And there would be strong and legitimate objections to any effort to allow suits to be brought not by but against an animal's owner. But insofar as owners are authorized to enforce existing law, we may not yet be in especially controversial territory. Many of those who ridicule the idea of animal rights believe in anticruelty laws, and with appropriate qualifications, they should support efforts to insure that those laws are actually enforced.

INCREASED REGULATION OF SCIENCE, FARMING, AND MORE

We might focus our attention not only on the "enforcement gap" but also on areas where current law offers little or no protection. In short, the law might consider appropriate regulation of scientific experiments, entertainment, and (above all) farming to safeguard against unnecessary and unjustified animal suffering. It is easy to imagine a set of initiatives that would do a great deal here, and indeed, European nations have moved in just this direction. There are many possibilities; some of them are reflected, to one or another degree, in existing practice.

Building on that practice, private institutions or the law might direct scientists to justify experiments on animals by showing, in front of some kind of committee or board, that (1) such experiments are actually necessary or promising and (2) the animals involved will not be subjected to unnecessary suffering. If dogs or chimpanzees are going to be used as test subjects in the development of some medical treatment, they should not be treated cruelly, and they should be decently fed and housed.

With respect to agriculture, controls might be similarly motivated. Of course, it would be best if such controls were instituted voluntarily. If cows, hens, and pigs are going to be raised for use as food, they should be treated decently in terms of food, space requirements, and overall care. The European Union has taken significant steps of this sort,[6] banning the standard bare wire cage for hens and requiring that they be provided with access to a perch and nesting box for laying eggs.[7] If we focus on suffering, as I believe we should, it need not be impermissible to kill animals for food, but it should be impermissible to show complete indifference to their interests while they are alive. So, too, for other animals on farms, even or perhaps especially if they are being used for the benefit of human beings. If sheep are going to be used in the manufacture of clothing, they should not live in conditions that involve gratuitous suffering.

I believe that steps in this direction deserve serious consideration. But here things become far more controversial. Partly this is because of sheer ignorance about what actually happens to animals in, say, farming and scientific experimentation. I am confident that greater regulation would be given consideration if current practices were widely known. To some extent, the controversy is a product of the sheer political power of the relevant interests, which intensely resist regulation. But sensible objections might be raised against some imaginable regulatory strategies, for one simple reason: the legitimate interests of animals and the legitimate interests of human beings can collide. Here, as elsewhere, additional regulation would be costly and burdensome. The relevant costs must be taken into account. It is possible to fear that regulating scientific experiments on animals would lead to less animal experimentation—and to less in the way of scientific and medical progress. If farms are regulated, the price of meat will rise. If the health of human beings could be seriously compromised by regulating experiments on animals and farming, there is reason to engage in some balancing before supporting that regulation.

At the very least, I suggest that animal suffering should count, and that any measures that impose suffering and harm should be convincingly justified. If animals are being made to suffer to produce cosmetics and hair dyes, the justification seems likely to be weak. To make a sensible assessment, it would be helpful to know a great deal about the facts, not only about values. An important dispute in the domain of scientific experimentation is whether and to what extent animal experiments really hold out a great deal of promise for medical progress. If scientists are able to develop treatments for AIDS and cancer, the claim is much stronger.

ELIMINATING CURRENT PRACTICES?

Suppose that animal suffering concerns us. Some people might be tempted to conclude that certain practices cannot be defended and should not be allowed to continue, if mere regulation will inevitably be insufficient and do little to alleviate animal suffering. To make that argument convincing, it would be helpful to demonstrate not only that the harms to animals are serious but also that the benefits to humans are insufficient to justify continuing these practices. Many of those who urge radical steps—for example, that people should not eat meat—do so because they believe that without such steps, the level of animal suffering will be unacceptably severe.

To evaluate this position, there is no choice but to go area by area. Consider greyhound racing. Greyhounds tend to live in miserable conditions, and many of them are put to death after their racing careers end. I believe that if possible, the preferred step should be to use the law to insure that greyhounds are afforded decent lives—and to hope that the racing industry will comply with the law that promotes that goal. But if the law cannot insure humane treatment, perhaps greyhound racing should be abolished. It is not obvious that the entertainment gain, for some people, is sufficient to justify significant suffering.

Of course, a key issue involves eating meat. I believe that meat eating would be acceptable if the animals used for food were treated decently. But if, as a practical matter, animals used for food are almost inevitably going to endure terrible suffering, then there is a good argument that people should not eat meat. No one doubts that a legal ban on meat would be radical and extreme, and I am certainly not arguing in its favor. Even more than Prohibition—the era from 1920 to 1933, when alcohol was banned in the United States—such a ban would have a series of adverse consequences. But the principle seems clear. People should be less inclined to eat meat if their refusal to do so would prevent significant suffering.

There is an objection, utilitarian in spirit, to steps of this kind. If people do not eat meat, or if they take other steps to prevent animals from suffering, fewer animals will be born and raised. In one view, it is objectionable to protect animals through measures that reduce the total number of animals. Perhaps it is better for animals to have lives, even difficult ones, than not to have lives. But this objection is weak. Our goal should be to improve the quality of animals' lives, not to increase their numbers.

My argument—that we should consider refraining from certain practices if this is the only feasible way to avoid widespread suffering—raises a host of questions. Shouldn't it be possible to reduce the level of suffering in scientific experiments by, for example, requiring animals to be adequately sheltered and fed? It would also be valuable to ask some factual questions. If vegetarianism were widespread, would human health be undermined (as many contend) or improved (as many others contend)? After the factual questions are resolved, disputes will remain about the weight to be given to the various interests.

THE QUESTION OF ANIMAL AUTONOMY

Some people go further. They focus not only, and perhaps not mostly, on relieving suffering. On one view, animals have rights, in the sense that they should not be subject to human use and control. This is not a Bentham-inspired point about the prevention and relief of suffering. It is instead a suggestion that animals deserve to have a kind of autonomy. This suggestion goes well beyond the view, which seems to me correct, that animals should be seen as ends rather than solely as means. Many people who own pets, or who use horses in shows or for racing, do not consider their animals to be mere means to human ends. They agree that animals have intrinsic value as well as instrumental value. But those who think that animals should not be subject to human control tend to reject all of these uses. They want all or most animals to be able to make their own choices, free from human control.

This claim raises many questions, and in the end, it seems to me extreme and unconvincing, mostly because it neglects the possibility that animals will have short and miserable lives under natural conditions, and much better lives with a degree of human control. The most obvious point is that it is not clear whether and how this position might be applied to pets. Dogs and cats have been bred specifically for human companionship, and most of them would not fare well on their own. Perhaps those who believe in animal autonomy would accept the idea that people should be able to have control over animals that have been bred to live with them. Perhaps the autonomy argument would apply only to wild animals, prohibiting human beings from hunting, trapping, and confining them.

But what if certain practices, such as confinement in zoos, science labs, and other facilities, can be undertaken in a way that insures decent lives for the relevant animals? What if some animals, including dolphins and elephants, would fare very well under human control? Nature can be very cruel, after all, and many animals live longer and better with human beings than in the wild. Of course, longer is not necessarily better. But good zoos have breeding programs that protect endangered species, provide good care to animals, and serve an important function (for nonhuman animals and human beings alike) in educating people about the nature and worth of animals. Indeed, we could imagine that many lions, elephants, giraffes, and dolphins would have far better lives with human assistance, even if confined, than in their own habitats.

If this is so, it is not easy to see what sort of response might be made by those who believe in animal autonomy. Perhaps autonomy advocates disagree on the facts, not on the theoretical issue, and think it highly unlikely, in most cases, that wild animals can have decent lives under human control. I do not believe that they are correct on the facts. In any case, the claim for animal autonomy ultimately must depend on an assessment of what will afford animals good lives.

ARE ANIMALS PROPERTY?

I have not yet explored the debate over the status of animals as property. What underlies this debate?

There is no obvious answer. Those who insist that animals should not be treated as property might be making a simple and modest claim, which is that human beings should not be able to treat animals however they wish. They seem to think that if you are property, you are, in law and in effect, a slave, wholly subject to the will of your owner. Mere property cannot have rights of any kind. A table, a chair, or a stereo can be treated as the owner likes; it can be broken or sold or replaced at the owner's whim. For animals, it might be thought, the status of property undermines any protection against cruelty and abuse.

Some people go so far as to urge that certain animals, at least, are "persons," not property, and should have many of the legal rights that human beings enjoy. Of course, this claim does not mean that those animals can vote or run for office. Their status would be akin to that of children—a status commensurate with their capacities. What that status is, exactly, remains to be spelled out. But at a minimum, it would seem to entail protection against torture, battery, and perhaps even confinement.

There is, however, a major puzzle here. What does it mean to say that animals are property and can be "owned"? As we have seen, animals, even if owned, cannot be treated however the owner wishes. The law already forbids cruelty and neglect. Ownership is merely a label, connoting a certain set of rights and duties, and without knowing a lot more, we cannot identify those rights and duties. A state could dramatically increase enforcement of existing bans on cruelty and neglect without turning animals into persons, or assigning them nonproperty status, or banning animal ownership.

To be sure, rhetoric matters, and most people do not consider animals to be property in the same sense that they do a table, a chair, or a stereo. But what matters is not rhetoric but conduct. The goal should be to protect animals against cruelty and abuse. The debate over whether animals are property is mostly a distraction.

CAN THEY SUFFER?

People do not see all animals as equal. They might agree that human beings should consider the interests of dogs, cats, horses, and dolphins, but they are unlikely to think the same about ants, mosquitoes, and cockroaches, and they do not much love rats and squirrels. It is often objected, to those who believe in animal rights, that their position would lead to truly ludicrous conclusions—to the suggestion that people cannot kill ants or mosquitoes, or rid their houses of rats and cockroaches.

There are two ways to answer this objection. The first, holding special appeal for those who stress autonomy, would inquire into the cognitive capacities of the particular animals involved. We would draw the line by seeing how well the animals in question think. But this view seems to me misdirected. Jeremy Bentham was right to place the emphasis on whether and to what extent the relevant animal is capable of suffering. In deciding whether animals are entitled to consideration, the question is whether they can suffer.

This claim need not be viewed as radical or extreme. Many people already take account of whether animals are suffering. In my view, ants and mosquitoes have no claim to human concern, and this is because they suffer little or not at all. When we are ridding our homes of mice, many of us do so in ways that do not maximize distress. Here we have some empirical questions about the capacities of various creatures. And we should certainly be willing to engage in a degree of balancing. If, for example, human beings are at risk of illness and disease from rats, there is no question that they have a strong justification for eliminating or relocating them.

ANIMAL RIGHTS WITHOUT CONTROVERSY?

Even the sharpest critics of animal rights support the anticruelty laws. The simple moral judgment behind these laws is that animal suffering matters. Most modestly, I have suggested that private suits should be permitted to prevent illegal cruelty and neglect, at least if those suits are brought by owners. There is no sufficient reason to give public officials a monopoly on enforcement; such a monopoly is a recipe for continued illegality. Less modestly, there is no good reason to permit the level of suffering that is now being experienced by millions—even billions—of living creatures.

I have also raised doubts about the radical idea that animals deserve to have autonomy, understood as a right to be free from human control and use. In my view, the real questions involve animal welfare and suffering, and human control and use may be compatible with decent lives for animals. But the emphasis on suffering, and on decent lives, has significant implications. Of course, it is appropriate to consider human interests in the balance, and human interests will often outweigh those of nonhuman animals. But the problem is both simple and serious. Far too much of the time, the interests of animals are not counted at all.

CHAPTER 6

MARRIAGE

The freedom to marry has long been recognized as one of the vital personal rights essential to the orderly pursuit of happiness by free men . . . Marriage is one of the basic civil rights of man, fundamental to our very existence and survival.

—*LOVING V. VIRGINIA*[1]

Modern marriage has lost its meaning—consequently one abolishes it.

—FRIEDRICH NIETZSCHE[2]

Is there a constitutional right to marry? On several occasions, the Supreme Court has said so.[3] But the very idea of a "right to marry" presents two sets of puzzles. The first involves the *content* of the right: what it provides for those who are entitled to it. The second set of puzzles involves the *scope* of the right to marry: the kinds of relationships that can claim it.

Begin with the first puzzle. As an official matter, marriage is no more and no less than a government-run licensing system. Why should governments license marriages? Some people are skeptical of the official institution of marriage and argue that it should be abolished—not by forbidding private arrangements, religious or otherwise, but by eliminating the special status that governments confer, including a unique set of legal benefits and burdens. Most people strongly favor this particular licensing system, and the doubts are not widely held, but they have cast in sharp relief the vast range of possibilities, with respect to human relationships, that the simple notions of "married" and "single" tend to erase.

But are states under a constitutional obligation to recognize an official institution called marriage? Does the Constitution really mean that the government must provide tax, Social Security, and other benefits to those who are lawfully married? Or does it mean, much more modestly, that states may not forbid religious and other organizations from performing "marriage ceremonies" and allowing those who go through such ceremonies to claim that status as a matter of personal choice?

And what relationships are included within the right to marry? People do not have a right to marry their dog, their cell phone, their house, their refrigerator, Afghanistan, July 21, a power plant, or a rose petal. At most, people have a right to marry people. But the Supreme Court cannot possibly have meant to suggest that "people" have a general right to marry "people"; it did not mean to say that, under the Constitution, any "person" has a right to marry a thousand other people, or five, or even two. We might conclude that the Court is saying (at most) that one person has a right to marry one other person. But if there is a right to marry, what is the basis for this particular limitation on the right? Does the Constitution require states to recognize same-sex marriages?

My initial suggestion is that the right to marry is best understood as an analogue to the right to vote. In both cases, states are under no obligation to create the relevant institutions; but once those institutions are created, the Constitution imposes large barriers to government efforts to deny people access to them. But what is the institution of marriage? It seems to have two characteristics: the *expressive legitimacy* that comes from the public institution of marriage, and the panoply of *material benefits*—both economic and noneconomic—that the marital relationship confers.

The right to marry, then, is a right of access to the expressive and material benefits that the state affords with the institution of marriage. Unless a compelling justification can be found, no one can be denied access to those benefits. This understanding of the right to marry suggests that so long as the official institution of marriage exists, the right to marry entitles people not to any particular set of expressive and material benefits but to exactly that panoply of benefits that the relevant state offers.

But what is the scope of that right? At a minimum, the right includes relationships between one man and one woman—the right, of one adult man and one adult woman, to enter into the marital relationship, with whatever expressive and material incidents the state affords, unless the relevant restriction is supported by compelling justifications.

This minimal understanding is fully consistent with the Supreme Court's decisions. It can also claim support in a tradition-centered approach to constitutional interpretation, one that attempts to root an understanding of liberty in longstanding practices. Under the minimal understanding, the bans on same-sex, bigamous, and polygamous marriages are legitimate, simply because such marriages do not involve one man and one woman.

The principal problem with the minimal understanding is that it seems to draw arbitrary lines. Why should the scope of the right be limited in that way? Compare a far-from-minimal understanding of the right to marry: a right, of two or more adults, to enter into the marital relationship, with its expressive and material incidents, unless the relevant restriction is supported by compelling justifications. This approach would essentially convert marriage from a closed licensing system into an open-ended one, allowing people to enter into marital agreements as they see fit. Such an approach might tailor its economic incidents to the particulars of the relationship—refusing, for example, to accord economic benefits when there is no sufficient reason for them.

From the constitutional point of view, the problem with this understanding is that it depends on a broad and unanchored understanding of "liberty," one that endangers restrictions on marriage that are at least time-honored (such as the ban on incestuous or polygamous marriages). One task is to produce an understanding of the scope of the right that lacks the arbitrariness of the minimal understanding without being unnecessarily broad.

I shall try to provide that understanding here. To get ahead of the story, I believe that there are no reasonable grounds for prohibiting same-sex marriages. That prohibition is a form of unacceptable discrimination. But this conclusion raises several puzzles about the nature of the marriage right and the role of the federal courts in a democratic society.

MARRIAGE AND THE SUPREME COURT

The constitutional right to marriage has deep roots. In 1888 the US Supreme Court described marriage as "the most important relation in life"[4] and called it "the foundation of the family and of society, without which there would be neither civilization nor progress." In *Meyer v. State of Nebraska*,[5] decided in 1923, the Court said that the Constitution protected the right "to marry, establish a home, and bring up children." In *Skinner v. State of Oklahoma ex rel. Williamson* (1942),[6] striking down a compulsory sterilization law, the Court described marriage as "fundamental to the very existence and survival of the race." *Griswold v. Connecticut*[7] (1965) held that states could not ban married couples from using contraceptives. The Court emphasized that it was dealing with "a right of privacy older than the Bill of Rights—older than our political parties, older than our school system. Marriage is a coming together for better or for worse, hopefully enduring, and intimate to the degree of being sacred." (So wrote Justice William O. Douglas, who was married four times.)

None of these cases, however, involved the right to marry as such. In its modern form, the right to marry is principally a product of three cases. The initial decision, in 1967, was *Loving v. Virginia*,[8] in which the Court struck down a ban on interracial marriage. Most of the Court's opinion spoke in terms of the equal-protection clause, seeing that ban as a form of racial discrimination. The Court could easily have stopped there. But in a separate and broader ruling, it also held that the ban was inconsistent with "the freedom to marry," which "has long been recognized as one of the vital personal rights essential to the orderly pursuit of happiness by free men." It added that "[m]arriage is one of the 'basic civil rights of man,' fundamental to our very existence and survival."

The second decision was *Zablocki v. Redhail* (1978).[9] There the Court invoked the equal protection clause to strike down a Wisconsin law forbidding people facing child support obligations to remarry unless they obtained a judicial determination that they had met those obligations and that their children were not likely to become public charges. The Court proclaimed that "the right to marry is of fundamental importance for all individuals," adding that "the decision to marry has been placed on the same level of importance as decisions relating to procreation, childbirth, child rearing, and family relationships."

The Court did say that it would uphold "reasonable regulations that do not significantly interfere with decisions to enter into the marital relationship." But it announced that any "direct and substantial" interference with the right to marry would be scrutinized carefully. In a concurring opinion, Justice John Paul Stevens underlined the point, urging that the Constitution would cast serious doubt on any "classification which determines who may lawfully enter into the marriage relationship." This suggestion appears to be extremely broad, applying to incestuous and same-sex marriages, among others—though it is most doubtful that Justice Stevens meant to suggest that states must recognize those marriages. In *Zablocki*, the Court concluded that the restriction could not be justified, for it was an unnecessarily intrusive means of ensuring compliance with child support obligations.

In *Turner v. Safley* (1987),[10] the Court followed and extended *Zablocki*, striking down a prison regulation that prohibited inmates from marrying unless there were "compelling reasons" to allow them to do so. "Compelling reasons" were understood to include pregnancy or the birth of an illegitimate child. In fact, the Court went beyond its previous decisions to spell out some of the foundations of the right to marry. It said that marriages, by inmates as by others, "are expressions of emotional support and public commitment," and emphasized that these are "important and significant aspects of the marital relationship." The Court added that marriages are often recognized as having spiritual significance, and that the "marital status often is a prerequisite for" a number of material benefits, including property rights, government benefits, and less tangible advantages.

WHAT IS THE RIGHT TO MARRY?

What, exactly, does it mean to say that there is a right to marry? Are states obliged to provide the institution of marriage? This is a more difficult question than it might seem. To answer it, we need to be clear on what that institution entails.

Imagine that a state abolishes the institution of marriage in the following sense: it says that it will not recognize anything called "marriage," nor will it provide marriage licenses in any form. It will not legitimate particular relationships through declaring them to be "marriages." Nor will it confer special benefits, economic and otherwise, on people who deem themselves to be "married." But the state will not forbid such private arrangements as people choose. Above all, it will allow private persons to organize their personal relationships as they see fit, subject to limitations stemming from the criminal law (such as the ban on sexual relations with children).

Religious ceremonies, constituting relationships that the parties may call "marriage," would not be abolished. If the parties follow the proper formalities for making contracts, their agreements would be enforceable under the ordinary terms of contract law. But as a matter of law, and apart from these points, there would be no such thing as "marriage" as an official matter of state licensing.

Does the "right to marry" mean that the abolition of official marriage would be unconstitutional? Under the Supreme Court's decisions, this would not be an implausible conclusion. Perhaps the Court is best read as having recognized the existence, within Anglo-American law, of the institution of marriage as one that the government recognizes and safeguards. But if there is a right to an official institution of marriage, what must the state do or provide? The initial question is what marriage actually entails. We need to distinguish here between material benefits on the one hand and expressive ones on the other.

Many material benefits, economic and noneconomic, accompany the marital relationship. Of course, state laws vary, but these benefits fall into six major categories.[11]

1. *Tax Benefits (and Burdens).* While a great deal of public attention is paid to the "marriage penalty," the tax system rewards many couples when they marry—at least if one spouse earns a great deal more than the other. There is a marriage "bonus" for couples in traditional relationships, in which the man is the breadwinner and the woman stays at home. The marriage penalty can be significant if the spouses both earn substantial incomes. Married couples can also file joint returns. Members of such couples are allowed to transfer property to each other without being subject to gain-loss valuation.
2. *Entitlements.* While the Obama administration took numerous steps to put unmarried same-sex couples on a plane of equality with married opposite-sex couples, federal law continues to benefit married couples through a

number of entitlement programs. Under the Family and Medical Leave Act, for example, employers must allow unpaid leave to workers who seek to care for a spouse; they need not do so for "partners." Veterans' programs provide some economic benefits (involving medical care, housing, and educational assistance) to the spouses, but not the partners, of veterans. Those who are married to federal employees can also claim certain benefits unavailable to those who are unmarried. Under state law, the entitlement to consortium protects spouses; the status of members of unmarried couples is unclear. With respect to same-sex couples, the law is evolving rapidly, but in general, married couples have significant advantages under entitlement programs.

3. *Inheritance and Other Death Benefits.* The surviving member of a married couple obtains a number of benefits at the time of a spouse's death. The rules favor wives and husbands for those who die intestate, or without a will, and many states forbid people to refuse to leave money to the person to whom they are married. Under the Uniform Probate Code, those who die intestate give much of their estate to their spouse, even if they had children. In wrongful death actions, spouses automatically qualify for benefits.
4. *Ownership Benefits.* Under both state and federal laws, spouses may well have automatic ownership rights that nonspouses lack. In community property states, people are given automatic rights to their spouses' holdings, and they cannot contract around the legal rules. Even in states that do not follow community property rules, states may presume joint ownership of property acquired after marriage and before legal separation.
5. *Surrogate Decision Making.* Members of married couples are given the right to make surrogate decisions of various sorts in the event of their spouse's incapacitation. More

generally, a spouse might be appointed formal guardian, entitled to make decisions about care, residence, and money, as well as about particular medical options.

6. *Evidentiary Privileges*. Federal courts, and a number of state courts, recognize marital privileges, including a right to keep marital communications confidential and to exclude adverse spousal testimony.

This is a large set of benefits. Some states do make them available to same-sex couples, but most do not. While there are sharp political constraints on any effort to rethink such benefits, the state is not constitutionally required to provide them. Suppose that Illinois altered a host of laws to place married people closer to, on the same plane as, or even below unmarried couples or single people. It defies belief to suggest that the alteration would be an unconstitutional violation of the right to marry.

But if the right to marry does not require economic benefits, what, exactly, does it entail? Perhaps it operates as a kind of precondition for certain familial rights that are, broadly speaking, associational in character—for example, the right to visit and make choices for a loved one in case of incapacitating illness. Under existing law, marriage may or may not be a literal precondition for these rights, but it usually makes their exercise significantly easier. Does the Constitution require states to provide the institution of marriage so as to recognize these rights? Suppose that a state abolishes official marriage and denies members of committed relationships the right to make decisions on behalf of their incapacitated partners in the hospital. The Constitution may well forbid states to take such (absurd) steps. But this point does not suggest that states must provide the institution of marriage as such. If official marriage were abolished, the Constitution might grant people a right to some of those benefits in any case—without requiring the institution of marriage.

But is that institution required for other reasons? Recall that in *Turner*, the Court stressed that marriages are "expressions of emotional support and public commitment." If a state says that people are married, then they are, in fact, married, and not only for purposes of financial and other benefits. They are married in the sense that the relationship is taken, by everyone who knows about it, to have a special quality as an official and public matter. In short, marriage has an important function in signaling the nature of the relationship. Quite apart from material benefits, the official institution of marriage entails an important form of public legitimation and endorsement. Perhaps states must provide the institution for that reason.

Consider two people who announce to the world that they are married, or who seem to act as married couples do, or both, but with one wrinkle: under state law, they are not, in fact, married. (Suppose, too, that they have not been married through any formal ceremony, religious or otherwise.) To be sure, people can become "engaged" simply by announcing that fact. But to be married as a matter of formal law, they have to go through certain official procedures. Does the right to marry mean that the Constitution requires states to make those procedures available? Perhaps it does.

But perhaps not. Constitutional rights usually do not require affirmative provision by the state. The right to choose abortion, for example, forbids the state to impose undue burdens on the right to choose, but it does not require the state to fund abortion. For most privacy rights, the Constitution requires government noninterference. It does not require government to provide money, institutional arrangements, or anything else.

Of course, this analogy is not decisive. We could imagine a ruling to the effect that the legal institution of marriage is so time-honored, and so important to family formation, that states must make it available. But this argument might end up falling on deaf ears in any situation in which official marriage really was abolished. To see why, note the difficulty, at the present time, of even imagining a state that has actually abolished the legal institution of marriage. This is difficult to imagine simply because most people cherish that institution. If a state did abolish marriage, it would be because most people, or most influential people, had come to believe that the official institution should be abolished. In those circumstances, the idea that there is a right to that institution would be difficult to accept. Whatever the content of the right to marry, it is not at all clear that it requires states to maintain an official licensing scheme for recognizing and legitimating marriage.

It follows that the "right to marry" entails *an individual right of access to the official institution of marriage so long as the state is providing that institution*. The best analogy is the right to vote. As the Constitution is now understood, states are not required to provide elections for state offices. But when elections are held, the right to vote qualifies as fundamental, and state laws that deprive people of that right will be carefully scrutinized and generally struck down. For both the right to marry and the right to vote, there is an unanswered question whether and when the state is required to create the practice in the first instance. But so long as the practice exists, the state must make it available to everyone.

LOVE AND MONEY

I have said that as a matter of state law, the institution of marriage contains both material and expressive features. And the discussion thus far should be enough to suggest that when the Supreme Court says there is a right to marry, it is establishing a right to *both* features. Suppose that a white person and an African-American seek to marry, and that a state says that such relationships can be formed as civil unions but not as marriages. Suppose, too, that civil unions have all the legal benefits of marriage. It is clear that under *Loving*, the state cannot deny interracial couples the right to marry merely by insisting that it is providing such couples with the right to the material incidents of marriage. (So, too, a state cannot say that unless people have met their child support obligations, they may enter into civil unions but not marriage.)

Just as a state could not grant the material benefits of marriage while denying the expressive benefits, it could not provide expressive benefits while denying the material benefits. Certainly a state could not say that mixed-race couples can marry but without receiving the material advantages that normally flow from marriage. The Court's opinions seem to mean that for those who enjoy it, the right to marry conveys a right of access to the expressive and the material benefits of marriage, so long as the institution of marriage exists.

THE MINIMAL RIGHT TO MARRY

But what is the scope of this right? Begin with a minimal understanding. By deeming the right to marry fundamental, the Court did not mean to suggest that it would question any law that departed from the traditional idea that a marriage is between (one) woman and (one) man. It meant to say only that when a man and a woman seek to marry, the state must have exceedingly good reasons for putting significant barriers in their path. The minimal understanding of the right to marry is that without very good reason, states may not deny an adult man and an adult woman access to the institution of marriage. This rationale would not question bans on same-sex marriages, polygamous marriages, or marriages between people and cats.

But the minimal understanding does have two serious problems. First, it might turn out to be less minimal than it appears, for one simple reason: it raises serious questions about bans on incestuous marriages. If this problem is deemed serious, two options are available. The right might be described more narrowly still: without very good reason, states may not deny an adult man and an adult woman access to the institution of marriage unless the marriage runs afoul of longstanding views about who may enter into a marital relationship. This understanding of the right to marry also fits with the Court's decisions, and it would insure that the Court would uphold any restriction that is not novel—a benefit for those who believe in a cautious judicial role in this domain. Alternatively, bans on incestuous marriages might be permitted only if they can be compellingly justified—and struck down if they cannot be. For example, an uncle might be prohibited from marrying his niece simply because of the risk of coercion and psychological harm. But a ban on marriage between cousins might well be struck down.

The second problem with the minimal understanding is much more formidable. It draws lines that seem arbitrary in principle. Why, exactly, should the right to marry be limited in this way? Why should the state be required to give a strong justification for any law that forbids marriage between one woman and one man—but not have to justify any other law that impinges on marital choices?

A possible answer would be that marriage is a legal status, with a scope that depends on nothing more than convention. On this view, the Court has not (until recently) been willing to revisit the question of what marriage is; it has worked entirely within the convention on that count. But are conventions really determinative? Suppose that a white person and an African-American seek to marry, and a state responds (in, say, 1961) that they cannot marry because marriage is defined as, or is conventionally understood as, a legal relationship between people of the same race. The mere fact that there is a convention to this effect cannot be decisive. The convention is constitutionally unacceptable. There are countless conventions, and their legal validity depends on whether they conform to the Constitution. Their status as conventions cannot resolve that question.

TRADITIONALISM

Apart from convention, what might be said in favor of the minimal understanding of the right to marry? One answer would endorse constitutional traditionalism. A decision to root constitutional rights in traditions might be the best way of reducing judicial mistakes and judicial burdens (in economic terminology, the costs of errors and the costs of decisions). Let us see how this argument might be spelled out.

Some members of the Supreme Court have been drawn to constitutional traditionalism simply as a way of disciplining themselves—of limiting judicial discretion. If judges follow traditions, they will not have to ask hard questions about basic values, and if judges are not good at answering such questions, traditionalism will have considerable appeal. An initial objection to this approach is that traditions are not self-defining; they do not come prepackaged for easy identification. It is tempting to object that constitutional traditionalism is a charade, in which the key value judgment—how should the tradition be defined?—ends up doing all the work. But the objection is overstated. We should be able to agree, for example, that in the United States, there is no tradition of respect for incestuous marriages or marriages that involve more than two people.

Many people believe that the discipline imposed by tradition is far from arbitrary. Suppose that with the great British statesman and theorist Edmund Burke,[12] we believe that simply because traditions represent the judgment of countless people over a long period of time, they are likely to be wise. If so, traditions have some of the advantages of free markets, reflecting as they do the assessments of many rather than few. This is not to say that longstanding practices are always justified. They might reflect prejudice or ignorance rather than wisdom. But perhaps practices are likely to be longstanding only if they make some sense and promote important goals. If so, there should be a presumption in their favor.

In any case, the question is a comparative one. If we believe that judges are prone to error, an effort to root constitutional understandings in traditions might well be better than any alternative. And even if we believe that judicial decisions have some advantages, we might agree that in the face of doubt, democratic judgments, especially in a federal system, deserve a measure of respect, in part because self-government is one of the rights to which people are entitled.

For all of these reasons, constitutional traditionalism is far from irrational or arbitrary, even if it produces bad results in particular cases. And if we are constitutional traditionalists, we might insist that if there is a right to marry, it includes only the time-honored form: one man and one woman.

RATIONALITY, ARBITRARINESS, INVIDIOUSNESS

To clarify the issue, imagine a much broader understanding of the scope of the right to marry: two or more people have a right of access to the marital relationship, with its expressive and material features, unless any restriction is supported by compelling justifications. And with the benefit of a little science fiction, it should not be so difficult for us to imagine a parallel world—unfamiliar to be sure, but perhaps not so unrecognizably different from our own—in which this understanding were accepted. In such a world, people could deem themselves married and receive the appropriate license from the state, so long as force and fraud were not involved. Should this understanding be accepted? What would be the implications?

Even under the broad understanding, prohibitions on nonconsensual marriages are plainly legitimate; so, too, are prohibitions on marriages involving people who are underage, as well as incestuous marriages (except perhaps if they involve cousins). There are only two differences between the minimal and the broad understanding. First, the latter eliminates the limitation to two people. Second, the latter eliminates the ban on same-sex marriages.

Put aside the fact that no federal judges seem even a little bit interested in ruling that states must recognize polygamous marriages. Is their skepticism justified? An affirmative answer might insist that many of the material benefits of marriage make sense only for couples, and no sense at all for groups of three or more. To come to terms with this justification, we would have to go through those benefits one by one. Perhaps states could compellingly justify the decision to withhold some—but not all—of the material incidents of marriage from polygamous relationships. But even if so, the broad understanding might nonetheless require states to recognize certain relationships as "marital" for expressive reasons.

But these points do not capture the real reason that polygamous relationships cannot be deemed "marriages." After all, most states not only refuse to recognize them as such but also impose criminal penalties on the people involved. The reason is that states believe that polygamous relationships cause individual and social harm—and, in any case, are immoral. Under the broad understanding, however, states must produce compelling justifications for prohibiting polygamous marriages. Should they be required to do so?

I do not believe so. A central reason involves the limited role of the judiciary in a democracy. The broad understanding would put courts in a position for which they are extremely ill-suited. It would require them to assume the exceptionally difficult task of policing the adequacy of official justifications for refusing to recognize marriages involving more than two people. Those justifications, which involve complex questions of both policy and morality, are best evaluated democratically, not judicially. If this objection is convincing, then we can imagine an intermediate understanding of the scope of the right to marry, one that puts the question of same-sex marriage in sharp relief: two adults have a right of access to the marital relationship, with its expressive and material incidents, unless the restriction is supported by compelling justifications.

I believe that this is the right principle, and that it is not possible to make a convincing defense of the prohibition on same-sex marriage. The principle is especially appealing in light of the fact that discrimination on the basis of sexual orientation has long been rooted in hostility and prejudice, and should therefore be carefully scrutinized by courts. What sorts of social harms would follow from recognizing marriages between people of the same sex? Some people argue that refusing to recognize same-sex marriage is a way of protecting the marital institution itself. But aside from purely semantic arguments, this is very puzzling. How do same-sex marriages threaten the institution of marriage? Extending the right to enter into the institution of marriage would hardly threaten traditional marriages—unless it were thought that significant numbers of heterosexuals would forgo traditional marriages if same-sex marriages were permitted (a difficult causal argument, to say the least). Or perhaps same-sex marriages would harm children. But what evidence supports that speculation?

Some people believe that the state can legitimately deny marriage to same-sex unions for expressive reasons. They do not want to "endorse" such unions or suggest that they are appropriate or legitimate, or have a standing similar to that of traditional marriage. But what is their justification? Why should states refuse to endorse such unions?

For those who believe, as I do, that the ban on same-sex marriages cannot be plausibly justified, the only questions involve the limited role of the judiciary in a democratic society. In 2013, the Supreme Court struck down the Defense of Marriage Act as discriminatory, but it declined to rule on bans on same-sex marriage as such. There have been legitimate prudential reasons for federal courts to hesitate before requiring states to recognize same-sex marriage, not least because that issue is under intense discussion at the local, state, and national levels. Committed minimalists (see chapter 10) would want judges to leave the question undecided, not because they are ambivalent about the underlying principle but because they believe in a modest role for the federal judiciary.

To be sure, the minimalist position raises questions and objections of its own. Should courts really hesitate to vindicate constitutional rights? When? Won't there come a time when courts should strike down unjustified discrimination? Why isn't that time now? This is not the place to answer these questions. The only point is that if judges are to hesitate, it is because of the claims of judicial humility, not because there is a good argument, in principle, for forbidding same-sex marriage.

RIGHTS AND DEMOCRACY

My goal has been to make progress on two questions. The first is the content of the right to marry. The second is the scope of that right.

I have suggested that like the right to vote, the right to marry is one of equal access to a publicly administered institution. It is a right of access to the expressive and material benefits that official marriage provides.

I have also identified competing understandings of the scope of the right to marry. The minimal understanding recognizes the right of access, by any couple consisting of one adult man and one adult woman, to the expressive and material benefits of marriage, so long as the institution of marriage exists. The chief advantage of the minimal understanding is that it promises to minimize judicial discretion and to rely on practices that, simply because they are time-honored, have a claim to social respect. Its chief disadvantage is arbitrariness. The disadvantage is serious. In principle, there is no convincing constitutional defense of the ban on same-sex marriage.

What about the marital institution itself? Like most people, I believe that it should be continued, if only because it provides the basis for a kind of precommitment strategy that is beneficial to adults and children alike. But this conclusion should not obscure a central point: official marriage is unambiguously a form of government intervention, and its future form should be a matter not of following supposed dictates of any kind, but of our own free choices.

CHAPTER 7

CLIMATE CHANGE JUSTICE

(WITH ERIC A. POSNER)

The problem of climate change raises difficult issues of science, economics, and justice. Of course, the scientific and economic issues loom large in public debates, and they have been analyzed in great detail. By contrast, the question of justice, while also playing a significant role in international debates, has received less sustained attention.

Several points are clear. The United States, which long led the world in greenhouse gas emissions, has been surpassed by China. The two leading emitters now account for over 40 percent of the world's emissions, but they have independently refused to accept binding emissions limitations, apparently because of a belief, on the part of influential political leaders, that the domestic costs of such limitations would exceed the benefits. President Obama did support a national cap-and-trade program, which was passed by the House of Representatives in 2009, but the Senate refused to act on it, and as of this writing, such a program does not appear likely to be enacted in the near future.

The emissions of the United States and China threaten to impose serious economic and environmental losses on other nations and regions, including Europe, India, and Africa. For this reason, it is tempting to argue that both nations are, in a sense, engaging in wrongful acts against nations that are most vulnerable to climate change. This argument might seem to have special force as applied to the actions of the United States. While its emissions are growing relatively slowly, and while China's are growing rapidly, the United States remains the largest contributor to the existing *stock* of greenhouse gases. Because of its past contributions, does the United States owe remedial action or material compensation to those nations, or those citizens, most likely to be harmed by climate change? Principles of corrective justice might seem to require that the largest emitting nation pay damages to those who are hurt—and that they scale back their emissions as well.

Questions of corrective justice are entangled with questions of distributive justice. The United States has the highest gross domestic product of any country in the world, and its wealth might suggest that it has a special duty to help to reduce the damage associated with climate change. Are the obligations of the comparatively poor China, the leading emitter, equivalent to those of the comparatively rich United States, the second-leading emitter? Does it not matter that the per capita emissions of China, which has more than four times the population of the United States, remain a small fraction of those of the United States? Perhaps most important: because of its wealth, should the United States be willing to sign an agreement that is optimal for the world as a whole—but not optimal for the United States?

The goal of this chapter is to answer these questions. Let us start with two reasonable but admittedly controversial assumptions.

First, the world, taken as a whole, would benefit from an agreement to reduce greenhouse gas emissions. This assumption is reasonable because mounting evidence suggests that the global benefits of imaginable steps—such as a modest worldwide carbon tax, growing over time—are significantly greater than the global costs.

Second, some nations, primarily the United States (and China as well), might not benefit, on net, from the agreement that would be optimal from the world's point of view. Suppose, for example, that the world settled on a specified carbon tax—say, $60 per ton. Such a tax would likely impose especially significant costs on the United States, simply because its per capita emissions rate is so high. Suppose, too, that America is less vulnerable to the serious health and agricultural consequences of climate change than are many other nations, such as India and sub-Saharan Africa.[1] Perhaps the optimal carbon tax, for the world, would be $60 per ton, but the United States would do better with a worldwide carbon tax of $40 per ton, or $30 per ton, or even $20 per ton.

If so, the standard resolution of the problem is clear: the world should enter into the optimal agreement, and the United States should be given side payments in return for participating. The reason for this approach is straightforward. The optimal agreement should be assessed by asking about the overall benefits and costs of the relevant commitments for the world. To the extent that the United States is a net loser, the world should act so as to induce it to participate in an agreement that would promote the welfare of the world's citizens, taken as a whole. With side payments to the United States (of the kind that have elsewhere induced reluctant nations to join environmental treaties), an international agreement could be designed so as to make all nations better off and no nation worse off. Who would oppose such a treaty?

A serious puzzle is that almost everyone does! No one is suggesting that the world should offer side payments to the United States. Indeed, even the United States is not insisting on side payments, perhaps on the grounds that the demand would be regarded as preposterous. One reason involves distributive justice. Many people would find it odd to suggest that the world's richest nation should receive compensation for helping to solve a problem faced by the world as a whole—and above all by poor nations.

On this view, wealthy nations should be expected to contribute a great deal to solving the climate change problem; side payments would be perverse. If we care about distributive justice, it might seem far more plausible to suggest that nations should pay China to take part in a climate change agreement. And indeed, developing nations, including China, were given financial assistance as an inducement to reduce their emissions of ozone-depleting chemicals. Some people think that a climate change agreement should build on this precedent; but no one seems to think that payments should go to the United States.

But claims about distributive justice are only part of the story. Corrective justice matters as well. The basic thought is that the largest emitters, including the United States, have imposed serious risks on other nations. Surely it cannot be right for nations to request payments in return for ceasing to harm others. Many people think that wrongdoers should pay for the damage that they have caused and should be asked to stop.

This chapter will raise serious questions about both accounts. There is a strong argument that rich nations and rich people should give resources to poor nations and poor people. But significant greenhouse gas reductions are not the best way of attempting to achieve redistributive goals. The arc of human history suggests that in the future, people are likely to be much wealthier than people are now. Why should wealthy countries give money to future (less) poor people rather than to current poor people?

In any case, nations are not people; they are collections of people. Redistribution from wealthy countries to poor countries is hardly the same as redistribution from wealthy people to poor people. Poor people in wealthy countries may well pay a large part of the bill for emissions reduction. A stiff tax on carbon emissions could have particularly severe effects on poor people, at least if steps are not taken to compensate them.

The upshot is that if wealthy people in wealthy nations want to help poor people in poor nations, emissions reductions are unlikely to be the best means by which to do so. A puzzle, then, is why many people take distributive justice to require wealthy nations to help poor ones in the context of climate change, when wealthy nations are not being asked to help poor ones in areas in which the argument for help is significantly stronger.

The discussion here will also accept, for purposes of argument, the view that when people in one nation wrongfully harm people in another nation, the wrongdoers have a moral obligation to provide a remedy to the victims. It might seem to follow that the largest emitters, and especially the United States, have a special obligation to remedy the harms they have caused (and certainly should not be given side payments). But this argument runs into serious problems. Nations are not individuals: they do not have mental states and cannot act, except metaphorically. Blame must ordinarily be apportioned to individuals.

If the United States wants to assist poor nations, reducing its greenhouse gas emissions is unlikely to be the best way to accomplish that goal. It is true that many people in poor nations are at risk because of the actions of many people in the United States, but the idea of corrective justice does not easily justify any kind of transfer from contemporary Americans to people now or eventually living in, say, India and Africa.

This conclusion should not be misunderstood. Nothing said here questions the proposition that an international agreement to control greenhouse gases, with American participation, is justified. Moreover, it is good if wealthy countries are willing to help vulnerable people in poor ones. Consider the example of genocide. If a nation could prevent genocide at a modest cost to itself, it should do so, even if that nation is a net loser. The goal here is not to question these propositions, or to suggest any particular approach to the climate change problem, but to show that contrary to widespread beliefs, standard ideas about distributive or corrective justice poorly fit the climate change problem.

ETHICALLY RELEVANT FACTS

There is voluminous literature on the science and economics of climate change. Let us concentrate on the facts that are most relevant to the questions of justice.

As noted, there is strong agreement with the view that the world would benefit from significant steps to control greenhouse gas emissions. If all of the major emitting nations agreed to such steps, the benefits would almost certainly exceed the costs. To be sure, there is continuing disagreement about the appropriate timing and severity of emissions reduction; perhaps aggressive reductions are justified in the near future. But as compared with "business as usual," much would be gained, and less lost, if at least some reduction policies were adopted soon, followed by larger ones over time.

There is also much agreement that if the world does undertake an effort to reduce greenhouse gas emissions, it should select one of two possible approaches.[2] The first is an emissions tax, designed to capture the externalities associated with climate change. A worldwide tax on carbon emissions might start relatively low—perhaps $10 per ton—and increase as technology advances. With this approach, it is generally assumed that the tax would be uniform. Citizens of Russia, China, India, the United States, France, and so forth would all pay the same tax, on the theory that the relevant amount reflected the social cost of the emissions. There is disagreement about the proper magnitude of the tax, and, as we shall see, different nations would gain and lose different amounts from any specified tax.

The second approach involves a system of cap and trade, under which nations might create a worldwide cap on aggregate emissions—calling for, say, a 3 percent reduction in worldwide emissions to start, with further reductions over time. A cap-and-trade system would require judgments about the appropriate cap as well as an initial allocation of emissions rights. In one version, existing emissions levels would provide the foundation for initial allocations; countries would have to reduce those existing levels by a certain percentage. The use of existing levels is highly controversial and, in a sense, arbitrary. But analytically, it is not very different from a uniform carbon tax; in both cases, current practices are the starting point for regulatory measures.

It is critical to see that an agreement to control greenhouse gas emissions would be most effective only if all or most of the major nations participate. If the United Kingdom, France, or Germany stabilized its emissions rate at 1995 levels, aggressive cuts by each would be required, but the effect on warming would be modest. One reason is the large existing stock of greenhouse gases; another is that global increases in greenhouse gas emissions would not be much affected if only one of those three countries stabilized its emissions. If the developed world acts while developing nations refuse to accept any emissions restrictions, the actual effect on anticipated warming will not be trivial, but it will be very far from what is required.

EMITTERS

To understand the issues of justice and the motivations of the various actors, it is important to appreciate the disparities in emissions across nations. We do not have clear data on the costs of emissions reduction for different nations, but it is reasonable to predict that the largest carbon emitters would bear the largest burdens from, say, a worldwide carbon tax.

As noted, the United States and China are the world's largest emitters, and China's emissions are growing at a truly explosive rate. Estimates suggest that the largest contributors are likely to continue to qualify as such but that major shifts will occur, above all with emissions growth in China and India. Next to China and America, the countries that have produced the highest emissions are India,

Russia, Japan, and Germany. Projections are in considerable flux, but by 2030, the developing world is expected to contribute at least 55 percent of total emissions, with at most 45 percent coming from developed nations. All by itself, China may well produce over half of the world's emissions before long.

These are points about flows: how much a given nation emits on an annual basis. Also relevant for claims of justice are the stocks: how much a given nation has, over time, contributed to the current accumulation of greenhouse gases in the atmosphere. The United States is the highest-ranked contributor, while China remains a distant fourth, and India is ninth.

The reason for the disparity is that greenhouse gases dissipate very slowly, so countries that industrialized earlier have contributed more to the stock than countries that industrialized later, even though today the latter group might contribute more on an annual basis. Carbon dioxide (CO_2) is the most important greenhouse gas, and about half of the CO_2 emitted in 1907 still remains in the atmosphere.[3] If the world suddenly stopped emitting CO_2 today, the stock of CO_2 in the atmosphere in 2107 would remain at about 90 percent of what it is now. This point matters greatly. It helps to explain why even significant emissions reduction will bring down anticipated warming but hardly halt it. We are now in a better position to see why unilateral action, even by the largest emitters, will accomplish relatively little. Such action cannot affect the existing stock, and by definition, it will do nothing directly about the rest of the flow.

VICTIMS

Which nations are expected to suffer most from climate change? The precise figures are greatly disputed. The extent of the damage in 2050 or 2100 cannot be predicted now, in part because of insufficient information about each country's ability to adapt to warmer climates. But it is generally agreed that the poorest nations will be the biggest losers by far.[4] The wealthy nations, including the United States, are in a much better position, for three independent reasons.[5] First, they have much more in the way of adaptive capacity. Second, a smaller percentage of their economies depend on agriculture, a sector that is highly vulnerable to climate change. Third, the wealthy nations are generally in the cooler, higher latitudes; this also decreases their vulnerability.

To be sure, any specific estimates must be taken with many grains of salt; they are at best only suggestive. Because regions are economically interdependent, significant adverse effects on India, Africa, and Europe would surely have a major impact on the United States, China, and Russia. But it is readily apparent that some nations are far more vulnerable than others.

India, for example, is expected to experience devastating losses in terms of both health and agriculture. In terms of health effects alone, the country has been projected to lose 3.6 million years of life from climate-related diseases such as malaria.[6] For Africa, the major problem involves health, with a massive anticipated increase in climate-related diseases.[7] Sub-Saharan Africa has been projected to lose 26.7 million years of life due to climate-related diseases, with 24.4 million coming from malaria.[8] The United States faces significant but more limited threats to both agriculture and health.

From these very brief notes, it seems useful to analyze the questions of justice by assuming that (1) the world would benefit from an agreement to control greenhouse gas emissions; (2) the United States would have to pay a significant amount to reduce its emissions; (3) some nations would benefit far more than others from worldwide reductions; and (4) the United States would not be the largest beneficiary and could possibly even turn out to be a net loser from a large uniform carbon tax or from a cap-and-trade program that requires very major reductions from existing emissions levels. A primary question is how to understand the moral obligations of the United States; also of interest are the proper approaches of and toward China.

CLIMATE CHANGE AND DISTRIBUTIVE JUSTICE

To separate issues of distributive justice from those of corrective justice, let us begin with a risk of natural calamity that does not involve human action at all.

THE ASTEROID

Imagine that India faces a serious new threat, in the form of impact from an asteroid. Imagine, too, that this potentially cataclysmic event will not materialize for a century. Finally, imagine that the threat can be eliminated today, but at such a high cost that it would devastate the country. As a practical matter, India lacks the resources to take the steps necessary to prevent the asteroid strike. But if the nations of the world act in concert, they can begin to build technology that will allow them to divert the speeding space rock, thus insuring that it does not collide with India a century hence. The cost is high, but it is lower than the discounted benefit of eliminating the threat. If the world delays, it *might* still be able to eliminate the threat or reduce the damage if the asteroid does strike. But many scientists believe that the best approach, considering relevant costs and benefits, is to start immediately to build technology that will divert the asteroid.

Are wealthy nations, such the United States, obliged to contribute significant sums of money to protect India from the asteroid? On grounds of distributive justice, it is certainly tempting to think so. But if we do reach that conclusion, how should we deal with India's contention that it could avert millions of premature deaths from disease and malnutrition if the United States came to its aid with some small fraction of the US gross domestic product? If one nation is threatened by malaria or a tsunami, other nations might well agree that it is appropriate to help; it is certainly honorable to assist those in need. But even altruistic countries do not conventionally think that a threatened nation receives their assistance as a matter of entitlement. To be sure, there are some philosophical puzzles here, but for those who believe that there is such an entitlement, the puzzle remains: Why is there an entitlement to help in the event of future harm from an asteroid, rather than to help to avert current harms?

True, the problem of the asteroid threat differs significantly from that of climate change, whose adverse effects are not limited to a single nation. To make the analogy closer, let us suppose that all nations are threatened by the asteroid, in the sense that it is not possible to project where the collision will occur. Scientists believe that each nation faces a risk. But the risk is not identical. Because of its adaptive capacity, its location, its technology, and a range of other factors, let us stipulate that the United States is less vulnerable to serious damage than are India and the nations of Africa and Europe. Otherwise the problem is the same. Under plausible assumptions, the world will certainly act to divert the asteroid, and it seems clear that the United States will contribute substantial resources for that purpose.

In this scenario, all nations favor an international agreement requiring contributions to a general fund. But because the United States is less vulnerable, it believes that the fund should be smaller than the one supported by countries in greater danger. From the standpoint of domestic self-interest, then, those nations with the most to lose will naturally seek a larger fund than those facing lower risks.

At first glance, it might seem intuitive that the United States should accept the proposal for the larger fund, simply because it is so wealthy. If resources should be redistributed from rich to poor, on the ground that redistribution would increase overall welfare or promote fairness, the intuition appears sound. But there is an immediate problem. If redistribution from rich nations to poor nations is *generally* desirable, it is not at all clear that it should take the particular form of a deal in which the United States joins an agreement that is not in its interest. Other things being equal, the more sensible kind of redistribution would be a cash transfer, so that poor nations can use the money as they see fit. Perhaps India would prefer to spend the money on education, or on AIDS prevention, or on health care in general. If redistribution is what is sought, a generous deal with respect to the threat of an asteroid collision seems a crude way of achieving it.

A second difficulty is that the asteroid will not hit Earth for another hundred years. If the world takes action now, it will be spending current resources for the sake of future generations, which are likely to be much richer. The current poor citizens of poor nations are probably much poorer than will be the *future* poor citizens of those nations. If the goal is to help the poor, it is odd for the United States to spend significant resources to help posterity while neglecting the present. Thus far, then, the claim that the United States should join what seems, to it, to be an unjustifiably costly agreement to divert the asteroid is doubly puzzling. Poor nations would benefit more from cash transfers, and the current poor have a stronger claim to assistance than the future (less) poor.

From the standpoint of distributive justice, there is a third problem. Even wealthy countries such as the United States have many poor people, just as poor countries such as India have many rich people. If the United States is paying a lot of money to avert the threat of an asteroid strike, it would be good to know whether that cost is being paid, in turn, by wealthy Americans or by poor Americans. Suppose, for example, that greenhouse gas reductions lead to a significant increase in energy costs. Any such increase—either from carbon taxes or from cap and trade—would be regressive, in that it would hit the poor harder than the wealthy. True, products should be priced at their full social cost, and an externality-correcting tax would have strong justifications here as elsewhere. But if the concern is to help people who need help, such a tax is hard to defend.

Because the median members of wealthy nations are wealthier

than the median members of poor nations, it is plausible to think that if wealthy nations contribute a disproportionally high amount to the joint endeavor, the redistribution of wealth will be not be entirely ineffective. Americans who are asked to make the relevant payments are, on average, wealthier than the Indians who are paying less. But asking Americans to contribute more to a joint endeavor is hardly the best way of achieving the goal of transferring wealth from the rich to the poor.

CLIMATE CHANGE: FROM WHO TO WHOM?

In terms of distributive justice, the problem of climate change is analogous to the asteroid problem, in the sense that it raises three questions:

1. Why should redistribution take the form of an in-kind benefit rather than a general monetary grant that poor nations could use as they wish?
2. Why should rich nations help poor nations in the future rather than poor nations now?
3. If redistribution is the goal, why should it take the form of action by rich nations that might turn out to hurt many poor people?

To sharpen these questions, suppose that an international agreement to cut greenhouse gas emissions would cost the United States $325 billion. If distributive justice is the goal, should America spend the money on climate change or on other imaginable steps to help people in need? In fact, the distributive justice argument is especially weak in the case of climate change. No one would gain from an asteroid collision, but millions of people are benefiting, and will benefit, from climate change. Many people die from cold, and to the extent that warming reduces cold, it will save lives. Warming will also produce monetary benefits in many places, mainly as a result of increased agricultural productivity in countries such as Russia.[9]

Many millions of rural Chinese continue to live in poverty despite the country's increasing prosperity as a whole. These people are among the poorest in the world. For at least some of them, climate change could well provide benefits by increasing agricultural productivity. In addition, many millions of poor people would bear the burdensome cost of emissions reduction in the form of higher energy bills, lost jobs, and increased poverty.

None of this means that climate change is in the world's interest; it is not. And to be sure, a suitably designed emissions reduction agreement would almost certainly help poor people more than it would hurt them, because disadvantaged people in Africa and India are at such grave risk. From the standpoint of distributive justice, such an agreement might well be better than the status quo. The only point is that there is a highly imperfect connection between distributive goals on the one hand and requiring wealthy countries to pay for emissions reduction on the other.

TWO COUNTERARGUMENTS

There are two tempting counterarguments. The first involves the risk of catastrophe. The second involves the fact that cash transfers will go to governments that may be ineffective or corrupt.

Catastrophe. On certain assumptions about the science, greenhouse gas reductions are necessary to prevent a catastrophic loss of life.[10] Suppose, by way of imperfect analogy, that genocide is occurring in some nation. For multiple reasons, it would not be sensible to say that rich countries should give that country financial assistance rather than act to prevent the genocide. Or suppose that a nation is threatened by a natural disaster that would wipe out hundreds of thousands of lives. If other nations could somehow eliminate the harms associated with such a disaster, it would be hard to object that they should offer cash payments instead. One reason is that if many lives are at risk, and they can be saved through identifiable steps, taking those steps would seem to be the most direct and effective response to the problem, while cash transfers would have little or no advantage.

Suppose that climate change threatens to create massive losses of life in various countries. In light of the risk of catastrophe, perhaps emissions reductions are preferable to other redistributive strategies. The catastrophic scenario is a way of saying that the future benefits of cuts in greenhouse gases could be exceptionally high rather than merely very high. If poor people in poor nations face a serious risk of catastrophe, then greenhouse gas abatement *could* turn out to be the best way to redistribute wealth (or, more accurately, welfare) to people who would otherwise die in the future.

Ultimately the strength of the argument turns on the extent of the risk, based on the scientific evidence. If it is high, and faced mostly by people living in difficult or desperate conditions, the distributive justice argument gains a great deal of force.

Ineffective or Corrupt Governments. As noted, development aid is likely to be more effective than greenhouse gas restrictions as a method of helping poor people in poor nations. But a legitimate argument for cutting greenhouse gas emissions is that this step bypasses the governments of poor states more completely than other forms of development aid do. This might be counted as a virtue because the governments of some poor states are, to a large degree, either inefficient or corrupt (or both), and partly for that reason, ordinary development aid has not always been effective.

At the same time, this form of redistribution does not, as we have stressed, help existing poor people at all; it can, at best, help poor people in the future. In addition, the claim that emissions reduction avoids political inefficiency or corruption overlooks the fact that emissions abatement does not occur by itself; it must take place through the activity of governments. In cap-and-trade systems, for example, the government of a poor country would be given permits, which it could then sell to industry, raising enormous sums of money that the government could spend however it chose. A corrupt or disreputable government might not spend this money to benefit its people. On the contrary, it might use the money to finance political repression, while also possibly accepting bribes from local industry that chooses not to buy permits, in return for nonenforcement of the country's treaty obligations. These points are speculative, to be sure, but they suggest that the risks associated with inefficient or corrupt governments cannot easily be avoided.

PROVISIONAL CONCLUSIONS

There are reasonable arguments to support the view that people in rich countries should be giving money to help people in poor ones. There are reasonable arguments on behalf of a uniform carbon tax. There are also reasonable arguments on behalf of a worldwide cap-and-trade program, designating existing emissions rates as the starting point. What is puzzling is the claim that on grounds of distributive justice, the best approach is for the United States to join an agreement that is not in its interest rather than to take more direct steps to help those who need it.

It is true, however, that if America does spend a great deal on emissions reduction as part of an international agreement, and if the agreement does give particular help to disadvantaged people, considerations of distributive justice support its action, even if better redistributive mechanisms are imaginable. It is even possible that desirable redistribution is more likely to occur through climate change policy than otherwise, or is likely to be accomplished more effectively through climate policy than through direct foreign aid.

The only claims are that aggressive emissions reductions on the part of the United States are not an especially effective method for transferring resources from wealthy people to poor people, and that if this is the goal, many alternative policies would probably be better. It should be clear that these claims apply broadly to efforts to invoke distributive justice to ask wealthy nations to participate in international agreements from which other nations might gain.

CORRECTIVE JUSTICE

Climate change differs from the asteroid example in another way. In the asteroid scenario, no one can be blamed for the fact that the asteroid is hurtling toward Earth and the threat that it poses to India (or the world). But many people believe that by virtue of its past actions and policies, the United States, along with other developed nations, is particularly to blame for the problem of climate change.

Corrective justice arguments are backward looking, focused on wrongful behavior that occurred in the past. They require us to look at stocks rather than at flows. Of course, a disproportionate share of the stock of greenhouse gases can be attributed to other long-industrialized countries as well, such as Germany and Japan, and so what is said here about the United States can be applied to those other countries too.

In the context of climate change, the corrective justice argument is that the United States has wrongfully harmed the rest of the world—especially low-lying states and others that are most vulnerable—by emitting greenhouse gases in vast quantities. Many people believe that corrective justice requires America to devote significant resources to remedy the problem. India, for example, might be thought to have a moral claim against the United States, one derived from the principles of corrective justice, and on this view, the United States has an obligation to provide a compensatory remedy to India. (Because India is especially exposed to climate change, that nation can be used as a placeholder for those at particular risk.)

This argument enjoys a great deal of support in certain circles and seems intuitively correct. The apparent simplicity of the argument, however, masks some serious difficulties. The most general point, summarizing the argument as a whole, is that the climate change problem fits the corrective justice model poorly, because the consequence of such thinking would be to force many people who have not acted wrongfully to provide a remedy to many people who have not been victimized.

THE WRONGDOER IDENTITY PROBLEM

The current stock of greenhouse gases in the atmosphere is a result of the behavior of people from the past. Many of them are now dead. The basic problem for corrective justice is that dead wrongdoers cannot be punished or held responsible for their actions, or forced to compensate those they have harmed. At first glance, holding Americans today responsible for the activities of their ancestors is not fair or reasonable on corrective justice grounds.

The best response to this point is to insist that all or most Americans today benefit from the emissions activities of US citizens from the past, and therefore it would not be wrong to require Americans today to pay for abatement measures. This argument is familiar from debates about slave reparations, where it has been argued that Americans today have benefited from the toil of slaves one hundred fifty years ago. To the extent that members of current generations have gained from past wrongdoing, it may well make sense to ask them to compensate those harmed as a result. On one view, compensation can help to restore the status quo ante—that is, put members of different groups in the positions they would have occupied if the wrongdoing had not occurred.

But this argument runs into serious problems. In the context of climate change, the most obvious difficulty is empirical. How many US citizens benefit from past climate change emissions, and how much do they benefit? Many Americans today are, of course, immigrants or children of immigrants, and therefore are not the descendants of greenhouse-gas-emitting Americans of the past. Nonetheless, such people may benefit from past emissions, because they enjoy the kind of technological advances and material wealth that those emissions made possible. But have they actually benefited, and to what degree? Further, not all Americans inherit their wealth, and even those who do would not necessarily have inherited less if their ancestors' generations had not engaged in the greenhouse-gas-emitting activities.

Suppose that these obstacles could be overcome and that we could trace, with sufficient accuracy, the extent to which current Americans have benefited from past carbon emissions. As long as the costs are being totted up, the benefits should be as well, and used to offset the requirements of corrective justice. If past generations of Americans have imposed costs on the rest of the world, they have also conferred substantial benefits. American industrial activity has produced products that are (and have long been) consumed in foreign countries, and helped produce technological advances from which citizens in other countries have greatly benefited.

True, many citizens in other nations have not benefited much from those advances, just as many citizens of the United States have benefited little from them. But what would the world, or India, look like if America had engaged in 10 percent of its level of greenhouse gas emissions, or 20 percent, or 40 percent? For purposes of corrective justice, a proper accounting would seem to be necessary, and it presents formidable empirical and conceptual problems.

THE CULPABILITY PROBLEM

Philosophers disagree about whether corrective justice requires culpability.[11] Intentional, reckless, or negligent action is usually thought to be required for a corrective justice claim. Because multiple persons and actions (including actions of the victim) are necessary for harm to have occurred, identification of the person who has "caused" the harm requires some assignment of blame. At a minimum, the case for a remedy is stronger when a person acts culpably rather than innocently, and so it is worthwhile to inquire whether the United States or Americans can be blamed for contributing to climate change. The idea that Americans are to blame by contributing excessively to climate change is an important theme in international debates.

Negligence. The weakest standard of culpability is negligence. If you negligently injure people, you owe them a remedy. Economists define negligence as the failure to take cost-justified precautions. Lawyers tend to appeal to community standards.

Today the scientific consensus holds that the planet is warming and that this warming trend is due to human activity. But the consensus took a long time to form. Greenhouse-gas-emitting activities could not have been negligent, under existing legal standards, until a scientific consensus formed and it became widely known among the public—a relatively recent occurrence.[12]

Even today, it is not clear when and whether engaging in greenhouse gas emitting activities is properly characterized as negligent. Suppose that a large company in New York emits a large volume of greenhouse gases. Is it negligent? It is easily imaginable that the costs of emissions abatement would be significant; it is clear that the benefits of emissions abatement, in terms of diminished warming, would be very low. Heating a house, driving a car, running a freezer, taking an airplane—are all of these activities negligent? Even though the warming effects of the relevant emissions are essentially nil? Recent work tries to identity a "social cost of carbon"; in the United States, the central value is now around $37.[13] Perhaps we could use that value to test the question of negligence. But if so, a great deal of activity that involves greenhouse gas emissions would not count as negligent.

Negligent Government? What about the US government? The argument would be that the government failed to take precautions that would have cost it a lot but benefited the rest of the world much more.

In the context of climate change, the problem is that, as noted above, it is not clear that America could have taken unilateral action that would have created benefits for the rest of the world greater than the cost to the United States. Unilateral reductions in greenhouse gas emissions would not have a large effect on overall climate change. Use of the social cost of carbon might help, but here, as in the case of individuals, a great deal of emissions activity would not be defined as negligence.

However appealing, corrective justice intuitions turn out to be a poor fit with the climate change problem—where the dispute is among nations, and where an extremely long period of time must elapse before the activity in question generates harm. This is not to say that a corrective justice argument cannot be cobbled together and presented as the basis of a kind of rough justice in an imperfect world. But such an argument would rely heavily on notions of collective responsibility that are not so easy to defend.

PER CAPITA EMISSIONS

Along with other developing nations, China has urged that the analysis ought to focus on a nation's per capita emissions, not its aggregate emissions.[14] This argument might even be linked to a general "right to development," on the theory that a worldwide carbon tax (for example) would make it harder for poor nations to achieve the levels of development already attained by wealthy nations. Perhaps an imaginable climate change agreement, one that would actually be effective and efficient, would violate the right to development.

With respect to China, the factual predicate for this argument is that its population is the largest on the planet. Notwithstanding its truly explosive emissions growth, the country's per capita emissions remain well below those of many nations. China has contended that its relatively low per capita emissions rate—below not only the United States but also Japan, India, Russia, Germany, the United Kingdom, and the Ukraine—should be taken into account in deciding on appropriate policy.

To clarify the claim, assume that the world consists of only two nations, one with two billion people and one with one million people. Suppose that the two nations have the same aggregate emissions rate. Would it make sense to say that the two should be allocated the same level of emissions rights, for purposes of a system of cap and trade? Intuition suggests not, and therefore China argues that all citizens should have a right to the same level of opportunity, which means that emissions rights should be allocated on a per capita basis.[15]

A LITTLE DOUBLESPEAK? OF "COMMON BUT DIFFERENTIATED RESPONSIBILITIES"

China's argument for taking account of per capita emissions is captured by its support for and understanding of the principle of "common but differentiated responsibilities,"[16] which has played a large role in international debates. On the surface, this principle means that a country's obligations on climate issues should be determined by two factors: its responsibility for climate change and its capacity to cut emissions. Beneath the surface, the principle means that developed nations have to spend a great deal to reduce their emissions, while developing nations do not.

Invoking this principle, Chinese officials have called on developed countries to take the lead in cutting their emissions, and have argued that developing countries such as China are bound merely to take account of environmental issues as they continue to insure that their economies grow.[17] While China's position is not static and may be evolving, its officials have insisted that raising their citizens' standard of living is their first priority.[18] With this point in mind, the country has emphasized that any actions it takes in regard to climate change will be "within its capability based on its actual situation."[19]

China also maintains that developed countries have an obligation to assist the developing world with the challenges of climate change, both through technology transfer to allow sustainable development and through financial assistance for adapting to the effects of climate change.[20] This moral obligation, China argues, arises because the developed world bears the greatest share of responsibility for climate change.[21] Developed countries should now use their wealth to help poor countries develop in a world where warmer climates are a serious threat.[22]

A CRUEL IRONY

Some of these arguments have considerable intuitive appeal. But to the extent that China claims that emissions rights should be allocated on a per capita basis, it is asking for massive redistribution from the developed nations—above all the United States—to the developing nations (most of all, to China). It is most puzzling to suggest that the redistribution should occur in the context of climate change policy.

To see the point, we need to distinguish between greenhouse gas taxes and a cap-and-trade program. Some people favor the latter. A large challenge for such programs is to decide on the initial allocation of entitlements. An obvious possibility would be to say that all of the major emitters must reduce their emissions by a stated amount, relative to what they emitted on a specified date—by, say, 3 percent relative to 2005. Analytically, this approach would be similar to a tax in terms of its distributional consequences: both take existing emissions rates as the starting point. An alternative possibility, based on per capita rates and obviously attractive to China, would be to say that each nation has a right to emit a specified amount per person. Using this approach, the United States (with over 300 million people) would have less than 30 percent of the emissions rights of either India or China (each of which has over 1 billion people). The key point is that such an approach would represent a massive transfer of resources from the United States to other nations. Indeed, the transfer would be worth hundreds of billions of dollars.

Suppose that total global emissions were capped at their 2005 levels, and that emissions rights were allocated on a per capita basis.

For the United States, such an approach would require American companies to purchase hundreds of billions of dollars in emissions rights from China and other nations. But there is no sign that the United States intends to give hundreds of billions of dollars to China or India. Any proposal that it should do so, in general or in the context of climate change, would be widely unpopular, to say the least, and domestic political constraints would doom any such proposal. And if the United States does decide to give hundreds of billions of dollars to poor nations, why should the gift take the form of emissions rights?

It is increasingly clear that an international agreement to control climate change is necessary to reduce the risk of serious and potentially catastrophic harm. If the United States agrees to participate in a climate change agreement on terms that help the world, there would be no reason to object. Compared with continued inaction, participation under those terms would be honorable. The cruel irony is that weak arguments from distributive and corrective justice, designed to promote participation by the United States and other wealthy nations, appear to be creating an obstacle to a sensible agreement—and are thus serving to harm poor nations most of all.

CHAPTER 8

SEX EQUALITY VERSUS RELIGIOUS FREEDOM?

In the United States and in many other nations, it is generally agreed that most ordinary law, both civil and criminal, can be legitimately applied to religious organizations. Thus, for example, the government may prohibit members of religious institutions from engaging in murder, kidnapping, assault, or cruelty to animals, even if those acts are claimed to be part of a religious ceremony or otherwise guided by or even mandated by religious precepts.

At the same time, it is generally agreed that governments should hesitate before applying the law of sex discrimination to religious organizations. States do not, for example, require the Catholic Church to ordain women as priests. Under existing law, religious institutions are plainly permitted to engage in acts of sex discrimination that would be unacceptable if carried out by a secular institution.[1]

Let us call this puzzle the "Asymmetry Thesis." According to the Asymmetry Thesis, it is acceptable to apply ordinary civil and criminal laws to religious institutions, but it is not acceptable to apply the law forbidding sex discrimination to those institutions. It is permissible to prevent priests from beating up women (or anyone else) as part of a religious ceremony, but it is unacceptable for the government to ban sex segregation in religious education or to prohibit religious groups from excluding women from certain domains.

What is the source of this asymmetry? Can it be defended? My discussion here is meant to be tentative, but I believe that there is no good defense of the Asymmetry Thesis.

PUZZLES AND CONFLICTS

To anchor the discussion, consider some potential conflicts between sex equality and freedom of religion, conflicts that arise in one form or another in many countries:

1. Certain Jewish synagogues educate boys separately from girls, and certain Jewish schools refuse even to admit girls. Some Jewish girls and their parents object that this is a form of sex discrimination that contributes to sex-role stereotyping, thus harming girls and undermining equality of opportunity.
2. A Catholic university refuses to tenure several women teachers in its canon law department. A disappointed faculty member complains that this is a form of employment discrimination.[2] The university responds that courts should not be allowed to intervene in a religious matter of this kind.
4. Certain Mormon employers allegedly engage in various practices of sex discrimination. It is claimed that they refuse to hire women for certain jobs, and that they believe that being male is an occupational qualification, imposed in good faith, for certain positions. These prac-

tices are undertaken in the private sector, in institutions that have and do not have explicitly religious functions.

5. A Western nation allows immigrant men to bring in multiple wives. It recognizes their polygamous marriages and various discriminatory practices (including arranged marriages between teenage girls and older men) that accompany certain religious convictions.

In the United States, as elsewhere, the laws that forbid sex discrimination usually contain important exemptions for religious institutions. Courts have said that the free exercise clause of the Constitution requires courts to refrain from adjudicating sex discrimination suits brought by ministers against the church or religious institution employing them—even though ministers could certainly complain of assault or rape.[3] This principle of religious immunity from secular law has sometimes been read quite broadly to apply to lay employees of institutions (including high schools and universities) whose primary duties consist of spreading the faith or supervising religious rituals.[4]

The puzzle created by the Asymmetry Thesis is not only obvious but also important, for there is good reason to believe that serious forms of sex discrimination may result from the practices of some religious institutions, which can produce internalized norms of inequality. Those internalized norms might undermine equality of opportunity itself, as when women scale back their aspirations to conform to those norms. The remedy of "exit"—the right of women to leave a religious group or order—is important, but in practice it may not be available. Indeed, exit will not be sufficient when girls have been taught in a way that makes it hard for them to scrutinize the practices with which they have grown up. Here in particular, the ideal of equal opportunity is compromised.

How should a free society, committed at once to religious freedom and sex equality, respond to this problem? The answer is not obvious.

THE *SMITH* PRINCIPLE: GENERALITY AND ADMINISTRABILITY

To explore the underlying questions, it is necessary to step back a bit and offer some more general words about the relationship between constitutional law and religious institutions. In the United States, there is a sharp and continuing debate about whether a state may apply "facially neutral" laws to religious institutions. A law is facially neutral if it does not aim specifically at religious practices or beliefs. For example, a law banning the nonpayment of taxes or the burning of animals is facially neutral. By contrast, a law banning the Lord's Prayer or the practice of Buddhism is facially discriminatory.

Under current law in the United States, courts are likely to uphold any facially neutral law, under the presumption that such laws are constitutionally acceptable.[5] The constitutional validity of all facially neutral laws may be deemed "the *Smith* principle," after the controversial Supreme Court opinion, written by Justice Antonin Scalia in 1990, that established it.

The *Smith* principle seems to be based on two distinct ideas. The first involves the political safeguards that are expected to accompany lawmaking in a democracy. If a law discriminates against a particular group—no public religious services for Catholics or Buddhists, for example—the ordinary political protections are not in play, because only one group is being targeted. Courts need to get involved because there is a serious risk that the majority is oppressing the minority. By contrast, secular law that is not so targeted and that is neutral on its face, is less likely to interfere with religious liberty, properly conceived. The very neutrality and generality of such laws reduces the risk of oppression, for when multiple groups are subject to a restriction, they are likely to mobilize against it and to prevent its enactment unless it is genuinely justified. By emphasizing the value of political protection, the *Smith* principle suggests that a requirement of generality provides a reliable check on unjustified interference with freedom.

The second basis for the *Smith* principle is judicial administrability. When the state contends that it has strong and legitimate reasons to interfere with religious liberty, how easily can courts assess or balance the opposing interests? True, we can imagine some easy cases. A neutral tax law would almost certainly be upheld against religious objections, because a tax system would be very hard to run if religious objectors could exempt themselves. But many cases would be exceedingly hard for courts to handle, simply because of the difficulty of evaluating the competing claims. The best defense of the *Smith* principle is that even if it protects religious liberty too little, it comes close to protecting religious liberty enough—and it does so with the only principle that real-world judges can apply fairly and easily.

A straightforward reading of the *Smith* principle would suggest that no less than other neutral measures, laws forbidding discrimination can be applied properly to religious institutions. Hence, the Asymmetry Thesis is not at all compelled by the *Smith* principle. On the contrary, the Asymmetry Thesis is in grave tension with that principle, which would seem to permit application of antidiscrimination laws, facially neutral as they are.

SEX DISCRIMINATION AND RELIGIOUS LIBERTY

With this background, let us ask why a state might be permitted to apply its ordinary civil and criminal laws to religious institutions, yet be prohibited from applying the law of sex discrimination to such institutions. Let us see, in short, how the Asymmetry Thesis might be defended.

Ordinary Civil and Criminal Laws Are Backed by Especially Powerful Justifications, as Sex Discrimination Law Is Not. The first possibility is that, in principle, a state should interfere with religious practices only when it has an especially strong reason for doing so (sometimes described as a "compelling interest"). Ordinary criminal and civil laws provide that reason, whereas the law forbidding sex discrimination does not. On this view, it is one thing for a state to prohibit murder or assault. It is quite another for a state to forbid sex discrimination.

There can be no doubt that a judgment of this kind helps explain current practice. In fact, it plays a large role in establishing the Asymmetry Thesis. And the idea might have some force if the ordinary criminal and civil laws always directed themselves against the most serious harms. But they do not. The ordinary law prohibits infliction of injuries that might be relatively modest, such as libel and defamation, and minor assaults that count as such even without physical contact. The state does not apply civil law to religious organizations only when grave injuries are involved.

Religious organizations are thus subject to civil and criminal laws prohibiting low-level harms. Why can't the law against sex discrimination be applied as well? The interests that justify prohibiting sex discrimination are important. It is not easy to explain why those interests are weaker than the interests that underlie various aspects of the ordinary civil and criminal laws. Sex discrimination should not be considered a low-level harm.

Ordinary Law Does Not Strike at the Heart of Religious Liberty, as Sex Discrimination Law Could. Perhaps a prohibition on sex discrimination would impose a substantial burden on religious beliefs and practices, or even strike at their heart, whereas the ordinary civil and criminal laws do not. On this view, the *Smith* principle is wrong: some exemptions from ordinary law are necessary in order to protect religious liberty.[6] The reason for any religious exemption is respect for religious freedom and autonomy—respect that can usually coexist with ordinary civil and criminal laws, but not with the law forbidding sex discrimination. For some religious institutions, a legal mandate of sex equality, forbidding discrimination, would be intolerable, whereas application of ordinary law fits comfortably, in general, with their own beliefs and practices. The Asymmetry Thesis might be defended squarely on these grounds.

The argument is hardly implausible. Sometimes ordinary civil or criminal law is entirely consistent with the norms of religious institutions. Importantly, much of that law grows directly or indirectly out of religious principles and norms. The prohibitions against murder, theft, and assault lie at the foundation of both religious and secular law. It is for this reason that application of ordinary civil and criminal laws causes no trouble for most religious organizations. Such prohibitions are compatible with—even in the service of—the goals of those organizations. And it is also possible to imagine requirements of sex equality that would threaten religious practices and convictions. Imagine a ban on sex discrimination in the priesthood. Perhaps the Asymmetry Thesis can be defended on the grounds that ordinary civil and criminal laws do not compromise religious beliefs and practices, whereas a ban on sex equality would.

But in its broadest form, this argument is quite fragile. Some aspects of ordinary civil and criminal laws do regulate practices and beliefs that are central to some religions. Consider, for example, laws forbidding animal sacrifice or the use of drugs, or even laws forbidding certain kinds of assault and imprisonment. And some aspects of the law of sex discrimination would not interfere at all with some religious beliefs and practices. For some religions, sex equality is permissible or even mandatory; in any case, it is practiced. Indeed, a commitment to sex equality can also be connected with deeply held principles of some religions.

To be sure, it is conceivable that as a class, ordinary civil and criminal laws are not in tension with religious practices and beliefs, whereas the law of sex discrimination is in tension with them. But to the extent that this is so, we would not endorse the Asymmetry Thesis. We would ask more specific questions about the relationship between the particular practice at issue and the particular legal intervention. In the end, the Asymmetry Thesis cannot be easily defended on the grounds that ordinary law is a lesser intrusion into religious autonomy than is sex equality law.

Balancing. It would be possible to defend the Asymmetry Thesis, or to make sense of potential conflicts between religion and secular law, with a commitment to balancing. More specifically, the suggestion would be that in order to know whether the government can interfere with religious practices, we need to consider two factors. The first is the legitimacy and strength of the state's interest; the second is the extent of the harmful effect on religion. Under a balancing approach, we might reach the following simple conclusions:

- An illegitimate state interest (in, say, weakening an unpopular religion) is entirely off-limits.
- A weak state interest (in preventing, let us suppose, libels that are not especially harmful) is not enough to justify any intrusion on religion at all.
- An exceedingly powerful state interest (in, for example, preventing murder or rape) would justify any intrusion, no matter how severe.
- A strong interest would justify most intrusions on religion, at least if the intrusion is not especially severe.

All of these terms would need to be defined, but under this approach, most cases would be easy. The hardest problems would arise where a strong interest was matched by a reasonable claim, on the part of a religious organization, that the interference would seriously jeopardize or injure it.

In principle, a standard of this sort seems sensible for a democratic social order to adopt. The major objection is that in order to accept it, we would need to have a degree of confidence in those who would be entrusted with administering it. Such a standard would require courts (or other institutions) to decide which aspects of the civil and criminal laws were sufficiently justified. For example, we could imagine reasonable judgments in favor of applying a ban on imprisoning people to religious institutions—but against applying a ban on peyote, on the ground that the government cannot defend the peyote ban with the force that it can defend a ban on imprisonment.

Under this approach, we would not accept the Asymmetry Thesis. The legitimacy of applying the law of sex discrimination to religious institutions would depend on an assessment of two factors: (1) the strength of the state interest and (2) the extent of the interference with religious institutions. In some cases, the claim that sex discrimination is central to religious practices will clearly be unconvincing. In other cases, that claim will have evident force.

Different outcomes would be imaginable in different contexts, and I do not mean to sort out all of the conceivable dilemmas. The basic point is that with a balancing approach of this kind, the asymmetry between most civil and criminal laws and the law banning sex discrimination could not possibly be sustained. Under the standard I am exploring, some ordinary laws would not legitimately be applied to religious institutions (because they would fail the balancing test), whereas some of the laws banning sex discrimination could be (because they would survive the balancing test). The legal standard would force a candid assessment of the nature of the intrusion and the strength of the underlying interest.

BARRIERS AND FREEDOMS

This conclusion means that there is no *general* barrier to applying the law of sex discrimination to religious institutions. Whether it is legitimate to do so depends on the extent of the interference with religious convictions and the strength of the state's justification. Reasonable people can reach different conclusions about particular cases. For those who endorse the Asymmetry Thesis, an especially serious problem is that discriminatory practices may have harmful effects on the development of beliefs and aspirations on the part of men and women alike.

To be sure, religious liberty deserves a central place in a free society, and it would be excessive to say that the law of sex discrimination should always or generally be applied to religious institutions. But there is no convincing justification for the Asymmetry Thesis.

CHAPTER 9

A NEW PROGRESSIVISM

The German psychologist Dietrich Dörner has conducted some fascinating experiments, via computer, to see whether people can engage in successful social engineering.[1] Participants are asked to solve problems faced by inhabitants of some region of the world. The problems may involve poverty, poor medical care, inadequate crop fertilization, sick cattle, or insufficient water. Through the magic of the computer, many policy initiatives are available (improved care of cattle, childhood immunization, drilling more wells), and participants can choose among them. Once particular initiatives are selected, the computer projects, over short periods and then over decades, what is likely to happen in the region.

In these experiments, success is entirely possible. Some initiatives will actually make for effective and enduring improvements. But most of the participants—even the most educated and professional ones—produce calamities. They do so because they do not see the complex, systemic effects of particular interventions. For example, they may see the importance of increasing the number of cattle, but once they do that, they fail to anticipate the serious risk of overgrazing. They may understand full well the value of drilling more wells to provide water, but they do not foresee the energy and environmental effects of the drilling, which then endanger the food supply. Only the rare participant is able to see a number of steps down the road—to understand the multiple effects of one-shot interventions into the system.

NOT A MIDPOINT

My goal in this chapter is to elaborate an understanding of the appropriate role of government, which I will call the New Progressivism. This understanding is developed with particular reference to the role of the nation-state in an era of globalization. The New Progressivism is an effort to combine an appreciation of a great lesson of the first half of the twentieth century (the failure of reliance on markets alone) with an appreciation of a great lesson of the second half of that century (the failure of economic planning).

I suggest that the New Progressivism offers simultaneously (1) a distinctive conception of government's appropriate *means*, an outgrowth of the late-twentieth-century critique of economic planning, and (2) a distinctive understanding of government's appropriate *ends*, an outgrowth of evident failures with complete reliance on market arrangements and largely a product of the mid-twentieth-century critique of so-called laissez-faire. For this reason, the New Progressivism should not be seen as a compromise between right and left or as an effort to seek some midpoint between those who believe in markets and those who reject them. Far from being a compromise or a midpoint, the New Progressivism offers both means and ends of its own.

With respect to means, the New Progressivism rejects approaches prominently associated with both social democracy and the New Deal, on the grounds that they are frequently ineffective or even counterproductive. To the New Progressivists, social democrats are too often like participants in Dörner's experiments. Those who endorse the New Progressivism are insistently focused on *consequences*. They know that initiatives designed to help people who need assistance might backfire in practice—and that good intentions are no excuse for bad outcomes. Above all, those who endorse the New Progressivism have learned from the past fifty years of experience with markets and with efforts to discipline and constrain markets. They are alert to the risk of surprise and unintended bad consequences. They do not favor social engineering. Wherever possible, they attempt to use market-oriented strategies, enlisting markets on behalf of human interests, above all because such strategies are likely to work.

It follows that New Progressivists are alert to the central role of civil society, and especially to the importance of social norms, which often drive private behavior and which can change, for better or worse, over time. They are highly skeptical of command-and-control regulation and of aggressive interference with the labor market. They want to supplement markets, not displace them. They favor initiatives such as the Earned Income Tax Credit (EITC) and housing subsidies for the poor, and they are cautious about a high minimum wage and rent-control legislation. They believe that environmental problems should be handled through economic incentives, not centralized mandates. They favor nudges, in the form of low-cost, choice-preserving initiatives (such as default rules). For example, the New Progressivism

- attempts to control problems associated with social norms, such as crime, obesity, and distracted driving, through democratic efforts at *norm management*, often involving public-private partnerships;
- places the highest possible premium on education and training;
- rejects economic protectionism;
- favors incentives rather than centralized governmental commands;
- attempts to insure flexibility in the labor market, in part

on the ground that flexibility helps low-income workers as well as others; and

- sees economic growth as a central (though far from exclusive) part of antipoverty policy.

So much for means; what of ends? Those who endorse the New Progressivism seek initially to achieve an *incompletely theorized agreement* on various practices and initiatives capable of attracting support from a wide range of theoretical perspectives. (See chapter 10.) Utilitarians, Kantians, those who begin from diverse theological positions, and numerous others can support the approaches described here. But to the extent that theoretical depth is required, New Progressivists will insist that free markets promote liberty, and indeed are centrally associated with it, but also that markets operate against a background that includes considerable injustice and also less than complete liberty. They think that, to a degree, complete reliance on market ordering will build on that unacceptable background.

Despite their enthusiasm for free markets, New Progressivists have considerable sympathy for some of the ideals associated with social democracy in Europe and the New Deal in the United States (see chapter 2): decent life prospects for all, good education, a social safety net for those at the bottom, environmental protection, workplace safety. But they believe that those ideals have often been quite murky and ill-defined—and also that they have been confused too often with a freestanding egalitarianism designed to promote equal economic outcomes as such. Those who believe in a New Progressivism do hope to produce an acceptable floor for everyone (largely by providing decent opportunities for all). But they are not much offended by large disparities in wealth—not because these are necessarily fair but because the much more important goal is to guarantee decent opportunities for all and because allowing at least some such disparities may well be necessary to provide appropriate incentives for economic growth. (Admittedly, this proposition raises empirical questions that require investigation.)

To those who believe in a New Progressivism, what is most necessary is to insure that basic *human capabilities* do not fall below a certain threshold.[2] With Franklin Delano Roosevelt, New Progressivists favor minimal security. (See chapter 2.) New Progressivists add a distinctive conception of equality, one that forbids second-class citizenship or lower caste status for members of any group. This anticaste principle makes sex equality a singularly high priority, as a means for economic development and an end in itself.

OF MESS AND MENACE

The great American law professor Karl Llewellyn is reported to have said, "Technique without morals is a menace; but morals without technique is a mess." This is a fitting criticism of some experiments in social democracy over the last several decades and a shorthand description of the failures of many participants in Dörner's experiments—failures with parallels in the experiences of twentieth-century planners of various stripes. But Llewellyn reportedly also made essentially the same statement with an intriguingly different emphasis: "Morals without technique is a mess; but technique without morals is a menace." This is an apt criticism not only of many twentieth-century experiments in social engineering but also of excessive reliance on free markets. The real task, for those interested in a New Progressivism, involves developing approaches and methods that are neither menace nor mess.

Longstanding debates have drawn attention to two possible strategies for dealing with markets: leave them alone or displace them. But the dichotomy is much too simple—in fact, damagingly so. First, the idea of "displacing" markets conceals a range of options, from nationalizing industries to blocking certain deals to providing information. Second, it is possible to complement markets rather than displace them—to provide institutions that do what markets do not do, and to help people who are failed by markets, an emphatically human institution. As economist Amartya Sen has written, very much in the spirit of the New Progressivism, "[I]t is possible to argue at the same time both (1) for *more* market institutions, and (2) for going *more beyond* the market."[3]

With respect to methods and strategies, that is what I will be suggesting here. Throughout this chapter, I will paint with an extremely broad brush, discussing many issues that could easily be treated in a short book (or even a long one). My hope is that the brisk and sometimes reckless treatment of many issues might make up for its otherwise unpardonable neglect of the trees, by providing a decent perspective on the forest—a perspective that perhaps continues to be absent from existing treatments of possible twenty-first-century "ways."

THE WAY OF MARKETS AND THE WAY OF PLANNING

If there is a New Progressivism, what is it opposing? There are two candidates. Let us understand the first to be a stylized version of the Ronald Reagan–Margaret Thatcher program, drawn from the work of the great Nobel Prize–winning economist Friedrich Hayek. Call this "the way of markets."

On this view, free markets are indispensable to both liberty and economic growth. The state's role is to create the preconditions for well-functioning markets by (1) establishing rights of private property and freedom of contract, (2) ensuring competition rather than monopoly, and (3) preventing force and fraud. Perhaps the government should also provide a social safety net, though a relatively weak one (to insure proper work incentives). But according to those who endorse the way of markets, government should not interfere with the labor market by requiring, say, high minimum wages or special protections for labor unions. And those who endorse the way of markets place the highest possible premium on both economic growth and a particular, market-based conception of liberty.

Of course, there is a spectrum of possible approaches here, from those who reject a social safety net to those willing to accept an ample set of protections for people at the bottom. What I mean to stress—captured in the ideas of "neoliberalism" and "liberalization"—is the primary emphasis on free markets and economic productivity.

As with the way of markets, the way of planning is actually a spectrum of ways, ranging from Soviet-style centralized planning to those forms of social democracy that are comfortable, in some areas, with nationalized industries, aggressively regulated markets, price and wage controls, and, most generally, "planning" of various kinds. For diverse examples, consider the following:

- laws that make it difficult for employers to discharge employees;
- laws that make it hard for landlords to evict tenants;
- state-created or state-protected monopolies;
- environmental regulations that specify the technology that must be used by industry;
- high minimum-wage requirements;
- high barriers to entry into certain jobs and professions;
- protectionism;
- tariffs;
- production requirements and quotas;
- public ownership of industry; and
- price-fixing or ceilings and floors on prices as a whole.

Of course, it is possible for a nation to adopt narrow or broad plans, or to be a planner in only a few small domains. A government that is generally skeptical of planning might conclude (whether rightly or wrongly) that it makes sense to have tariffs in some areas, or that agriculture should be protected with price supports, or that certain workers should be protected from arbitrary discharge, or that technological requirements are properly placed on new cars, to reduce levels of air pollution.

PROBLEMS AND STRESSES

Let us now explore briefly some of the problems in both of these ways. For those who seek the way of markets, the initial difficulty is that while markets help to protect and promote liberty, they should not be identified with it. Markets operate against the backdrop set by existing distributions of resources, opportunities, and talents. When a disabled employee receives substandard wages and works under terrible conditions, it is wrong to say that liberty is sufficiently respected if we simply respect the deal. To the extent that starting points and existing distributions are products of a lack of liberty, market ordering may be a problem, not the solution. Whether the deal should be disrupted is another question. But from the standpoint of liberty, what markets generate should not always come with an automatic stamp of approval.

An equally fundamental problem is that the consequences of market ordering may not be so wonderful for many people. In any large nation, reliance on free markets alone—even if the markets are policed by prohibitions on force and fraud—will predictably produce a situation in which millions of people end up working long hours in shabby conditions for little pay (if they end up employed at all). Certainly a social safety net can help. But even if it is generous, it is not going to do all of what must be done. It will not, for example, protect people against unsafe working conditions, sexual harassment, pollution, or unfair discrimination. Market failures must be corrected. (See chapter 3.) And to the extent that the economic catalogue of market failures may not include certain forms of injustice (such as discrimination), free societies nonetheless take steps to counteract injustice.

But planning faces severe difficulties of its own. One problem is that it is likely to be vulnerable to pressures from self-interested private groups with stakes in a particular outcome. Environmental regulation might be turned into a mechanism for distributing benefits to groups that have precious little interest in environmental protection. An even more fundamental problem involves the unintended adverse consequences of even the most well-motivated plans. As Hayek emphasized, planners lack complete knowledge and are constantly surprised. The "knowledge problem" poses a constant and often insuperable challenge for planners. To take two simple examples, a law that makes it hard for employers to discharge employees is likely to make employers reluctant to hire people in the first instance. Similarly, a high minimum wage is likely to decrease employment. The problem is pervasive. We can understand it a bit better in light of Dörner's work, showing the unfortunate and sometimes catastrophic effects of one-shot interventions. Economic and social orders are *systems*, and the difficulty with plans is that their architects are frequently unable to foresee the consequences of their actions. The great advantage of incentives, rather than commands, is that they reduce the knowledge problem.

Planners commonly refer to the unfairness of markets, and they are often right. But an emphasis on unfairness does not justify laws that actually do no good. As Amartya Sen and Jean Drèze write in their book *India: Development and Participation*, "The rhetoric of 'equity' has often been invoked to justify governmental interventions without any scrutinized political assessment of how these powers will be exercised and what actual effects they will have. In practice, these ill-directed regulations have not only interfered often enough with the efficiency of economic operations (especially of modern industries), they have also failed fairly comprehensively to promote any kind of real equity in distributional matters."[4] An overriding problem with the way of planning is that the consequences of plans are often really bad, not least from the perspectives of well-meaning planners themselves.

THE ROLE OF GLOBALIZATION

Thus far, I have said nothing about globalization. (By that term, I mean to refer, very simply, to the increasing mobility of persons, information, and products from one area of the globe to another.)

What is the effect of globalization on the way of planning and the way of markets?

It is best to think of global markets as like ordinary domestic markets in exaggerated form. The major effect of global pressures is to intensify competition, so that stringent national regulation might well leave companies within a country at a disadvantage both abroad and at home. In fact, such companies might decide to do business in other nations. If the effect of regulation is to cause companies to exit, it might cause serious harm—among other things, by reducing both growth and employment. Strict environmental controls might be objectionable for this reason. If a rule is designed to control greenhouse gas emissions, it might not be so helpful if polluters leave and continue to pollute where they do business. True, such risks might be reduced through protectionist measures, but these create familiar problems of their own, because they hurt local consumers by increasing prices and are likely, generally speaking, to damage the national economy.

In some respects, globalization increases the problems associated with both of the two ways. Insofar as markets produce unfairness and negative results for millions of people, global pressures can increase the difficulty. (Of course, such markets also produce many benefits for poor people as well as for everyone else, especially insofar as they promote growth, create jobs, and cut prices.) If a nation's workers have to compete with everyone in the world—or, in any case, with a much larger class of people—those without training and skills are going to be left further behind. At the same time, global pressures will inevitably confound ill-considered plans. Because markets are frequently global, the effect of plans will often be very different from what was sought and anticipated. This is a particular problem if, for example, an effect of stringent regulation of the labor market is to reduce the demand for domestic labor, thus hurting domestic workers.

These points hardly mean that states are incapable of governing in a global era. There is a great deal that they can do. The increased mobility of capital has not disabled national regulation. But the problems with both of the two ways are simultaneously intensified by the existence of global markets.

THE ROLE OF COSTS

Those who favor markets and those who favor planning often make a sharp distinction between "negative rights" and "positive rights." The former are said to be barriers to government action, and to that extent costless. The latter are entitlements to government protection, and to that extent costly. Market enthusiasts argue for the former and against the latter. Planners tend to argue for both.

From the standpoint of the New Progressivism, both views suffer from a problem that is both conceptual and practical: there is no categorical difference between negative and positive rights. Both consist of entitlements to government action, and both are costly. Compare, for example, the right to freedom of speech with the right to a minimum-income guarantee. In a state of anarchy, or in a state without money, neither right can exist. Of course, the minimum-income guarantee needs taxpayer support. But the same is true for the right to free speech. Without institutions (including a judiciary) willing to protect people from both public and private intrusions on free speech,[5] that right cannot exist. Without a sufficiently funded state willing and able to prevent public marauders from silencing opposition, free speech is a chimera. Without public protection from private acts of violence against those who make controversial statements, free speech is weakened.

What is true for free speech is true for much of the universe of supposedly negative rights.[6] Consider, for example, two rights that are central to a market economy: the right to private property and the right to freedom of contract. Both of these depend on government protection. (See chapter 2.) Private property does not exist in the state of nature, at least not in its current form. It is a taxpayer-subsidized right, justified on the grounds that it benefits individuals and society as a whole. True, people can make contracts without a strong state, but unless a taxpayer-subsidized legal system stands ready and able to insure that contracts are enforced, how much force are mere words likely to have?

Those who believe in a New Progressivism know that all rights have costs and that a poor state cannot adequately protect rights. One reason why they favor a strong economy and economic growth is that these are important preconditions for ample rights protection. In a rich or poor state, it follows that a central task for democratic self-government is to obtain the necessary funds and to insure that they are allocated in a way that reflects sensible priority setting. The field of public finance is not separable from the field of democratic theory.

SOCIAL MEANING AND SOCIAL NORMS

Those who endorse the way of markets may not have a lot to say about the relationship between government and civil society. Market enthusiasts tend to rely on existing norms and preferences; this is part of their conception of laissez-faire. Those who endorse the way of planning may also have little to say about civil society, sometimes treating it as a domain that must be enlisted in the interest of social goals. A better approach would emphasize several points:

1. the crucial importance of social norms in producing both desirable and undesirable behavior;
2. the likely role of government in helping to constitute such norms;
3. the dependence of social norms on current information;
4. the often rapid change in social norms over time;
5. the extent to which highly visible, or cognitively "available," examples and events can alter norms and behavior; and

6. the possible use of government to move norms in desirable directions.

These points suggest promising possibilities for controlling many social problems, including crime, obesity, HIV/AIDS, discrimination, distracted driving, and environmental degradation. What I will be emphasizing here is the significance of *social cascades*, including *norm cascades*, in which social interactions can lead behavior in dramatic directions. (See chapter 1.) Sometimes these cascades are induced by new beliefs; sometimes they are induced by new understandings of the meaning of certain actions. Since people take their cues from the actions of others, and since they care about their reputations, certain policies can backfire, while others can have wide-ranging desirable effects.

PROBLEMS WITH BANS

When government seeks to discourage certain conduct, what should it do? Those committed to planning generally have a simple answer: forbid it. Those committed to markets respond similarly, though they are reluctant to ask government to discourage private behavior falling outside the basic categories of force and fraud. Those who believe in a New Progressivism think that the shared answer—"forbid it"—is too simple and misleading, and potentially even damaging.

New Progressivists do believe that incentives are important, and for anyone who believes this, it seems natural to think that if conduct is banned, there will be less of it. But bans create problems of their own. In some (admittedly unusual) circumstances, they can be self-defeating, leading to more of the behavior that they seek to reduce. The reason is that behavior is often driven by social norms and by the signal that the behavior carries; a ban can amplify the signal and increase the conduct. Suppose, for example, that people are engaging in certain harmful conduct precisely because it is a way of defying authority and offering certain signals to relevant people. You might smoke, for example, because smoking is, in some places, an act of rebellion; so, too, with engaging in unsafe sex; so, too, with a decision to commit a crime. In short, actions have meanings, and the *social meaning* of an action is an important determinant of what people will do and when they will do it. Consider the finding that when people are paid to engage in a certain desirable activity (cleaning up, for example, or arriving on time to pick up children from school), they will sometimes actually engage in that behavior less rather than more—because the payment reduces the effect of the norm, which would otherwise have the deterrent effect of the payment.[7]

Bans may also have a high degree of rigidity and impose significant costs. In some cases, it is possible to identify approaches that are more flexible, have high benefits, and impose lower burdens. "Nudges," in the form of small steps that maintain freedom of choice, may be less costly and more effective than mandates and benefits.[8] Consider automatic enrollment in savings plans, which is highly effective in increasing participation rates—potentially more effective, in fact, than significant economic incentives.

DOING WHAT OTHERS DO

Those who seek a New Progressivism are especially interested in enlisting an understanding of social norms and social meanings in the service of improved policies. They emphasize that in many domains, people think and act because of what they think (relevant) others think and do. Here are some examples:

- Employees are more likely to file suit against their employer if others on the job have done so.[9]
- Teenage girls who see that other teenagers are hav-

ing babies are more likely to become pregnant themselves.[10]

- Littering and nonlittering appear to be contagious behaviors.[11]
- The same is true of some kinds of crime.[12]
- Those who know other people who are on public assistance are more likely to go on public assistance themselves.[13]
- If people are informed of how their energy use compares with that of their neighbors, they consume less energy.[14]
- The behavior of proximate others affects the decision whether to recycle.[15]
- A good way to increase the incidence of tax compliance is to inform people of high levels of voluntary tax compliance.[16]
- Students are less likely to engage in binge drinking if they think that most of their fellow students do not engage in binge drinking, so much so that disclosure of this fact is one of the few successful methods of reducing binge drinking on university campuses in the United States.[17]

As we saw in chapter 1, social influences affect behavior by means of two different mechanisms. The first is informational. If many other people support a particular candidate or refuse to use drugs, observers receive a signal about what it makes sense to do. The second mechanism is reputational, as group members impose sanctions on perceived deviants, and would-be deviants anticipate the sanctions in advance.[18] Even when people do not believe that what other people do provides information about what actually should be done, they may think that the actions of others provide information about what other people *think* should be done. Reputational considerations may lead people to do or not do the following: obey the law, smoke, drive while drunk, and help others.

The central question is how understanding these points might lead policies in better directions. What is especially promising is the possibility of achieving a "tipping point," at which large numbers of people start moving in novel directions. People typically have different thresholds for choosing to believe or do something new or different. As those with low thresholds come to a certain belief or action, people with somewhat higher thresholds join them, possibly to a point where a critical mass is reached, making groups tip. The result can be to produce snowball or cascade effects, as small or even large groups of people end up believing or doing something simply because other people seem to believe that it is true or worth doing. Many real-world phenomena have a great deal to do with cascade effects.[19] Consider, for example, smoking, participating in protests, striking, recycling, using birth control, choosing what to watch on television,[20] even leaving bad dinner parties.[21] We can understand certain people, in the private and public sectors, as "norm entrepreneurs," seeking to give certain signals to many people, and, in the process, helping to shift norms in a desirable direction.

All this is quite abstract. The central question remains: How might government induce tipping, or social cascades?

EDUCATION AND INFORMATION

Suppose that people are engaging in an activity that involves harm to themselves or to others; for simplicity, assume that the activity is not itself criminal. From the standpoint of the New Progressivism, the first prescription is simple: inform people. With respect to cigarette smoking, obesity, and unsafe sex, a great deal of risky behavior comes simply from a lack of information. Evidence shows that by itself, information, if it can be made salient and vivid, can produce substantial changes in behavior. In Thailand, a revelation that 44 percent of sex workers in Chiang Mai were infected with HIV appears to have contributed to a substantial increase in the use of condoms. Growth in condom use in the United States in the 1980s was driven largely by information. Public information campaigns, use of the mass media, and face-to-face education and training programs can help.[22]

This should hardly be surprising. But there is a somewhat more subtle point. It is possible to produce *information-induced norm cascades*, in which social norms—and social meanings—change dramatically as a result of changes in beliefs. In the United States, this has happened with large-scale shifts in judgments about cigarette smoking and, in the early 1990s, with large-scale shifts in judgments about both sexual harassment and unsafe sex. One of the causes and consequences of these shifts has been a change in the relevant social meaning.

Whereas smokers were once thought to be doing something entirely normal, so that objecting nonsmokers were bossy intermeddlers, smokers are now thought to be doing something aggressive and possibly harmful (as a result of secondhand smoke), so that they are expected to refrain or to apologize and to ask permission. What once seemed abnormal and even bold—a request to refrain—now seems normal and unobjectionable. With respect to buckling seat belts, something similar has happened. At one point, those who buckled their belts seemed to be accusing the driver or confessing cowardice; that was the social meaning of their decision to buckle. As norms shifted, the act of buckling had no such meaning.[23] A general question is when and whether dissemination of more information about harm-producing activity can produce large-scale changes in behavior. Often it seems to do precisely that. In the areas of obesity and distracted driving, we might hope for significant changes in the future.

COSTS AND NORMS

Of course, information may not do enough. People who engage in risky behavior often know that their behavior is risky. People who text while driving, or who pollute or who otherwise impose environmental harm, often know what they are doing. People who engage in discrimination may mistake no facts. In such circumstances, New Progressivists will be willing to consider initiatives that will increase the benefits or decrease the (pecuniary or nonpecuniary) costs of desirable behavior, and decrease the benefits or increase the (pecuniary or nonpecuniary) costs of undesirable behavior. Efforts to influence norms might play a role in these efforts.

In the context of risk-taking behavior, it is often easy to think of steps in this vein. People might, for example, be required to wear seat belts, or to use helmets when riding motorcycles. Such programs impose sanctions on violators. Sometimes subsidies are better than sanctions. In the context of the HIV/AIDS crisis, condom marketing programs have often been demonstrably successful. Especially when high-risk areas and poor households are targeted, such programs have been exceedingly beneficial, producing significant increases in condom sales and use.

It can also be important to alter the social meaning of risk-producing activity, partly through creative private-public partnerships. In some places in the world, condom use is an accusation or a confession. But in other cultures, the failure to use a condom reflects a kind of irresponsibility—a willingness to endanger the life of another person. The most promising policies make condom use appear routine and responsible, and hardly an act of cowardice or a violation of the goals of the underlying activity.

Norms are changed most easily when the relevant population is young. With respect to HIV/AIDS, obesity, distracted driving, environmental harm, and crime, many people are in the process of developing their own norms. To the extent that government can work with this population, helping to create norms that produce benefit rather than harm, there is much to be gained. For HIV/AIDS in particular, an absolutely central goal should be to insure equality on the basis of gender with respect to sexual relations—an idea that calls for prohibitions, through law and norms, on sexual coercion of all kinds (principally rape, but other forms of force as well). "No" should be understood to mean "no"; "only with a condom" should be understood to mean exactly that. Obesity and distracted driving are especially high-priority items for the future, and here norms are crucial.

CRIME: ORDER MAINTENANCE AND CONTAGION

Why do people commit crimes? No simple answer would make sense. For some, poverty and desperation are part of the answer. But part of the answer also lies in people's perceptions of what other people do. Criminality and law-abiding behavior appear to be contagious.

If most people think that many people are engaging in crime, it will increase. If most people think that few people are criminals, criminal activity will be less likely. The bad news is that all societies are vulnerable to "crime cascades," as people take their cues from others. The good news is that this fact can be enlisted in the service of crime prevention. In both the United States and England, efforts have been made, with considerable success, to use order maintenance and community policing in the interest of "legality cascades." In various contexts, an understanding of group polarization can help explain the underlying social dynamics.

In the 1990s, for example, New York saw a dramatic decrease in crime—not merely in murder (40 percent) but also in burglary (over 25 percent) and robbery (over 30 percent). A contributing factor can be seen in light of the "fixing broken windows" approach to crime prevention. The basic idea is that both law-abiding citizens and potential lawbreakers learn a great deal from the presence of order or disorder. People who obey the law are less likely to use the streets in the presence of disorder, and prospective criminals are more likely to engage in criminal activity, taking disorder as a signal of what is possible. But if minor problems—such as begging, graffiti, prostitution, loitering, littering, and broken windows—are sharply reduced, the signals will be different, and more serious crimes will decline too. Efforts to stop or reverse a crime epidemic at the very start, through seemingly small changes in context, can bring about sizeable benefits.

This is the core of the "order maintenance" approach to crime. In 1993, New York took new steps to maintain social order, and to give new signals to prospective criminals, by focusing on seemingly small criminal actions, such as aggressive begging, public drunkenness, prostitution, and vandalism. Prospective criminals, and prospective victims, act on the basis of their perceptions of what other people are going to do. When people think that crime is increasing, cascade effects are possible. Happily, the opposite can happen when people are given signals that crime is decreasing.

EMPLOYMENT AND POVERTY: SUPPLEMENTING, NOT DISPLACING, MARKETS

Let us turn from social norms to issues of deprivation and poverty and in particular to three ways of responding to certain problems in the employment market. These ways are associated respectively with markets, planning, and New Progressivism. My general suggestion is that a New Progressive government should generally refuse to block exchanges between contracting parties. It should respond instead by providing *economic help directly to those who need help*. These "market supplementing" approaches are preferable to "market displacing" approaches characteristic of the way of planning.

Those who favor the way of markets tend to respond to poverty either with nothing or with a social safety net, and not a very generous one at that. Those who favor the way of planning respond with high minimum wages, aggressive regulation of the labor and housing markets, and a generous social safety net. Those who endorse the New Progressivism reject both approaches. They place the highest premium on three strategies: (1) education and training, (2) taxpayer-supported wage and housing subsidies, and (3) incentives to companies to increase the likelihood that they will relocate to poor areas and hire people who would otherwise lack work ("empowerment zones" and "enterprise zones").

Above all, they believe that no citizen should be poor if she is willing and able to work; that to the extent feasible, everyone should be *able* to work; and that in the absence of special circumstances (disability, obligations to others), everyone should be *willing* to work. This is the sense in which New Progressivists endorse the old idea that there should be "no rights without responsibilities."

BLOCKED EXCHANGES AS MESS

Well-motivated planners often try to protect people by "blocking exchanges," through, for example, minimal rights that employees, consumers, and tenants must enjoy, and may not waive, even through voluntary agreements. In the market, and particularly in the labor market, a common justification for this form of regulation is *redistribution*—particularly redistribution to those who need help.

National legislatures often impose controls on the market to prevent what they see as exploitation or unfair dealing by employers, who seem to have a competitive advantage over workers, especially poor workers. Those who favor a New Progressivism do not lack sympathy with the goals here, but they believe that this approach suffers from many of the problems faced by Dörner's planners. New Progressivists thus have a presumption against this approach, because they do not believe that it is, in general, a good way to help people who need help. The presumption is certainly rebuttable; in some cases, it is reasonable to block exchanges. But New Progressivists generally seek to help workers through different means, such as the Earned Income Tax Credit, other forms of income supplementation, subsidized housing, and education and training.

To be sure, some agreements between employers and employees are harsh, and the claim for redistribution is often strong as a matter of basic principle. Some workers enter into deals that do not seem terrific, simply because their options are so few. In fact, market wages and prices depend on a wide range of factors that are or may be morally irrelevant: historical injustice; supply-and-demand curves at any particular point; variations in family structure and opportunities for education and employment; existing tastes; and even differences in initial endowments, including talents, intelligence, or physical strength. The inspiration for minimum-wage legislation, for example, is easy to identify. Some workers have very low wages, and if minimum-wage legislation can help them, it seems attractive. Similarly, rent-control legislation prevents tenants from being subject to unanticipated price increases and perhaps thrown into much worse housing. Implied warranties of habitability protect tenants from living in disgraceful and even dangerous apartments.

In all these cases, however, regulation may well be a poor mechanism for helping people, precisely because it can be self-defeating. The problem is that if everything else is held constant, the market will frequently adjust to regulation in a way that will harm many people, including the least well-off. The claim need not be that markets have any special moral status; it is that blocking exchanges is often a doomed way of doing what well-motivated planners seek to do: help poor people. Dörner's planners are highly relevant here.

For example, it is a mistake—we might even call it a defining mistake of planners—to assume that regulation will directly transfer resources or create only after-the-fact winners and losers (an idea exemplified by the assumption that the only effect of the minimum wage is to raise wages for those currently working, or that the only effect of protecting tenants against eviction is to allow poor tenants to retain housing). An important consequence of a high minimum wage may well be to increase unemployment by raising the price of marginal labor. Those at the bottom of the ladder—the most vulnerable members of society—are the victims. In a wealthy nation with a growing economy, a relatively high minimum-wage law might not do much harm, and might do enough good to be justified on balance. And indeed, recent evidence suggests that in the United States, modest increases in the minimum wage have not had adverse effects on employment. But in a country that is poor and has a high unemployment rate, there is reason to question high minimum-wage requirements, because they do not simply redistribute resources from employers to poor workers (which would be good), and because they end up hurting the poorest people of all, who end up without jobs.

In fact—and this is a separate problem with blocking exchanges as a method of redistribution—a minimum wage is not directly aimed at poor people at all. Many of the people who benefit from minimum-wage increases have other sources of income, and they would not qualify for programs that would be specifically designed to help those who need financial assistance.[24] Of course, minimum-wage workers are usually far from wealthy, and many of them are indeed poor. But the problem with regulations that block exchanges is that the poor are not specifically or necessarily targeted. The regulations help some people who do not need help, or who do not have the strongest claim to help, and thus use resources that might be better used elsewhere.

I have said that blocking exchanges is not always a bad idea. Minimum-wage legislation does, after all, raise the wages of the working poor, and as noted, some studies suggest that modest increases in the minimum wage do not increase unemployment. But there can be little doubt that interference with the labor market will produce losers as well as winners. Efforts to redistribute resources through regulation can therefore have perverse results. The point bears on regulation of the labor market, the housing market, and the market for ordinary goods and services. It counsels against anything that looks like price-fixing as a redistributive strategy.

ALTERNATIVES

Thus far, I have discussed what the New Progressivism opposes. What does it support?

New Progressivists believe in a social safety net. But they emphasize approaches that will give people an ability to help themselves, through education, training, and job opportunities, fueled by economic incentives in the form (for example) of tax credits to employers and employees alike. They seek to supplement markets rather than displace them.

Consider a study of South Africa, based on 1996 data, demonstrating the enormous importance of education to employment prospects.[25] The study shows that high ratios of teachers to students dramatically increase the likelihood of employment—with a statistically significant effect for males, and a very large effect for females. The authors conclude that the apartheid "system continues to profoundly influence the life chances of many Black Africans, through its long-lasting effects on the country's education system. Many Black Africans currently in the labor force attended schools with inadequately trained teachers, insufficient textbooks, and pupil-teacher ratios above 80 children per class." The result of all this is to decrease both years in school and employment prospects. Better education and training are a direct and effective way of helping people to obtain jobs and decent wages. Similarly, an impressive study in the United States shows that good teachers have extremely significant long-term effects in improving students' economic prospects—and, indeed, that good teachers have such effects even in early grades.[26]

For many people, of course, other steps are required. A central New Progressivist approach is to develop initiatives to supplement low wages. Well-designed initiatives neither discourage employers from hiring people nor discourage prospective workers from seeking employment. Many countries have experimented with some variation on the Earned Income Tax Credit. (The program may or may not be limited to people with children.) Under this approach, low-wage workers obtain a tax credit from the government, sufficient to raise their total compensation to a decent level. In the United States alone, the EITC has been a terrific success, lifting millions of people from poverty. In one year, for example, EITC took 4.6 million people, including 2.4 million children, out of poverty.[27]

Compared to planning-type initiatives, the EITC approach has three large advantages. First, it does not make labor more costly for employers and thus does not decrease employers' desire to hire people. Second, it increases people's incentives to work by making employment more remunerative. Third, the EITC genuinely and specifically targets the poor. In the United States, for example, nearly three-quarters of those who benefit from the EITC are poor or near poor. The EITC is the model of a New Progressivism antipoverty program.

Creative policy makers could easily build on this model and use it as an alternative to well-motivated but crude plans. Old-style planners interested in protecting tenants might, for example, impose ceilings on rent increases. Other such planners might try to protect consumers by imposing price ceilings. If the government is interested in ensuring that tenants cannot be evicted for nonpayment of rent, planners might impose large procedural hurdles to eviction. If decent housing is unavailable, government might build housing on its own. These strategies are all associated with planning, and while it is possible that they might do some good, New Progressivists are skeptical of these approaches and would hunt for market-friendly alternatives. For example, they might seek to provide housing vouchers to poor people, or to provide food to those who are unable to buy enough to eat.

New Progressivists would also urge government to promote empowerment zones or enterprise zones in poor communities by giving businesses a tax credit, or direct subsidies, to the extent that they are willing to locate in areas that need help and to employ people who need jobs. These are market-oriented strategies, deploying markets in the interest of human goals. Learning from the failures and half-successes of planning, those who adopt such strategies attempt to be like the successful participants in Dörner's experiments, whose interventions are alert to the potentially harmful side effects of intrusions into systems.

COMMAND AND CONTROL REGULATION: A PRESUMPTION AGAINST

In controlling pollution and other social harms, a number of nations, even some of the most proudly capitalist, have engaged in a form of planning through command-and-control regulation. Such regulation involves centralized regulatory requirements imposed on dozens, hundreds, thousands, or even millions of producers. As examples, consider "best available technology" (BAT) requirements, imposed on polluting firms. Similar approaches can also be found in the area of occupational safety, where national authorities sometimes specify the safety technologies and approaches that must be used by all or most firms in a nation.

It is important to acknowledge that in many countries, command-and-control regulation has hardly been a complete failure. In the United States, it has helped to reduce levels of air pollution dramatically. Relying on markets alone would have been far worse. In this domain, the way of planning is far better than the way of markets. But for several reasons, New Progressivists raise serious objections to the basic approach.

The first problem is that it can be unnecessarily expensive, even wasteful, for government to prescribe the means for achieving social objectives. As Hayek emphasized, the information held by planners is likely to pale in comparison to the dispersed information of the public. At least as a general rule, it is especially inefficient for government to dictate technology. One of the many problems with BAT strategies, for example, is that they ignore the enormous differences among plants and industries and among geographic areas. It is questionable to impose the same technology on industries in diverse areas, regardless of whether they are polluted or clean, populated or empty, or expensive or cheap to clean up. BAT strategies often require all new industries to adopt costly technology, and allow more lenient standards to be imposed on existing plants and industries. Through this route, BAT strategies actually penalize new products, thus discouraging investment and perpetuating old, dirty technology. The result is inefficient investment strategies, inefficient innovation, and inefficient environmental protection.

In general, governmental specification of the means of achieving desired ends is a good way of producing unnecessarily high costs. Instead of permitting industry and consumers to choose the means—and thus to impose a form of market discipline on that question—government sometimes selects the means in advance. The governmentally prescribed means is often the inefficient one.

Command-and-control approaches are also deficient from the standpoint of democracy. The focus on the question of means threatens to increase the power of well-organized private groups, by allowing them to press environmental and regulatory law in the service of their own parochial ends. The BAT approach, for example, insures that citizens and representatives will be focusing their attention not on what levels of reduction are appropriate but on the less central and sometimes impenetrable question of what technologies are now available. Because of its sheer complexity, this issue is not easily subject to democratic resolution. Moreover, the issue is not the most important one for democratic politics, which is the appropriate degree and nature of environmental protection.

New Progressivists do not rule mandates and bans off-limits, but their preferred approach is much simpler: (1) use "nudges," in the form of low-cost, choice-preserving approaches, such as informing people about risks, including environmental risks, or enlisting default rules; and (2) impose a cost on harmful behavior and let market forces determine the response to the increased cost. Such a system would also reward rather than punish technological innovation in pollution control, and do so with the aid of private markets.

Nudges and economic incentives could and should be applied in many areas. With respect to savings, energy, environmental protection, and health insurance, both information and default rules can do a great deal of good. The United States, the United Kingdom, and many other nations are using nudges—sometimes from the private sector, sometimes from the government.[28] In these domains, there is far more to be done.

With respect to incentives, workers' compensation plans help to increase workplace safety. According to a careful study, "If the safety incentives of workers' compensation were removed, fatality rates in the United States economy would increase by almost 30 percent. Over 1,200 more workers would die from job injuries every year in the absence of the safety incentives provided by workers' compensation."[29] This figure contrasts with a mere 2 percent to 4 percent reduction in injuries from the Occupational Safety and Health Act (OSHA), an amount that links up well with the fact that annual workers' compensation premiums are more than a thousand times greater than total annual OSHA penalties.

The international movement toward the use of economic incentives, a central part of the New Progressivism, is continuing. A great deal has occurred in the environmental area. In the United States, an important series of administrative initiatives has brought about "emissions trading," especially under the Clean Air Act.[30] Under certain policies of the Environmental Protection Agency (EPA), a firm that reduces its emissions below legal requirements may obtain "credits" that can be used against higher emissions elsewhere. In its early years, the program was far less expensive than a command-and-control system would have been, producing total private-sector savings of between $525 million and $12 billion.[31] By any measure, this is an enormous gain. On balance, moreover, the environmental consequences have been beneficial.

As part of the process for eliminating lead from gasoline—a decision that was strongly supported by a cost-benefit study (see chapter 3)—the EPA also permitted emissions trading. Under this policy, a refinery that produced gasoline with lower-than-required lead levels could earn credits that could be traded with other refineries or banked for future use. Until the termination of the program in 1987, when the phasedown of lead ended, emissions credits for lead were widely traded. The EPA concluded that the program produced savings of about 20 percent over alternative systems, amounting to total savings in the hundreds of millions of dollars. There have been similar efforts with water pollution and ozone depletion.[32]

In the United States, perhaps the most ambitious program of economic incentives can be found in the 1990 amendments to the Clean Air Act. The act explicitly creates an emissions trading system for the control of acid deposition. In these amendments, Congress made an explicit decision about total emissions of the pollutants that cause acid deposition (a "cap"). The program has turned out to be an extraordinary success.[33] It has achieved dramatic pollution reductions, and it has done so while costing billions of dollars less than the command-and-control alternatives. The program has also proved able to handle significant and unanticipated changes over time, in a tribute to Hayek's emphasis on the advantages of the price system in handling new and unexpected developments. In many respects, the acid deposition program should reflect the way of the future.

ECONOMIC GROWTH, CAPABILITIES, AND SEX EQUALITY

Thus far, I have dealt with New Progressivist means—stressing the need to attend to both incentives and norms, and to avoid the rigidity, harmful unintended consequences, and costs associated with many plans. It is now time to turn to the question of ends.

For the last decades, many people have evaluated national well-being in terms of economic growth. Indeed, this approach has been characteristic of those who emphasize the way of markets, and much of the time, it has been adopted by those who attempt the way of planning as well. On this view, a country's performance is assessed by asking about gross domestic product and by seeing its movement over time.

GDP is an exceedingly important and useful figure, for it bears a close relationship to important social goals. If we think of income as an all-purpose means—as something that people want regardless of what else they want—we will indeed want to attend to GDP. Growth does matter for achieving a wide range of vital ends. As we saw in chapter 4, increases in GDP are closely correlated with increases in subjective well-being (and without an evident point of "satiation"). A study of antipoverty measures in the United States, by someone well disposed to government programs and not especially enthusiastic about reliance on markets alone, announces as lesson one, "A strong macroeconomy matters more than anything else."[34] Well-protected property rights and freedom of contract, safeguarded by state institutions, are quite central to economic growth.[35] They are at least as important in poor countries as in rich ones.

While GDP has central importance, there are a number of problems with relying on it as the exclusive measure of well-being.

- If income is distributed unequally, a high GDP may disguise the fact that many people are living bad or even desperate lives. For example, the United States has the highest per capita real GDP in the world. But in recent years, it has also had a higher rate of childhood poverty than any other wealthy country in the world. The percentage of children living in poverty is significantly higher than that of the industrialized nations taken as a whole (and much higher than that in Western Europe). In recent years, about half of African-American children in the United States have lived in poverty. While white Americans, if taken separately, would rank first on the Human Development Index of the United Nations Development Program (UNDP), African-Americans, if taken separately, would rank somewhere in the thirties. These crucial economic facts are undisclosed by GDP.
- GDP sometimes seems to be a general placeholder for a number of diverse indicators of social and economic well-being. But in fact, it may not be closely correlated with some important indicators. Consider two major

social goals: reducing poverty and reducing unemployment. Of course, GDP growth is an important factor in counteracting both unemployment and poverty. But it is not impossible for GDP increases to be accompanied by increases in unemployment and, in turn, poverty (which is closely correlated with unemployment). Indeed, this phenomenon has occurred. Physical security is surely an important ingredient in well-being, but it is only reflected indirectly in GDP. Nor is there an inevitable connection between GDP and life expectancy. Some countries have a relatively low GDP but long life expectancy and low rates of infant mortality, while other countries with a high GDP fare poorly in promoting longevity. Education is an important part of a good life, whether or not educated people accumulate wealth; but the association between education and GDP, while real, is far from perfect.

- GDP also fails to account for free goods and services, including some that are closely associated with economic well-being. For example, unpaid domestic labor is not a part of GDP. Many environmental amenities, such as clean air and water, are not reflected in GDP. The GDP figure thus fails to capture either the benefits of a healthy environment or the costs of environmental degradation. There are other gaps in what GDP measures. It does not, for example, reflect changes in leisure time, but it is clear that any increase in leisure is a gain even in economic terms, since leisure is something for which people are willing to pay, sometimes a great deal. Most generally, a serious problem with GDP is that the figure excludes all social costs and benefits that do not have prices.

The broadest point is that GDP does not fully capture what a good society is concerned to promote. Responding to these points, many people have attempted to come up with other measures of national well-being. Of these, the United Nations Development Program's effort is the most well known. The UNDP uses an index of well-being based on per capita income, educational attainment, and longevity

Of course, any "index" is bound to have a degree of arbitrariness. What is important is that a nation with a relatively low GDP can provide its citizens pretty long lives and pretty good educations—and that a country with a high GNP can give many of its citizens a poor education and relatively low life expectancies. (The United States is an unfortunate case in point, with an extremely high per capita income but one of the lowest life expectancies among comparable countries.) The theoretical roots of one effort to go beyond GDP lie in the "capabilities approach," which attempts to assess "what people are actually able to do and to be."[36]

It should not be contentious to urge that certain capabilities are necessary for a decent human life. These include the ability to have good health, to participate in political choices that affect one's life, to be educated, to hold property.[37] When people lack one or more of these abilities, they suffer from "capability failure," and this is a problem to which government should respond. The minimal responsibility of a New Progressivist government is to try to insure that all citizens are able to rise above a certain threshold.

Insofar as the Human Development Index and related efforts go beyond GDP to provide a simple, salient, easily understood figure by which to facilitate international comparisons and changes over time, they are a good place to start. They also provide a great deal of help with priority setting. In some nations, for example, it is clear that a large premium should be placed on improving longevity; in some places in the world, citizens have relatively short life expectancies, partly as a result of high crime levels and low standards of health care. By contrast, other nations should concentrate on increasing economic growth; they provide decent education and relatively long lives, but their citizens are relatively poor.

THE ANTICASTE PRINCIPLE—AND THE CENTRALITY OF SEX EQUALITY

Caste and Anticaste. For New Progressivists, I have suggested that it is important to insure that everyone has decent life prospects and also that everyone comes over a "capability threshold." A separate goal is to prevent some people, defined in terms of a morally irrelevant characteristic, from being treated as second-class citizens or turned into members of a lower caste. Thus an *anticaste principle*, undergirding a constitutional equality norm, plays a large role in New Progressive thinking.

The anticaste principle is not thoroughly egalitarian. It is compatible with large disparities in wealth and resources. But it insists that morally irrelevant characteristics, such as race, religion, and gender, should not be turned into a basis for second-class citizenship. New Progressivists see one of the most serious inequality problems in the practice of seizing on a characteristic lacking moral relevance and using it as the basis for the systematic subordination of certain social groups. Sometimes formal law helps to create a caste system. Sometimes a caste-like system is a product of social norms and private decisions.

Sex Equality as a Central Goal, as a Means and an End. For developing and wealthy countries alike, an end to sex-based inequality is an especially high priority—as both a means and an end. With respect to many problems—HIV/AIDS, crime, economic growth, overpopulation—there are few higher priorities. Indeed, any generalized attack on poverty must be combined with an attack on sex inequality. The two problems are closely intermingled.

Note first that sex equality is an important means to human development, as Amartya Sen and others have shown with their particular emphasis on "women's agency."[38] A nation in which girls and women have a chance to do and be what they want is far more likely to develop. A country with severe sex inequality will suffer economically and in other ways. In fact, a commitment to equality on the basis of sex is likely to redress many problems not normally thought to be associated with it, such as overpopulation and the individual and social problems that come from unwanted children. When women have a range of opportunities, and when their choices are not foreclosed by (or a product of) deprivation, these problems are sharply diminished. If women have agency, the economy will do better, simply because more people are willing and able to do good work. If women have agency, there will be an immediate and substantial reduction in the transmission of AIDS, simply because women will be able to engage in sexual relations only when they want and on their terms. This is a potentially enormous benefit for men, women, and children.

This idea has many implications. It means that education and training for girls are crucial. It also means that by law and by norms, girls and women should be allowed to decide when and whether to become mothers—which means, among other things, that sexual relations should always be a choice, not a requirement. Here there is an evident link to the earlier discussion of norms and norm cascades, and a particular link to the problems of crime and HIV/AIDS. In fact, a social policy directed against sexual subordination in multiple spheres is highly likely to combat both problems.

MARKETS AND BEYOND

Markets are emphatically human products—not natural but conventional, created by law and to be evaluated in terms of their consequences. The question is what they do to and for the people who are subject to them. Free markets are an engine of both prosperity and freedom. But from the standpoint of freedom and justice, markets do not accomplish enough. From the standpoint of economics, this was a great lesson of the first half of the twentieth century.

At the same time, economic planning is often futile and counterproductive, partly because of the inevitability of unintended consequences, and partly because of the immense difficulty of foreseeing the systemic effects of interventions. In its many forms, planning tends to invite maneuvering by interest groups and produces unanticipated damage, notwithstanding the good intentions of many planners. This was the great lesson of the second half of the twentieth century.

To be worthy of use, any New Progressivism should not be understood as a compromise measure or as steering between two poles. It is unapologetically committed to a certain understanding of the goals associated with the New Deal in the United States. (See chapter 2.) These do not include egalitarianism, understood as equal or roughly equal economic outcomes. But they do include decent life prospects for all, a social safety net, political equality, and an anticaste principle, in the form of opposition to second-class citizenship for members of any social group. Those who endorse a New Progressivism reject the idea that reliance on markets is sufficient to promote liberty at the same time that they seek to go beyond the sometimes sloppy and diffuse set of goals associated with the way of planning. They also place the highest premium on ending sex inequality.

New Progressivists see many planners as analogous to the hapless participants in Dietrich Dörner's experiments, designing ill-conceived interventions with consequences that confound the expectations of their designers. New Progressivists insist on the importance of civil society and, above all, the norms that often drive behavior. Alert to the possibility of social cascades, those who seek a New Progressivism favor the provision of information and also urge seemingly small steps that can, under favorable conditions, have large effects on behavior.

There is no policy blueprint here, since no country is exactly like any other. But the problems with the way of markets and the way of planning are pervasive. New Progressivism promises to draw on both of the great lessons of the twentieth century, and to build policy on a more secure sense of government's appropriate ends, and of the means that are most likely to promote those ends.

CHAPTER 10

MINIMALISM

Many people, including many politicians and judges, embrace minimalism. They want to avoid broad pronouncements and theoretical ambition. My goal in this chapter is to attempt to understand the justifications for this desire and to explore their limitations. As we shall see, modest ambition has an important place in law, politics, and everyday life within governments, companies, and families.

SHALLOWNESS AND NARROWNESS

When people are confronted with a difficult decision, they often move in the direction of minimalism. Minimalists prefer small steps to large ones. This preference operates along two distinct dimensions.

First, minimalists want to proceed in a way that is *shallow rather than deep*. In deciding what to do with a political or legal question, minimalists want to leave the biggest and most foundational issues undecided. They want to decide what to do today or tomorrow or next month without resolving the deepest questions, and without accepting some large account of how the political or legal question should be handled.

Second, minimalists want to proceed in way that is *narrow rather than wide*. They want to decide what to do about next month's vacation, or a current problem in the workplace, without deciding how to handle many future vacations or what to do about problems in the workplace in general. They want to settle a legal dispute—say, about the rights of a student who claims that she has been unfairly silenced—without settling the rights of all students, including all those who claim that they have been unfairly silenced.

In ordinary life, minimalism, in the form of shallowness and narrowness, can provide a great deal of help with difficult situations. Sensible people often take small steps for that reason. But for those who embrace minimalism, there is an evident problem. Sometimes we need to make a large-scale decision about a political problem. Sometimes it is best to settle on a course of action for the workplace—and even for vacations—rather than to rest content with a series of small decisions. Minimalism might be easiest in the short run, but in the long run, it can be destructive—in part because it exports the burdens of decision to the future, in a way that might produce a great deal of trouble. However difficult a large decision may be, it may be best to make it, and sooner rather than later.

Despite these objections, minimalism plays an exceedingly important role in life, politics, and law. Some judges favor shallow rulings. Such rulings attempt to produce rationales and outcomes on which diverse people can agree, notwithstanding their disagreement on fundamental issues. For example, people vigorously debate the purpose of the free-speech guarantee. Should it be seen as protecting democratic self-government, or the marketplace of ideas, or individual autonomy? Minimalists hope not to resolve these disputes. They seek judgments and rulings that can attract support from people who are committed to one or another of these different understandings—or who are unsure about the foundations of the free-speech principle.

Minimalist judges also like narrow rulings, which do not venture far beyond the problem at hand. They focus on the particulars of the dispute before the court. Consider in this light Chief Justice John Roberts's suggestion that a big advantage of unanimous decisions from the US Supreme Court is that unanimity leads to narrower rulings. In his words, "The broader the agreement among the justices, the more likely it is a decision on the narrowest possible grounds."[1] The nine justices have diverse views, and if they are able to join a single opinion, that opinion is likely to be narrow rather than broad. This, in the chief justice's view, is entirely desirable, as he explained with an aphoristic summary of the minimalist position in constitutional law: "If it is not necessary to decide more to dispose of a case, in my view it is necessary not to decide more."

Note that shallowness and narrowness are very different. We could imagine a decision that is *shallow but wide*. Consider, for example, the proposition that racial segregation is always forbidden, unaccompanied by any deep account of what is wrong with racial segregation. We could also imagine a decision that is *deep but narrow*, such as a ban on censorship of a particular political protest, accompanied by an ambitious account of the free-speech principle but limited to the specific situation in which censorship has been imposed. A decision might be both shallow and narrow or both wide and deep—but the two distinctions point in different directions.

It should be clear that both distinctions are ones of degree rather than of kind. In almost all contexts, courts should not decide important cases without giving reasons, and reasons insure at least some degree of depth. No one favors rulings that are limited to people with the same names or initials as those of the litigants before the court. But among reasonable alternatives, minimalists show a persistent preference for the shallower and narrower options, especially in hard situations, or (in the case of judges) problems at the frontiers of constitutional law. Minimalists fear that people lack relevant information and do not have a full sense of the many situations to which a broad rule might apply. Minimalists also fear the potentially harmful effects of decisions that reach far beyond the case at hand.

HOLLOWNESS, SHALLOWNESS, AND CONCEPTUAL DESCENTS

It seems clear that people can often agree on legal and political practices, and even on constitutional rights, when they cannot agree on underlying theories. In other words, well-functioning social orders try to solve problems through *incompletely theorized agreements.*

Sometimes these agreements involve abstractions, accepted as such amidst severe disagreements on particular cases. Such agreements are common in Congress. The national legislature might able to agree that occupational safety should be protected "to the extent feasible," or that the air should be made clean to the extent "requisite to protect public health," without knowing exactly what these words mean. If members of Congress were forced to specify their meaning, serious disagreements might break out, and perhaps the legislation could not pass.

This phenomenon is common in constitutional law. Authors of a constitution can agree on abstractions without agreeing on the specific meanings of those abstractions. They might accept a principle of freedom of speech, even though they cannot specify its scope. People who disagree on whether a constitution should protect incitement to violence and hate speech can accept a general free-speech principle. Those who disagree about whether a constitution should protect same-sex relationships can accept an abstract anti-discrimination principle. We might think of incompletely theorized abstractions as "hollow," in the sense that they must be filled with some kind of specification.

A pragmatic argument on behalf of hollowness, in the form of incompletely theorized abstractions, is this: *nothing else is feasible*. Perhaps an effort at specification will prove too contentious. Citizens will support the abstraction but not the specification. Or perhaps constitutional framers lack the information that would give them reason for confidence in any specification. If so, the best way to proceed may be to set out a general norm and allow posterity to fill it in as seems fit.

But sometimes incompletely theorized agreements are the mirror image of hollowness, because they involve concrete outcomes rather than abstractions. In some cases, people might be able to agree that a certain practice is constitutional, even when the theories that underlie their judgments diverge sharply. In the day-to-day operation of constitutional practice, shallow rulings help to promote clarity about what the law is, even amidst large-scale disagreements about what, particularly, accounts for those rulings. Narrow decisions, limited to the case at hand or to a small subset of imaginable cases, have similar virtues.

These points suggest a general strategy for handling some of the most difficult decisions. In ordinary life, we might attempt to bracket the fundamental issues and decide that however they are best resolved, a particular approach makes sense for the next month or year. We have not settled on our career, our romantic future, our investments. We do the best we can to resolve the questions at hand, and only those. We favor shallowness and narrowness. So, too, in law, politics, and morality. When people disagree or are uncertain about an abstract issue—Is equality more important than liberty? Does free will exist? Is utilitarianism right? Does punishment have retributive aims?—they can often make progress by moving to a level of greater particularity. They attempt a *conceptual descent*.

This phenomenon has an especially notable feature: it enlists silence on certain basic questions as a device for producing convergence despite disagreement, uncertainty, limits of time and capacity, and diversity of views. In short, silence can be a constructive force. Incompletely theorized agreements are an important source of successful constitutionalism and social stability. They also provide a way for people to demonstrate mutual respect.

Consider a few examples. People may believe that it is important to protect religious liberty while having quite diverse theories about why this is so. Some people may stress what they see as the need for social peace; others may think that religious liberty reflects a principle of equality and a recognition of human dignity. Some may invoke utilitarian considerations, while others think that religious liberty is itself a theological command. Similarly, people may invoke many different grounds for their shared belief that the Constitution should insure an independent judiciary. Some think that judicial independence helps insure against tyranny; others think that it makes government more democratic; and still others think that it leads to greater efficiency in economic terms.

Often people can accept an outcome—banning racial segregation, protecting sexually explicit art—without understanding or converging on an ultimate ground for that acceptance. Often people can agree not merely on the outcome but also on a rationale offering low-level or midlevel principles on its behalf. But what ultimately accounts for the outcome, in terms of a full-scale theory of the right or the good, is left unexplained.

There is an extreme case of incomplete theorization, offered when disagreement is especially intense: *full particularity*. This phenomenon occurs when people agree on a result but without concurring on any kind of supporting rationale. They announce what they want to do without offering a reason for doing it. Any rationale—any reason—is by definition more abstract than the result that it supports. Sometimes people do not offer reasons at all, because they do not know what those reasons are, or because they cannot agree on reasons, or because they fear that their reasons would turn out, on reflection, to be inadequate and misused in the future. Juries usually do not offer reasons for verdicts, and negotiators and mediators sometimes conclude that something should happen without saying why it should happen.

My emphasis on incompletely theorized agreements is intended partly as descriptive. These agreements are a pervasive phenomenon in politics and law. Such agreements are crucial to the effort to make decisions amidst intense disagreement. But I mean to defend such agreements as well. In the public and private sectors, there are real virtues to avoiding large-scale theoretical conflicts, and to resolving the problem at hand while leaving other problems for another day.

CONVERGING ON PRACTICES

It seems clear that people may agree on a *correct* outcome even though they do not have a theory to account for their judgments. You may know that dropped objects fall, bee stings hurt, hot air rises, and snow melts without knowing exactly why these facts are true. You may know that slavery and genocide are wrong, that government may not stop political protests, and that every person should have just one vote, without knowing exactly why these things are so. Moral judgments may be right or true even if they are reached by people who lack full explanations for those judgments. People can know *that X* is true without entirely knowing *why X* is true.

In American constitutional law, diverse judges may agree that *Roe v. Wade* (1973),[2] protecting the right to choose abortion, should not be overruled, though the reasons that lead each of them to that conclusion diverge sharply. Some people think that the Court should respect its own precedents; others think that *Roe* was rightly decided as a way of protecting women's equality; others think that the case was rightly decided as a way of protecting privacy; others think that the decision reflects an appropriate judgment about the social role of religion; still others think that restrictions on abortion are unlikely to protect fetuses in the world, and so the decision is good for pragmatic reasons.

Rules and analogies are the two most important methods for resolving constitutional disputes without agreeing on fundamental principles. Both of these devices—keys to public law in many nations—attempt to promote a major goal of a heterogeneous society: to make it possible to obtain agreement where agreement is necessary, and to make it unnecessary to obtain agreement where agreement is impossible.

People can often agree on what the rules are, including the

Constitution's rules, even when they agree on very little else. Their substantive disagreements, however intense, are usually irrelevant to their judgments about the meaning and the binding quality of those rules. And in the face of persistent disagreement or uncertainty about what justice and morality require, people can reason about particular constitutional cases by reference to analogies. They point to cases in which the legal judgments are firm. They proceed from those firm judgments to the more difficult ones. In fact, this is how ordinary people tend to think.

We might consider in this regard United States Supreme Court Justice Stephen Breyer's discussion of one of the key compromises reached by the seven members of the United States Sentencing Commission.[3] As Breyer describes it, a central issue was how to proceed in the face of very different views about the goals of criminal punishment. Some people wanted the commission to base punishment on "just deserts"—an approach that would rank criminal misconduct in terms of severity. But different commissioners had diverse views about how different crimes should be ranked. Agreement on a rational system would be unlikely to follow from efforts by the seven commissioners to rank crimes in terms of severity.

Other people urged the commission to use a model of deterrence. There were, however, major problems with this approach. No good empirical evidence links all possible variations in punishment to prevention of crime. In any case, the seven members were highly unlikely to agree that deterrence provides a full account of the aims of criminal sentencing.

Under these circumstances, what route did the commission follow? In fact, the members abandoned large theories altogether. They adopted no general view about the appropriate aims of criminal sentencing. Instead, the commission abandoned high theory and adopted a simple rule—one founded on precedent. It based the guidelines mostly on the average past practice. The decision to adopt this approach must have been based on a belief that the average practice contained sense rather than nonsense—a belief that can be supported by reference to the frequent "wisdom of crowds."[4]

Justice Breyer sees this effort as a necessary means of producing agreement and rationality within a diverse, multimember body charged with avoiding unjustifiably broad variations in sentencing. Thus his colorful oral presentation: "Why didn't the Commission sit down and really go and rationalize this thing and not just take history? The short answer to that is: we couldn't. We couldn't because there are such good arguments all over the place pointing in opposite directions . . . Try listing all the crimes that there are in rank order of punishable merit . . . Then collect results from your friends and see if they all match. I will tell you they don't."[5]

The example suggests a more general point. Through both analogies and rules, it is often possible for participants in constitutional law to converge on both abstract principles and particular outcomes without resolving large-scale issues of the right or the good. The recognition of rights is often possible for this reason. Consider the growth of a norm against genocide, which attracted international support without much in the way of theory.[6] Indeed, the Universal Declaration of Human Rights was produced through a process akin to that described by Justice Breyer, with a refusal to engage high theory and, instead, an effort to build on widespread understandings.[7] The basic enterprise operated by surveying the behavior of most nations and then building a "universal declaration" on the basis of shared practices. A philosophers' group involved in the project "began its work by sending a questionnaire to statesmen and scholars around the world."[8] The Universal Declaration of Human Rights emerged from this process. Thus Jacques Maritain, a philosopher closely involved in the Universal Declaration, said famously, "Yes, we agree about the rights, but on condition no one asks us why."[9]

If such processes work better than imaginable alternatives, it is because they reduce the costs of decisions and the costs of errors. Theoretical depth is often difficult and costly to achieve, certainly when a number of people are asked to agree to a controversial proposition. By insisting on shallowness, people can also avoid the kinds of mistakes to which theory builders are prone. An incompletely theorized agreement may limit the costs of making decisions while simultaneously reducing the risk of errors.

INCOMPLETE THEORIZATION AND SILENCE

Some people think of incomplete theorization as quite unfortunate—as embarrassing, or reflective of some important problem, or a failure of nerve, or even philistine. When people theorize, by raising the level of abstraction, they do so to reveal bias, or confusion, or inconsistency. Surely participants in politics and constitutional law should not abandon this effort.

There is important truth in these usual thoughts. It would be senseless to celebrate theoretical modesty at all times and in all contexts. Sometimes people have enough information, and enough agreement, to be very ambitious. Sometimes they have to reason ambitiously in order to resolve cases. If the theory-building capacities of judges (or others) are infallible, theoretical ambition would be nothing to lament. But judges are hardly infallible, and incompletely theorized judgments help make constitutions and constitutional law possible. They even help make social life possible. Silence—on something that may prove false, obtuse, or excessively contentious—can help minimize conflict, allow the present to learn from the future, and save a great deal of time and expense. What is said and resolved may be no more important than what is left out. There are four points here.

First, a degree of shallowness may be necessary for social stability. Incompletely theorized agreements are well suited to a world—and especially a political and legal world—containing social divisions on large-scale issues. Stability would be difficult to obtain if fundamental disagreements broke out in every case of public or private dispute. In many nations, stable constitutions and laws have been possible only because the meaning of broad terms has not been specified in advance.

Second, incompletely theorized agreements can promote two

goals of a constitutional democracy and a liberal legal system: to enable people to live together, and to permit them to show one another a measure of reciprocity and mutual respect. The use of low-level principles or rules allows people to find a common way of life without producing unnecessary antagonism. At the same time, incompletely theorized agreements allow people to show one another a high degree of mutual respect, civility, reciprocity, or even charity.

Frequently, ordinary people disagree in some deep way on an issue—what to do about the Middle East, pornography, same-sex marriages, the war on terror—and sometimes they agree not to discuss that issue much, as a way of deferring to one another's strong convictions and showing a measure of reciprocity and respect (even if they do not at all respect the particular conviction that is at stake). If reciprocity and mutual respect are desirable, it follows that public officials or judges, perhaps even more than ordinary people, should not challenge their fellow citizens' deepest and most defining commitments, at least if those commitments are reasonable and if there is no need for them to do so. Indeed, we can see a kind of political charity in the refusal to contest those commitments when life can proceed without any such contest.

True, some fundamental commitments are appropriately challenged. Some such commitments are ruled off-limits by the Constitution itself. Many provisions involving basic rights have this function. Of course, it is not always disrespectful to disagree with someone in a fundamental way; on the contrary, such disagreements may reflect profound respect. When defining commitments are based on demonstrable errors of fact or logic, it is appropriate to contest them. So, too, when those commitments are rooted in a rejection of the basic dignity of all human beings, or when it is necessary to undertake the contest to resolve a genuine problem. But many controversies can be resolved in an incompletely theorized way, and this is the ordinary stuff of politics and law; that is what I am emphasizing here.

Third, incompletely theorized agreements have the crucial function of reducing the political cost of enduring disagreements. If participants in a disagreement disavow large-scale theories, then losers in particular cases lose much less. They lose a decision but not the world. They may win on another occasion. Their own theory has not been rejected or ruled out of bounds. When the specific result is disconnected from abstract theories of the good or the right, the losers can submit to political or legal obligations, even if reluctantly, without being forced to renounce their most deeply held ideals.

Fourth, incompletely theorized agreements are especially valuable when a society seeks moral evolution and even progress over time. Consider the area of equality, where considerable change has occurred in the past and will inevitably occur in the future. A completely theorized judgment would be unable to accommodate changes in facts or values. If a culture really did attain a theoretical end state, it would become rigid and calcified; we would know what we thought about everything.

Incompletely theorized agreements are central to debates over equality, with issues being raised about whether discrimination on the basis of sexual orientation, age, disability, and other characteristics is analogous to discrimination on the basis of race. Such agreements have the important advantage of allowing a large degree of openness to new facts and perspectives.

Something similar is true in ordinary life. At a certain time, you may well refuse to make decisions that seem foundational in character—about, for example, whether to get married within the next year; or whether to have two, three, or four children; or whether to live in London or Paris. Part of the reason for this refusal is the knowledge that your understandings of both facts and values may well change. Indeed, your identity may itself change in important and relevant ways, and a set of firm commitments in advance—something like a fully theorized conception of your life course—would make no sense. Political systems and legal systems are not altogether different.

NARROWNESS AND ITS DISCONTENTS

My emphasis thus far has been on shallowness; it is time to reintroduce narrowness. A court might rule that one exercise of presidential power is unconstitutional, without saying much about other imaginable exercises of presidential power. A court might conclude that sex segregation is impermissible in one domain, without saying much about whether sex segregation might be impermissible in other domains. Recall here Chief Justice Roberts's suggestion that if it is not necessary for a court to say more to decide a case, it is necessary for a court not to say more to decide a case.

Why would sensible politicians or judges embrace narrowness? We can isolate several reasons. First, institutional reality may require it. On a multimember court consisting of several (strong-willed?) people, it might be possible to reach a consensus on a particular outcome but not on a wide rule. Second, wide rulings might impose serious burdens on judges, even if the institutional problem could be overcome. To issue a wide ruling that resolves numerous disputes about presidential power to reduce the risks of terrorist attacks, or about constitutional protection of speech on the internet, judges may have to ask and answer questions for which they lack relevant information. Third, wide rulings might turn out to be embarrassing in the future in light of unanticipated scenarios and changes over time. If politicians or courts are in a poor position to generate rules that fit novel situations, their efforts to do so might produce serious blunders.

For judges, there is a fourth point, involving democratic self-government. In the constitutional domain, narrow rulings preserve a great deal of space for continuing discussion and debate. Imagine, for example, that a court is asked to issue some wide ruling involving the rights of disabled people or the authority of the president. A refusal to issue that ruling, and a narrow decision focused on particulars, allow room for continuing debate among citizens and their representatives.

These various points suggest that in many contexts, a narrow ruling (not less than a shallow one) can minimize the costs of decisions and the costs of errors. By definition, narrow rules impose lower decision-making burdens on judges. At the same time, they might help judges to avoid errors, certainly if the judges lack the information that would justify width.

Of course, we can imagine contexts in which this defense of shallowness is inadequate. If the Constitution is clear—for example, because basic rights are at risk—the argument for narrowness is much weakened. Or suppose that a court is operating in an area in which predictability is extremely important—perhaps because the issue comes up often, and it is simply too messy to have to proceed without a sense of what the law is. If this is so, narrow rulings will impose significant decision-making burdens on others, and very possibly increase the costs of decisions on balance. If the result of narrow rulings is to make a mess of the law, posterity might be harmed rather than helped.

We can see here a potential problem with Chief Justice Roberts's embrace of unanimous rulings. Roberts favors such rulings in part on the ground that they promote predictability. If the court is not fractured, everyone will know what the law is. But as Roberts also contends, a unanimous ruling is more likely to be narrow simply because a wide ruling is unlikely to attract a consensus. The problem is that a unanimous but narrow ruling might offer significantly less guidance than a divided but wide ruling. From the standpoint of promoting predictability, it may be better to have a 7–2 ruling in favor of some general proposition than a 9–0 ruling in favor of some narrow proposition, limited to particular facts.

CONCEPTUAL ASCENTS: FROM SHALLOWNESS TO DEPTH

Borrowing from the British philosopher Henry Sidgwick's writings on ethical method,[10] a critic of shallowness might respond that constitutional law should frequently use ambitious theories.[11] Concrete judgments about particular cases can prove inadequate for morality or constitutional law. Sometimes people do not have clear intuitions about how cases should come out. Sometimes their intuitions are insufficiently reflective. Sometimes seemingly similar cases provoke different reactions, and it is necessary to raise the level of theoretical ambition to explain whether those different reactions are justified, or to show that the seemingly similar cases are different after all. Sometimes people simply disagree.

By looking at broader principles, we may be able to mediate the disagreement. When modest judges join an opinion that is incompletely theorized, they must rely on a reason or a principle, justifying one outcome rather than another. The opinion itself must refer to a reason or principle; it cannot just announce a victor. Perhaps the low-level principle is wrong because it fails to fit with other cases or because it is not defensible as a matter of (legally relevant) political morality.

In short, the incompletely theorized agreement may be nothing to celebrate. If a judge is reasoning well, he should have before him a range of other cases, in which the principle is tested against others and refined. At least if he is a distinguished judge, he will experience a kind of "conceptual ascent," in which the more or less isolated and small low-level principle is finally made part of a more general theory. Perhaps this would be a paralyzing task, and perhaps our judge need not attempt it often. But perhaps it is an appropriate aspiration for evaluating judicial and political outcomes. On this view, judges and politicians who insist on staying at a low level of theoretical ambition are philistines—even ostriches.

Return to ordinary life. If someone is unsure what to do with a relationship or a medical problem, he might not do so well if he avoids the foundational questions. If he can answer those questions well, he might be able to choose far more wisely than he will do if he plods along with decisions that are at once narrow and shallow. Something similar may be true in the constitutional domain.

Indeed, we might go beyond necessity and speak instead of opportunity. Perhaps it is best to see constitutional provisions as inviting a degree of depth, and therefore to celebrate those occasions when courts announce the nature of the foundational commitments that underlie one right or another.

At least if moral and constitutional reasoners have time and competence, they might need or want to attempt a degree of theoretical ambition. In democratic processes, it is appropriate and sometimes indispensable to challenge existing practice in abstract terms. The same is true in constitutional law.

This challenge to incompletely theorized agreements should not be taken for more than it is worth. Its force depends on the context—on the kinds of information that judges have and on whether they have reason for confidence in deep rulings. We need to investigate the costs of decisions and the costs of errors. As I have noted, incompletely theorized agreements have many virtues. They promote stability, reduce the costs of disagreement, and demonstrate humility and mutual respect. A conceptual ascent might be appealing in the abstract, but if those who ascend will blunder, they might better stay close to the ground.

INCOMPLETELY THEORIZED AGREEMENTS, DISAGREEMENT, AND STABILITY

In law, as in politics, disagreement can be a productive and creative force, revealing error, showing gaps, and moving discussion and results in good directions. Many political systems place a high premium on "government by discussion," and real discussion requires a measure of disagreement. Agreements may be a product of coercion, subtle or not, or of a failure of imagination.

Social consensus is hardly a consideration that outweighs everything else. Usually it would be much better to have a just outcome, rejected by many people, than an unjust outcome with which all or most agree. A just constitution is more important than a constitution on which everyone agrees. Consensus or agreement is important largely because of its connection with stability, itself a valuable but far from overriding social goal. It may well be right to make an unjust constitutional order a bit less stable. We have seen that incompletely theorized agreements, even if stable and broadly supported, may conceal or reflect injustice.

It would be foolish to say that no general theory about constitutional law or rights can produce agreement, even more foolish to deny that some general theories deserve support, and most foolish of all to say that incompletely theorized agreements warrant respect, whatever their content. What I am suggesting here is more modest. In the face of serious disagreement, minimalism may provide the best path forward—even the only path forward. It deserves a respected place in law, politics, and ordinary life.

CHAPTER 11

TRIMMING

Lord Halifax was the original trimmer. He defended trimming in the following way:

> Why, after we have played the foole with throwing *Whig* and *Tory* at one another, as boys do snowballs, doe we grow angry at a new name, which by its true signification might do as much to put us into our witts, as the others have been to put us out of them? The Innocent Word *Trimmer* signifieth no more than this, that if men are together in a Boat, and one part of the Company would weigh it down on one side, another would make it lean as much to the contrary, it happneth there is a third Opinion, of those who conceave it would do as well, if the Boat went even, without endangering the Passengers . . . [T]rue Vertue hath ever been thought a *Trimmer*, and to have its dwelling in the middle, between the two extreams.[1]

Notwithstanding Halifax's understanding of virtue, the idea of trimming has become a pejorative. Consider these words, meant to describe Dante's "neutrals," or "trimmers":

> These innumerable seekers of safety first, and last, who take no risk either of suffering in a good cause or of scandal in a bad one, are here manifestly, nakedly, that which they were in life, the waste and rubble of the universe, of no account to the world, unfit for Heaven, and barely admitted to hell. They have no need to die, for they "never were alive." They follow still, as they have always done, a meaningless, shifting banner that never stands for anything because it never stands at all, a cause which is no cause but the changing magnet of the day. Their pains are paltry and their tears and blood mere food for worms.[2]

The tears and blood of trimmers may or may not be "mere food for worms," but no one marches proudly under the trimmers' banner. No one feels delighted or honored to be called a trimmer. A presidential candidate is not likely try to attract votes by proclaiming that he loves to trim, and a Supreme Court nominee will not announce at her confirmation hearing that she is a trimmer. But in this chapter, I shall attempt to show that in many domains, there are powerful arguments on behalf of trimming.

Sometimes trimming is a sensible rule of thumb, helping us to identify what is best. Sometimes trimming is a reasonable effort to identify and to preserve the best arguments and the deepest convictions on all sides. Sometimes trimming helps to reduce social conflict and public outrage. Sometimes trimming can be defended as a means of insuring that no one is excluded, humiliated, or hurt. Often trimming produces reasonable outcomes, and it also produces a degree of approval, or at least acquiescence, from all sides.

HISTORICAL NOTES

The trimmer's instinct is to see what diverse people have to say and to explore whether something might be drawn from their perspectives. As we will see, trimmers avoid the extremes, but they reject minimalism. Unlike minimalists, they do not bracket hard questions or attempt to leave such questions undecided.

To understand trimming, it will be useful to begin with some brief historical notes. Though the original trimmers have been largely lost in contemporary political and legal debates, we can learn a great deal from what they had to say.

The first mention of a "trimmer" in print was in *The Character of a Trimmer, Neither Whigg nor Tory*, published in 1682.[3] The text was written by the most influential trimmer, George Savile, the Marquis of Halifax, who left public office in February 1690[4] and died in April 1695.[5] After the publication of Lord Halifax's essay, trimmers were mentioned frequently in the popular press for the next three years and occasionally thereafter, until 1689.[6] Trimmers appeared frequently in Roger L'Estrange's widely read London newspaper, the *Observator*, in which political dialogues that had previously taken place between Whig and Tory were changed in November 1682 to be between a trimmer and a character named Observator.[7] To L'Estrange, anyone who did not follow the strictest of Tory policies could be termed a trimmer.[8] He summarized the defining trimmer characteristics as follows:

> Trim. And what Is a Trimmer at last?
>
> Obs. Why a Trimmer is a Hundred Thousand Things; A Trimmer I tell ye, is a man of Latitude, as well in Politiques as Divinity: An Advocate, both for Liberty of Practice in the State, and for Liberty of Conscience in the Church.[9]
>
> Obs. But then you must Consider that there are Severall sorts of Trimmers; as your State-Trimmer, Your Law-Trimmer; Your Church-Trimmer, Your Trading-Trimmer, &c.[10]

Others characterized trimmers as nonconformists who went to church and were not sufficiently in favor of punishing Protestant dissenters, the more moderate sort of Tories, or "secret Whigs."[11] As we shall see, the important point that "there are Severall sorts of Trimmers" applies no less in the twenty-first century than it did in the seventeenth.

Notwithstanding the frequent and explicit references to trimmers in the relevant period, historians continue to debate the existence of an actual group of thinkers and officials who deserved the label. In the first half of the twentieth century, historians assumed that there was such a group and that it was led by Halifax; the *Oxford English Dictionary* gave the definition of *trimmer* as "Lord Halifax and those associated with him (1680–1690)."[12]

In the 1960s and 1970s, however, some scholars began to question whether Halifax was associated with the trimmer movement during his lifetime, and even to doubt whether there was an actual trimmer movement with which to associate. According to a prominent 1964 essay by Donald Benson in the *Huntington Library Quarterly*, "The pamphlets of the Trimmer controversy give no indication that Halifax was identified in any way with the Trimmers during the period. He is not mentioned in the controversy by name or, apparently, by implication."[13] According to Benson, "it seems unlikely that a Trimmer party was ever more than a fiction of political controversy."[14]

Whatever we make of the controversy, Lord Halifax was certainly a self-identified trimmer who argued for "dwelling in the middle, between the two extreams."[15] He rejected the fixed positions of both Tories and Whigs; he believed that the government should make a place both for royal authority and for a strong parliament. He wondered, "Why do angry men aile to rayle so against Moderation? Doth it not looke as they were going to some very scurvy Extream, that is too strong to be digested by the more considering part of mankind?"[16]

For trimmers, moderation is a signal virtue, and it entails a sympathetic understanding of what is best in and least dispensable to the "extreams." In politics, Halifax favored a balance between the monarchy and the commonwealth, urging that the monarch must be constrained by law, that a constitutional order should protect civil liberties, and that parliaments should play a large role.[17] On his account, the trimmer is especially enthusiastic about the law, seeing legal rules as "the Chaines that tye up our unruly passions."[18] In religion, Halifax sought "a mutuall Calmnesse of mind" between Protestants and Catholics, "overlooking of all veniall faults."[19] With respect to longstanding social divisions, the trimmer "is not eager to pick out the sore places in History against this or any other party; on the contrary, is very solicitous to find out any thing that may be healing, and tend to an agreement."[20]

As England's Glorious Revolution of 1688 developed, Halifax insisted on maintaining contacts with both sides.[21] William III, who ascended the throne as a result of the revolution, practiced what he called trimming by including both Whigs and Tories in government, and he often said that he wanted to "'go upon the bottom of the trimmers' or [be] 'the middle party.'"[22] In an important effort to rehabilitate Halifax, the British politician and historian Thomas Babington Macaulay wrote with evident sympathy, "He had nothing in common with those who fly from extreme to extreme and regard the party which they have deserted with an animosity far exceeding that of consistent enemies. His place was on the debatable ground between the hostile divisions of the community."[23] In Macaulay's account, Halifax "was therefore always severe upon his violent associates, and was always in friendly relations with his moderate opponents. Every faction in the day of its insolent and vindicate triumph occurred his censure; and every faction, when vanquished and persecuted, found in him a protector."[24] As we shall see, this conception of Halifax has close parallels in the approach to law and politics that I mean to describe here.

My goal, however, is not one of intellectual biography or historical recovery. For purposes of contemporary law and politics, we can draw inspiration from Halifax and his associates, but for us, trimming is to be made, not found. The initial task is to show exactly why people might choose to trim.

COMPROMISERS, PRESERVERS, AND MODERATES

Two Kinds of Trimmers. Some trimmers are "compromisers." They identify the extremes and attempt to steer between them. Seeking to reduce social conflict, hoping to avoid public outrage, and believing that the middle position should be presumed to be best, compromisers try to give something to both sides. Other trimmers are "preservers." They attempt to identify and to preserve what is most essential, most intensely felt, and most valuable in the competing views. Seeking to learn from those views, such trimmers give sympathetic scrutiny to apparent antagonists and seek to vindicate what is most appealing in both sides' positions.

What makes preservers distinctive is that they insist on identifying what is most reasonable in competing positions, with a particular desire to insure that, to the extent possible, no one is or feels rejected or repudiated. Preservers care both about judgments that are actually most essential (in their independent judgment) and also about judgments that are most deeply felt (in the subjective views of the antagonists). These different emphases may, of course, press in different directions. Preservers who emphasize what is most essential might not end up in the same position as preservers who emphasize what is felt most intensely. At first glance, preservative trimming seems attractive or at least plausible. It is not so easy to identify a principled argument for compromising as such (though I will try).

Compromisers and preservers can be found in many domains. Consider, for example, the view that restrictions on abortion are justified only if they do not amount to an "undue burden" (suitably specified) on freedom of choice; that obscenity is protected unless it runs afoul of a test that pays close attention to community standards and social values; and that whether public displays of the Ten Commandments are constitutional depends on the specific context. In some of these cases, the prevailing view might be an effort to steer a middle course. In others, the prevailing view may be a product of a principled belief that trimming recognizes, and makes space for, the most legitimate claims of the competing sides.

Problems and Concerns. From these examples, it should be clear that what counts as the best form of trimming, and what qualify as the poles between which trimmers steer, will not always be self-evident. Trimmers might disagree with one another about the proper way to trim; two or more approaches might legitimately count as trimming. And what are the poles that interest trimmers? If influential leaders say that members of an unpopular religious group should be exterminated, and other leaders say that such people should be left alone, we would not admire trimmers who conclude that members of that religious group should be allowed to live but be incarcerated for life.

It would seem to follow that sensible trimmers should be prepared to evaluate, and not simply to observe, the competing positions—a view that will lead from compromise to preservation. It might also seem to follow that nearly any position could be characterized as trimming, because any position is likely to be between at least some imaginable poles. I will return to these problems below.

Moderates Versus Trimmers. It is important to distinguish between ideological moderates and trimmers, even though it will not always be easy to tell them apart in practice, and even though they will often agree. Moderates might simply believe that commercial advertisements are entitled to some constitutional protection, but less so than political speech. Moderates might not care about what other people think and might hold their positions in a social vacuum. This just happens to be their preferred interpretation of the Constitution, one that makes them moderates under current conditions.

Such moderates are not trimmers, because they do not much care about the competing positions and are not trying to steer between them. They are neither compromisers nor preservers. They might well refuse to compromise with others, or lack the slightest interest in investigating polar positions to preserve what is deepest and best in such positions. For moderates, it might not be especially important to insure that no one is humiliated or hurt. But some moderates might also turn out to be trimmers. For example, they might compromise by choosing to accept a position halfway between their moderate position and that of one of the extremists.

REASONS TO TRIM

Why would anyone want to trim? In answering that question, I will focus on judges, but most of the arguments apply to others as well, whether they are inside or outside government.

Trimming as Best in Principle. After sympathetic investigation of the contending positions, a judge might conclude that the best views steer between the poles. Consider the question of affirmative action in education. Maybe a judge believes that rigid racial quota systems are beyond the pale, but that it is acceptable to treat race as a "factor" in admissions decisions. A judge of this kind would produce a form of constitutional trimming for the affirmative action debate. Indeed, the US Supreme Court has taken exactly this approach in that domain; affirmative action is an area in which trimming has reigned triumphant.[25] Judges who reach this conclusion might be moderates rather than trimmers. But we could certainly imagine preservers and even compromisers who end up with this conclusion.

Trimming as a Rule of Thumb. A humble judge might believe that trimming is a good rule of thumb—a kind of heuristic for what is right. Unsure what to do, a judge might think that if he trims, he is most likely to avoid a mistake. It is here that we can understand why some trimmers are compromisers. Consider the fact that human beings typically demonstrate "extremeness aversion."[26] Suppose that you are confronted with a menu of options: a set of possible cell phones or television sets. Suppose, too, that you have incomplete information and that you are not sure what you want. If so, you might want to avoid the poles, trying to identify and to select the middle option. Indeed, jurors themselves have been found to trim, in the sense that they steer between the extremes. For this reason, the prosecutor's selection of criminal counts can greatly matter in what the jury ends up doing.

At first glance, people's tendencies here might seem puzzling. Why, exactly, is the middle choice the best one? This is a good question, but under certain assumptions, extremeness aversion is perfectly reasonable, because it reflects a sensible rule of thumb, above all for those who are unsure how to proceed. Suppose that a politician is confronted with a problem on which intelligent people are divided—say, whether there should be a big increase in the minimum wage. Suppose that some people urge one extreme course: no increase at all in the minimum wage. Suppose that other intelligent people urge another extreme course: a large increase in the minimum wage. If the politician is not sure which position is right, she might choose to trim, with the thought that the truth probably lies in between.

A judge who is disposed to compromise might have the further thought that by trimming, she can avoid the most serious dangers associated with both of the extremes. A judge who wants to avoid the worst risks might select trimming if each side is able to offer persuasive warnings about the hazards that would accompany the course suggested by the other. For those who believe that moderation is usually wiser, less dangerous, or both, trimming makes a lot of sense.

Those who adopt trimming as a rule of thumb might be either compromisers or preservers. They might not have the time or the capacity to think carefully about which position is right—or having thought carefully, they might not be sure. If so, trimming might seem to be the prudent course. If they are preservers, trimmers will also ask: On both sides, what commitments are most attractive, or most deeply held, or essential?

Strategic Trimming. A more confident person might trim for purely strategic reasons. Suppose that a judge believes that affirmative action is always unconstitutional or that the Constitution does not protect a right to privacy. Such a judge is not so moderate, and she may not be humble. But she might conclude that other judges cannot be persuaded to accept her position. Trimming might be an indispensable method for building a majority on behalf of the best outcome that is realistically possible.

Here, then, we can find grounds for trimming as a form of (strategic) compromise. The strategic trimmer is trying to obtain the best available result in light of the constraints produced by practical realities on a multimember court. Of course, strategic trimmers play a big role in national legislatures. Congress could not easily do its job without them. Coalitions are possible here among moderates, principled trimmers, and their strategic siblings. Some judges may believe that trimming leads to the best result, while others sign on because trimming is the best that they can get.

Trimming and Precedent. Judges must, of course, follow precedents, at least as a general rule. A judge might believe that trimming is the only way to proceed while respecting this requirement. Indeed, a system based on precedent is likely to produce a doctrine that is replete with a kind of trimming. Both compromisers and preservers might accept this proposition.

Suppose that a judge believes that as a matter of principle, it would be best if the First Amendment were interpreted not to protect commercial advertising at all, or if the Constitution were not taken to protect the right to choose abortion. Confronted with unwelcome precedents, the judge might attempt to limit the protection of commercial advertising—perhaps by allowing the government to regulate misleading advertising—and might conclude that the right to choose does not include partial-birth abortion. In fact, this kind of trimming occurs all the time. Judges do not like certain precedents, but they respect them, trying to confine their reach. Judges of this kind might hope to move the law, by degrees, in their preferred directions, but they will have to settle for a high degree of trimming.

Social Conflict and Trimming. A judge might not know which result is best and might trim in order to protect the court as an institution. When Chief Justice John Roberts cast the decisive vote to uphold the Affordable Care Act in 2012, he was engaged in a form of trimming. He might well have been trying to avoid an intense social conflict over the role of the Court—a conflict from which the Court might not have emerged unscathed.

More generally, the trimmer might seek to minimize social conflict and conclude that trimming is the best way of accomplishing that task. In politics or on a court, a trimmer might be particularly concerned about intense public outrage. The trimmer might believe the following: if the Court strikes down the Affordable Care Act, it will cause a sharp and enduring split in the nation, making the role of the Court—and perhaps the judges' political leanings—a central part of national debates. Or if the Court rejects an individual's right to own guns, its decision will cause polarization and agitation, and perhaps trigger a large public reaction, conceivably affecting the result of a presidential campaign. Alert to the potentially harmful consequences of certain rulings, a trimmer might be seeking to minimize the damage.

Or the trimmer might think that if the public would be outraged by one decision or another, perhaps the decision is wrong, because the people's intensely held beliefs offer some clues about what decisions would be wrong or right. If the public became agitated about the creation or denial of a certain right, it is at least possible that a judge can learn from the anticipated public agitation. Perhaps this is not true of judges. Even if it is not, it might be true of other public officials.

To the degree that public outrage is their concern, trimmers might be accused of being weak, passive, or cowardly. Return to these words: "They follow still, as they have always done, a meaningless, shifting banner that never stands for anything because it never stands at all, a cause which is no cause but the changing magnet of the day." In some contexts, the accusation is warranted. If judges allow racial oppression because of the intense desires of the oppressors, the changing magnet of the day has far too much power. But in difficult cases in which reasonable people differ, trimming can be understood to have moral foundations, captured in the idea that people should be respected and included, and should be neither humiliated nor hurt. When trimmers attempt to take on board the deepest commitments of legal or political adversaries, they are attempting to show respect to all sides—and to reduce the risk that any side will feel offended, diminished, or aggrieved.

AGAINST TRIMMING

Thus defended, trimming runs into some serious objections. As before, I will focus on the role of judges, but with suitable adjustments, the objections apply to others as well.

BLUNDERING TRIMMERS

The Supreme Court's most important obligation is to interpret the Constitution correctly. Some of the time, trimming might seem to violate that obligation. Why, it might be asked, should judges believe that trimming will yield the correct interpretation? Similar questions could be asked of those involved in politics.

This question could be pressed with equal vigor by skeptics

armed with competing accounts of constitutional interpretation. Justices Antonin Scalia and Clarence Thomas are originalists; they believe that the original understanding of the Constitution settles the document's current meaning. Originalists might well believe that trimming will yield bad interpretations. In their view, judges should not trim; they should construe the founding document to fit with the original understanding. Justice Oliver Wendell Holmes Jr. believed that judges should uphold acts of Congress unless the violation of the Constitution is plain. Trimmers will often violate Holmes's injunction, because they will vote to invalidate congressional enactments even when the violation is far from plain.

Still other people believe that the Constitution should be given a "moral reading," in the sense that judges should invest the document with the best moral principles, consistent with precedent.[27] In many cases, trimming will produce an inferior moral reading. Those who favor moral readings will ask, "Why should judges split the difference rather than interpret the disputed provisions in the morally best way?" And whatever our preferred account of constitutional interpretation, we can certainly find areas in which trimming would be unacceptable.

In politics, the problem is not obscure. If some people say that all suspected terrorists should be tortured, and other people say that no one should be tortured, we might not be enthusiastic about the view that half of all suspected terrorists should be tortured. Or suppose that a judge is presented with these alternatives: (1) strike down school segregation in all circumstances; (2) never strike down school segregation; and (3) strike down school segregation only when racial separation is demonstrably unequal, in the sense that the schools attended by white students are better. The trimming solution is the third, but the first is clearly preferable. In 1954 the Supreme Court chose (1) in its famous decision in *Brown v. Board of Education*. It would not have been right for the Court to choose (3)—even though reasonable people disputed the constitutional question and even though (1) left many segregationists feeling humiliated and not treated with respect.

The examples could easily be multiplied. They show that trimming is unacceptable when it produces an incorrect or implausible interpretation of the Constitution. We can easily think of political analogues.

CONFUSED TRIMMERS

What are the extremes that concern trimmers? And what, exactly, is the solution that counts as trimming? Might not many solutions qualify? So long as judges are sane, it might seem inevitable that they will trim, in the sense that they will steer between imaginable poles. In this light, how can we know whether judges are trimming?

On a court with a number of members, we might begin with the suggestion that its judges determine the extremes. If two of them are to the far left and two are to the far right, then the conscientious trimmer can start to find her bearings. This possibility demonstrates that no court could consist solely of trimmers. The reason is that if all judges are trimmers, then none will be able to find her place, because the very practice of trimming depends on being able to identify a number of people who are not trimmers at all.

Notwithstanding this point, there is a certain logic, at least on the Supreme Court, in focusing on the distribution of views on the tribunal. Suppose that the trimmer believes that those views reflect something important about the distribution of views within the nation. Perhaps justices are selected in a way that insures representation of reasonable positions among specialists. If so, the tribunal is hardly an arbitrary source of diverse perspectives. And again, the same point might be made about political institutions.

It is not entirely clear, however, that judicial trimmers should focus on their tribunal. Suppose that the court is to the right or the left of the nation, so that the distribution of opinions within that court is skewed compared to the distribution of opinions within the country at large. Perhaps the trimmer should look to society as a whole, not to the judiciary. Or suppose that the court is to the right of where it was twenty years ago, and the trimmer believes that the relevant extremes are best identified by examining the range of views in a previous era. Should the trimmer work on the basis of the contemporary range, rather than an earlier one—or should the trimmer think about the range of views that is likely to prevail in about a decade?

The answers to such questions will depend on why, exactly, the trimmer trims, and also on the distinction between compromisers and preservers. If trimmers seek to diminish public outrage and social conflict, they are likely to look to the range of views in society, not on the court. If the trimmers trim because trimming is a good rule of thumb and is likely to lead to good results, the choice between the tribunal and the public depends on the judge's theory of interpretation. Suppose that the judicial trimmer thinks that the meaning of the Constitution depends on some mix of respect for precedent and the original understanding. If so, the views of the public will not be relevant. What matters is the distribution of views within the group of people who are entrusted with interpreting the Constitution and who have relevant expertise.

MANIPULABLE TRIMMERS

The Problem. For both compromisers and preservers, what count as the extremes, and what counts as trimming, depends on the alternatives that are presented. As the philosopher Robert Goodin has objected, the trimmers' procedure "is outrageously sensitive to the choice of end points. Tack Saint Thomas Aquinas onto the one end or the Marquis de Sade onto the other, and the midpoint shifts wildly."[28]

The point is familiar in marketing. In order to get people to buy their products, self-interested sellers can exploit people's aversion to extremes and desire to seek the middle. Shrewd sellers might introduce some really high-cost items in order to make a moderately costly item seem to be the compromise choice. Prosecutors can do the same thing. Alert to extremeness aversion and intent on obtaining a conviction, they can bring an especially severe charge in order to help insure a conviction on a less severe one. The upshot is that trimmers can be manipulated by those who select or identify the range of options.

It is clear that trimmers have to be self-conscious about this risk; they must take steps to guard against their own vulnerability. We might distinguish between naive trimmers, who are easily exploited by others, and sophisticated trimmers, who, in deciding whether to trim, are alert to others' strategic incentives and whose very alertness diminishes those incentives. Naive trimmers are vulnerable here, and sophisticated ones may have to do a great deal of work to acquire the necessary information.

Arbitrary Poles? Even if preservers can overcome the problem of manipulation, a related problem remains: arbitrariness. What is the midpoint? It depends on what the end points are. If the end points are arbitrary, then the midpoint is arbitrary as well. If no justification is given for the end points, then there is no justification for the midpoint that they establish. Preservers are in a position to correct this problem because they will provide some scrutiny to the end points, insuring that they contain something to preserve. Preposterous readings of the Constitution—for example, the view that the president can censor speech however he sees fit—can be ruled out of bounds and are uninformative for purposes of trimming.

The problem of arbitrariness seems harder for the compromiser to solve. But suppose that the trimmer believes that the current distribution of views is no accident and that it was produced by a set of mechanisms that insures against arbitrary extremes. If the trimmer is concerned about the distribution of views on the Supreme Court, he might believe that political processes and professionalization ensure that the extremes are not genuinely arbitrary. And if he does not believe that, he might consult the nation more generally, believing that in a free and democratic society, the range of opinion is not a bad guide to what is reasonable. Of course, preservers might be skeptical on this count.

LAWLESS TRIMMERS

Trimmers are influenced by a set of concerns that might not be relevant, certainly in the domain of constitutional law and perhaps more generally. True, trimming can reduce social conflict and the intensity of public outrage at judicial decisions. But trimming is often inferior to minimalism on this count, simply because trimmers will not decline to decide. And even if trimming is a good way of reducing outrage, why should judges care about public outrage? Should they refuse to issue the best interpretation of the Constitution simply because the public would be angered by their decision? It is also true that trimming can be defended on strategic grounds. But should judges really be strategic? Should they attempt to persuade their colleagues by pressing for an interpretation of the Constitution that they do not endorse on principle?

Perhaps the least controversial defense of trimming involves respect for precedent. Sometimes judges will have to yield in their preferred interpretation in deference to past rulings. But this defense is limited, because it applies only when precedents impose an obstacle to selecting the favored approach. In some settings, no precedents require trimming. In other settings, the precedents are opaque, and judges can proceed with their preferred interpretations without trimming.

POLITICAL TRIMMERS

On one view, trimming is a quintessentially political act. For all of the reasons given thus far, legislators and other policy makers might want to trim. Indeed, trimming is a pragmatic necessity in the political domain. This point raises a distinctive objection. Why shouldn't judges simply respect, and uphold, whatever form of trimming emerges from politics? And if this question can be answered, another one remains: Why should we think that judges are good at trimming?

It is true that if the political process produces ideal trimming, judges might respect the results. But what emerges from politics is sometimes legitimately challenged on constitutional grounds, and the constitutional complaint raises issues that might not have been handled adequately politically. If so, judges must decide what to do. A distinguished tradition holds that so long as the Constitution is unclear, judges should respect whatever emerges from the political process. But this view is highly controversial, and those who reject it might decide to trim. To the objection that judges might not know enough to trim, the best response is that preservers attempt to obtain the information that would justify their judgments, and that compromisers act as they do precisely because of their own humility.

TAKING STOCK

These are formidable objections; they show that it would be foolish to adopt trimming as one's only response. But the objections should not be read for more than they are worth. They fail to show that trimming has no place in politics or constitutional law. Here, as in the case of minimalism, we need to investigate the costs of decisions and the costs of errors, and the investigation may argue in favor of trimming.

It is true that if judges are confident that the best interpretation of the Constitution forbids trimming, they should not trim. They should endorse the best interpretation. But suppose that judges are not confident about which interpretation is best, and they seek to trim on the ground that trimming is a reasonable rule of thumb. If so, they should be expected to spend some time on the merits, to insure that the result is defensible, that manipulation has not led them astray, and that a reasonable rule of thumb has not produced an error in the particular case. If they are convinced on those counts, they might do best to trim.

The objections to trimming downplay both the possibility that judges lack confidence on the right outcome (which might justify trimming) and the force of precedent (which might require trimming). It is true that once judges have decided to trim, they will not know exactly what to do; several possible approaches might count as trimming. But at least some approaches will be ruled out, and the range of attractive options will be defined and narrowed.

Because judges are specialists, they should not be mere compromisers, steering between the poles on the basis of their own ignorance. Some of the best arguments for trimming emphasize the importance of preserving the most essential and deeply held components of competing points of view. Preservers can maintain that they trim not out of cowardice, but on the ground that an investigation of the merits has persuaded them that the result of trimming is best. And if trimming insures that those with competing views do not feel humiliated or hurt, it is better still.

With suitable adjustments, all of these points apply in the political domain as well. Representatives may have clarity on what is best, and they may not want to trim. If experts are clear that a certain air pollutant is hazardous, or that certain equipment badly endangers workers, representatives should probably follow the experts rather than trim. But in the face of reasonable dispute, trimming has its attractions, not least because it makes solutions possible.

MINIMALISTS VERSUS TRIMMERS

Trimmers and minimalists seem to be cousins. Both groups seek to reduce the most intense social conflict and public outrage, and some of the arguments that support minimalism support trimming as well. No less than trimmers, minimalists are motivated by a principle of civic respect. But while minimalists leave hard issues for another day, trimmers do no such thing. Minimalists celebrate the virtues of not deciding; trimmers want to decide. Who's right?

Against Minimalism: On Predictability and Exporting Costs. In chapter 10, we saw that minimalism might be easiest in the short run, but in the long run, it can prove destructive, in part because it exports the burdens of decision to others in a way that might produce a great deal of trouble. However difficult a decision may be, it may be best to make it, and sooner rather than later. Wide rulings can reduce the overall burdens of decision; they can also reduce mistakes. And if enduring social controversy is a legitimate cause for concern, then wide rulings might be defended on the ground that such controversy will be diminished or muted if the court settles a range of issues at once.

Shallowness has its virtues, but as we have also seen, it is sometimes best to resolve foundational issues. Some cases cannot be decided at all unless judges make a relatively large-scale decision about constitutional law. And even if depth is not strictly required, judges may reasonably opt for it. They might conclude that they have enough understanding and experience to offer, right now, an ambitious account of the free-speech or equal-protection principle. If so, why should they hesitate?

Alert to these objections, trimmers are eager to rule widely in a way that will minimize confusion and conflict for the future. In especially sensitive areas, they insist that wide rulings will simultaneously create more stability and less controversy. They are perfectly comfortable with clear rules, laid down in advance. They are also willing to think hard about the foundations of constitutional law—about the appropriate constitutional method and about the grounds of one right or another. Trimmers refuse to export decisions to posterity.

It should now be clear why and when minimalists and trimmers disagree. In a dispute involving a gun control measure, a minimalist would be tempted to focus on the particular measure in a way that would leave a great deal undecided. A trimmer, by contrast, would try to decide many of the key questions in a way that would produce a high degree of predictability. A committed minimalist would prefer a narrow decision, limited to the measure in question. The minimalist would ask the trimmer, "Why decide issues that are not squarely presented?" The trimmer would respond, "Why leave so much uncertainty?"

The debate between minimalists and trimmers involves two familiar factors: the costs of decisions and the costs of errors. Trimmers tend to believe that their approach has the key advantage of clear rules—namely, the specification of outcomes in advance. Minimalists think that their approach has the key advantage of open-ended standards—namely, flexibility in the face of an uncertain future. The choice between the two approaches depends on the context, which will tell us about the costs of decisions and the costs of errors. We could easily imagine a situation in which minimalism should be preferred to trimming because politician or judges lack the information to justify wide or deep rulings; consider novel First Amendment questions involving new technologies. We could also imagine situations in which trimming should be preferred to minimalism, because the problem arises so frequently that uncertainty is intolerable; consider regulation of commercial advertising or sexually explicit speech.

Over time, minimalist rulings might produce a regime of trimming. As cases accumulate, minimalism is highly likely to prove unstable. Narrow rulings with respect to obscenity, commercial advertising, and sex equality will eventually produce a degree of width. Depth is also likely. To decide whether one case is analogous to another, judges have to offer reasons, and as problems become more confusing and difficult, those reasons will become more ambitious.

HUMILITY AND HONOR

Many trimmers are compromisers. They think that if we steer between the poles, we will probably do better than if we choose one or another. Other trimmers are preservers. They attempt to identify and preserve what it is deepest, most intensely held, and best in competing positions.

Because of their sympathetic attention to all sides, trimmers can claim a degree of humility. To the extent that they are preservers, trimmers are willing to scrutinize the poles and not simply observe them. For that reason, preservers are less subject to manipulation, and, in the end, they have reason for confidence that their decision is correct, not merely a way of splitting the difference. By their very nature, trimmers are motivated by a desire to reduce social conflict, to show a kind of civic respect, and to insure that no side feels excluded, humiliated, or hurt.

It is possible, of course, that any form of trimming will produce a bad or even indefensible result. It is also true that trimmers can be manipulated. If the poles are arbitrary, the trimming solution will be arbitrary too. But I hope that I have said enough to show that trimming is not only a pervasive practice but also an honorable one. In many areas, it is superior to the reasonable alternatives.

ACKNOWLEDGMENTS

I am grateful to a lot of people for help with this book. Special thanks to Martha Nussbaum, Eric Posner, Richard Posner, and Adrian Vermeule for excellent suggestions and advice on many of the chapters. My agent, Sarah Chalfant, provided valuable guidance. Thomas LeBien made terrific editorial suggestions. Daniel Kanter provided superb research assistance. My wife, Samantha Power, was a source of support throughout.

I am particularly grateful to Adrian Vermeule, coauthor of the original version of chapter 1; and Eric Posner, coauthor of the original version of chapter 7. I have made significant revisions in both chapters. Because the changes in chapter 1 were substantial, and because he was not involved in them, Vermeule is not listed as a coauthor, but he deserves full credit for development of the central argument. In both cases, the original essays may be worth consulting for a fuller sense of the emphases and content that emerged from genuinely joint work.

After this book was completed, and when it was in final page proofs, President Obama appointed me to the Review Group on Intelligence and Communications Technology. Nothing said here reflects an official position in any way.

The chapters in this book grow out of earlier publications, and in some cases (especially chapter 2), I have reduced the references and footnotes, which can be found in the original sources. I am very grateful to the original publishers for permission to draw on them here:

Chapter 1: "Conspiracy Theories: Causes and Cures," *Journal of Political Philosophy* 17, no. 2 (June 2009): 202–27.

Chapter 2 draws from *The Second Bill of Rights: FDR's Unfinished Revolution and Why We Need It More Than Ever* (New York: Basic Books, 2004).

Chapter 3: "If 'Misfearing' Is the Problem, Is Cost-Benefit Analysis the Solution?" in *The Behavioral Foundations of Public Policy*, ed. Eldar Shafir (Princeton, NJ: Princeton University Press, 2013), 231–42.

Chapter 4: "Illusory Losses," *Journal of Legal Studies* 37, no. S2 (January 2008): S157–94.

Chapter 5: "The Rights of Animals," *University of Chicago Law Review* 70 (Winter 2003): 387–401.

Chapter 6: "The Right to Marry," *Cardozo Law Review* 26, no. 5 (April 2005): 2081–120.

Chapter 7: "Climate Change Justice," *Georgetown Law Journal* 96, no. 5 (June 2008): 1565–612.

Chapter 8: "Should Sex Equality Law Apply to Religious Institutions?" in *Is Multiculturalism Bad for Women?* ed. Susan Moller Okin (Princeton, NJ: Princeton University Press, 1999), 85–94.

Chapter 9: "A New Progressivism," *Stanford Law & Policy Review* 17 (2006): 197–232.

Chapter 10: "Beyond Judicial Minimalism," *Tulsa Law Review* 43, no. 4 (Summer 2008): 825–41.

Chapter 11: "Trimming," *Harvard Law Review* 122, no. 4 (February 2009): 1049–94.

NOTES

CHAPTER 1: CONSPIRACY THEORIES

1. Zogby International, "Half of New Yorkers Believe US Leaders Had Foreknowledge of Impending 9-11 Attacks and 'Consciously Failed' to Act; 66% Call for New Probe of Unanswered Questions by Congress or New York's Attorney General, New Zogby International Poll Reveals," August 30, 2004, http://web.archive.org/web/20081217161036/http://www.zogby.com/search/ReadNews.dbm?ID=855.

2. Thomas Hargrove and Guido H. Stempel III, Scripps Howard News Service, "Third of Americans Suspect 9-11 Government Conspiracy," August 2, 2006, http://web.archive.org/web/20060805052538/http://www.scrippsnews.com/911poll.

3. Ibid.

4. Reuters, "One in 5 Canadians Sees 9/11 as U.S. Plot—Poll," September 11, 2006.

5. Matthew A. Gentzkow and Jesse M. Shapiro, "Media, Education and Anti-Americanism in the Muslim World," *Journal of Economic Perspectives* 18, no. 3 (Summer 2004): 117.

6. Ibid., 120.
7. Sander van der Linden, "Moon Landing Faked!!!—Why People Believe in Conspiracy Theories," *Scientific American* (April 30, 2013), www.scientificamerican.com/article.cfm?id=moon-landing-faked-why-people-believe-conspiracy-theories.
8. See Richard McGregor, "Chinese Buy Into Conspiracy Theory," *Financial Times*, September 26, 2007, www.redicecreations.com/article.php?id=1907.
9. See Terry Ann Knopf, *Rumors, Race and Riots*, 2nd ed. (New Brunswick, NJ: Transaction Publishers, 2006).
10. Karl R. Popper, "The Conspiracy Theory of Society," in *Conspiracy Theories: The Philosophical Debate*, ed. David Coady (Farnham, Surrey, UK: Ashgate Publishing, 2006), 13.
11. Brian L. Keeley, "Of Conspiracy Theories," in *Conspiracy Theories: The Philosophical Debate*, ed. David Coady (Farnham, Surrey, UK: Ashgate Publishing, 2006), 46, 56–57.
12. Quoted in ibid., 57.
13. Quoted in Christopher Hodapp and Alice Von Kannon, *Conspiracy Theories and Secret Societies for Dummies* (Hoboken, NJ: Wiley Publishing, 2008), 22.
14. A relevant study, not involving conspiracy theories, is Leon Festinger, Henry W. Riecken, and Stanley Schachter, *When Prophecy Fails: A Social and Psychological Study of a Modern Group That Predicted the Destruction of the World* (New York: Harper and Row, 1964).
15. See Brendan Nyhan and Jason Reifler, "When Corrections Fail: The Persistence of Political Misperceptions," *Political Behavior* 32, no. 2 (June 2010): 303. On the general point, see Edward Glaeser and Cass R. Sunstein, "Why Does Balanced News Produce Unbalanced Views?" (working paper 18975, National Bureau of Economic Research, Cambridge, MA, April 2013), www.nber.org/papers/w18975.
16. Martin Bruder et al., "Measuring Individual Differences in Generic Beliefs in Conspiracy Theories Across Cultures: Conspiracy Mentality Questionnaire," *Frontiers in Psychology* 4, no. 225 (April 30, 2013), www.ncbi.nlm.nih.gov/pmc/articles/PMC3639408.

17. Ibid.
18. Michael J. Wood, Karen M. Douglas, and Robbie M. Sutton, "Dead and Alive: Beliefs in Contradictory Conspiracy Theories," *Social Psychological and Personality Science* 3, no. 6 (November 2012): 767–73.
19. Ibid.
20. Stephan Lewandowky, Klaus Oberauer, and Gilles E. Gignac, "NASA Faked the Moon Landing—Therefore, (Climate) Science Is a Hoax: An Anatomy of the Motivated Rejection of Science," *Psychological Science* 24, no. 5 (May 2013): 622.
21. Karen M. Douglas and Robbie M. Sutton, "Does It Take One to Know One? Endorsement of Conspiracy Theories Is Influenced by Personal Willingness to Conspire," *British Journal of Social Psychology* 50, no. 3 (September 2011): 544–52.
22. See Viren Swami, Tomas Chamorro-Premuzic, and Adrian Furnham, "Unanswered Questions: A Preliminary Investigation of Personality and Individual Difference Predictors of 9/11 Conspiracist Beliefs," *Applied Cognitive Psychology* 24, no. 6 (September 2010): 749–61; Viren Swami et al., "Conspiracist Ideation in Britain and Austria: Evidence of a Monological Belief System and Associations Between Individual Psychological Differences and Real-World and Fictitious Conspiracy Theories," *British Journal of Psychology* 102, no. 3 (August 2011): 443–63.
23. Daniel Jolley and Karen M. Douglas, "The Social Consequences of Conspiracism: Exposure to Conspiracy Theories Decreases Intentions to Engage in Politics and to Reduce One's Carbon Footprint," *British Journal of Psychology* (2013), http://onlinelibrary.wiley.com/doi/10.1111/bjop.12018/abstract?deniedAccessCustomisedMessage=&userIsAuthenticated=false.
24. Russell Hardin, "The Crippled Epistemology of Extremism," in *Political Rationality and Extremism*, eds. Albert Breton et al. (Cambridge, UK: Cambridge University Press, 2002), 3, 16.
25. See Alan B. Krueger, *What Makes a Terrorist: Economics and the Roots of Terrorism* (Princeton, NJ: Princeton University Press, 2008), 75–82.
26. See Diane E. Goldstein, *Once Upon a Virus: AIDS Legends and Vernacular Risk Perception* (Logan: Utah State University Press, 2004); Seth Kalichman, *Denying AIDS: Conspiracy Theories, Pseu-*

doscience, and Human Tragedy (New York: Copernicus Books, 2009).

27. For a relevant discussion, see Duncan J. Watts, *Everything Is Obvious (Once You Know the Answer)* (Atlantic Books, 2011).
28. A clear outline can be found in David Hirshleifer, "The Blind Leading the Blind: Social Influence, Fads, and Informational Cascades," in *The New Economics of Human Behavior*, eds. Mariano Tommasi and Kathryn Ierulli (Cambridge, UK: Cambridge University Press, 1995), 188.
29. See Erik Eyster and Matthew Rabin, "Rational and Naive Herding" (working paper, Department of Economics, University of California—Berkeley, Berkeley, CA, June 15, 2009), http://emlab.berkeley.edu/~rabin/rationalnaiveherdingUSA.pdf; Erik Eyster and Matthew Rabin, "Naive Herding in Rich-Information Settings" (working paper, UC Berkeley, Berekley, CA, March 24, 2010), www.econ.as.nyu.edu/docs/IO/14395/Eyster_20100413.pdf.
30. See Chris Bell and Emily Sternberg, "Emotional Selection in Memes: The Case of Urban Legends," *Journal of Personality and Social Psychology* 81, no. 6 (December 2001): 1028.
31. See Cass R. Sunstein, *Going to Extremes: How Like Minds Unite and Divide* (New York: Oxford University Press, 2009); Roger Brown, *Social Psychology*, 2nd ed. (New York: Free Press, 2003), 202–26.
32. See David Schkade, Cass R. Sunstein, and Reid Hastie, "What Happened on Deliberation Day?" *California Law Review* 95, no. 3 (June 2007): 915.
33. Brown, *Social Psychology*, 223–24.
34. Roderick M. Kramer, "The Sinister Attribution Error: Paranoid Cognition and Collective Distrust in Organizations," *Motivation and Emotion* 18, no. 2 (June 1994): 199–230.
35. Thomas Gilovich, Victoria Husted Medvec, and Kenneth Savitsky, "The Spotlight Effect in Social Judgment: An Egocentric Bias in Estimates of the Salience of One's Own Actions and Appearance," *Journal of Personality and Social Psychology* 78, no. 2 (February 2000): 211–22, http://psych.cornell.edu/sites/default/files/Gilo.Medvec.Sav_.pdf.
36. William Weir, "Damage Control: State Department Officer

Works to Dispel Lies, Conspiracy Theories and Urban Legends That Harm U.S. Image," *Hartford Courant*, October 16, 2006, D1.

37. Nicholas DiFonzo and Prashant Bordia, *Rumor Psychology: Social and Organizational Approaches* (Washington, DC: American Psychological Association, 2007), 225.

38. Ibid., 217–22; see also Ben Yandell, "Those Who Protest Too Much Are Seen as Guilty," *Personality and Social Psychology Bulletin* 5, no. 1 (January 1979): 44–47.

39. David Dunbar and Brad Reagan, eds., *Debunking 9/11 Myths: Why Conspiracy Theories Can't Stand Up to the Facts* (New York: Hearst Communications, 2006): 60–61.

40. See, for example, Jim Hoffman, "Video of the Pentagon Attack: What Is the Government Hiding," http://911research.com/essays/pentagon/video.html (last visited November 14, 2006).

41. For evidence of why this might be so, see Charles G. Lord, Lee Ross, and Mark R. Lepper, "Biased Assimilation and Attitude Polarization: The Effects of Prior Theories on Subsequently Considered Evidence," *Journal of Personality and Social Psychology* 37, no. 11 (1979): 2098.

42. John W. McHoskey, "Case Closed? On the John F. Kennedy Assassination: Biased Assimilation of Evidence and Attitude Polarization," *Basic and Applied Social Psychology* 17, no. 395 (1995).

43. Carol Morello, "One Man's Unorthodox Ideas About the 9/11 Attack on the Pentagon Go Global in a Flash. Welcome to the Internet, Where Conspiracy Theories Flourish," *Washington Post*, October 7, 2004, B1.

44. Jim Dwyer, "U.S. Counters 9/11 Theories of Conspiracy," *New York Times*, September 2, 2006, B1.

45. Neil MacFarquhar, "At State Dept., Blog Team Joins Muslim Debate," *New York Times*, September 22, 2007, A1.

46. See Glaeser and Sunstein, "Balanced News."

47. See the overview in David K. Sherman and Geoffrey Cohen, "The Psychology of Self-Defense: Self-Affirmation Theory," in *Advances in Experimental Social Psychology*, vol. 38, ed. M. P. Zanna (San Diego: Academic Press, 2006): 183.

CHAPTER 2: THE SECOND BILL OF RIGHTS

1. There are some significant qualifications, including the view that property may be managed by stable institutions of self-government. See Elinor Ostrom, *Governing the Commons: The Evolution of Institutions for Collective Action* (Cambridge, UK: Cambridge University Press, 1990).
2. See F. A. Hayek, *The Road to Serfdom: Text and Documents—The Definitive Edition*, ed. Bruce Caldwell (Chicago: University of Chicago Press, 2007 [1944]), 88.
3. See "Annual Message to the Congress," January 3, 1938, *1938 vol., The Continuing Struggle for Liberalism*, in *The Public Papers and Addresses of Franklin D. Roosevelt* (New York: Macmillan Company, 1941), 14, http://name.umdl.umich.edu/4926315.1938.001.
4. For a relevant discussion, see generally Amartya Sen, *Development As Freedom* (New York: Knopf, 1999).

CHAPTER 3: IF "MISFEARING" IS THE PROBLEM, IS COST-BENEFIT ANALYSIS THE SOLUTION?

1. The best discussion is Daniel Kahneman, *Thinking, Fast and Slow* (New York: Farrar, Straus & Giroux, 2011).
2. See Cass R. Sunstein, *Valuing Life* (Chicago: University of Chicago Press, 2014).
3. Table 5.9, in *Regulatory Impact Analysis for the Final Revisions to the National Ambient Air Quality Standards for Particulate Matter* (Research Triangle Park, NC: US Environmental Protection Agency, Office of Air Quality Planning and Standards, Health and Environmental Impacts Division, December 2012), www.epa.gov/ttn/ecas/regdata/RIAs/finalria.pdf.
4. For discussion, see Cass R. Sunstein, *Simpler: The Future of Government* (New York: Simon & Schuster, 2013).
5. See Roger G. Noll and James E. Krier, "Some Implications of Cognitive Psychology for Risk Regulation," *Journal of Legal Studies* 19, no. 2 (June 1990): 747, 749–60.
6. See Amos Tversky and Daniel Kahneman, "Judgment Under Uncertainty: Heuristics and Biases," in *Judgment Under Uncertainty: Heuristics and Biases*, eds. Daniel Kahneman, Paul Slovic,

and Amos Tversky (Cambridge, UK: Cambridge University Press, 1982), 3, 11 (describing the availability heuristic).

7. Amos Tversky and Daniel Kahneman, "Extensional Versus Intuitive Reasoning: The Conjunction Fallacy in Probability Judgment," *Psychological Review* 90, no. 4 (October 1983): 293, 295.
8. Jonathan Baron, *Thinking and Deciding*, 2nd ed. (Cambridge, UK: Cambridge University Press, 1994), 218.
9. See Thorsten Pachur, Ralph Hertwig, and Florian Steinmann, "How Do People Judge Risks: Availability Heuristic, Affect Heuristic, or Both?" *Journal of Experimental Psychology: Applied* 18, no. 3 (September 2012): 314.
10. See Neal Feigenson, Daniel Bailis, and William Klein, "Perceptions of Terrorism and Disease Risks: A Cross-National Comparison," *University of Missouri Law Review* 69, no. 4 (Fall 2004): 991.
11. See Timur Kuran and Cass R. Sunstein, "Availability Cascades and Risk Regulation," *Stanford Law Review* 51, no. 4 (April 1999): 683.
12. See David Hirshleifer, "The Blind Leading the Blind: Social Influence, Fads, and Informational Cascades," in *The New Economics of Human Behavior*, eds. Mariano Tommasi and Kathryn Ierulli (Cambridge, UK: Cambridge University Press, 1995).
13. See Kuran and Sunstein, "Availability Cascades," 683.
14. Yuval Rottenstreich and Christopher K. Hsee, "Money, Kisses, and Electric Shocks: On the Affective Psychology of Risk," *Psychological Science* 12, no. 3 (May 2001): 185.
15. See Ali Siddiq Alhakami and Paul Slovic, "A Psychological Study of the Inverse Relationship Between Perceived Risk and Perceived Benefit," *Risk Analysis* 14, no. 6 (December 1994): 1085, 1094–96.
16. See George F. Loewenstein et al., "Risk as Feelings," *Psychological Bulletin* 127, no. 2 (March 2001): 267.
17. W. Kip Viscusi, "Alarmist Decisions with Divergent Risk Information," *Economic Journal* 107, no. 445 (November 1997): 1657–59.
18. Ibid.
19. See C. Boyden Gray, "The Clean Air Act Under Regulatory Reform," *Tulane Environmental Law Journal* 11 (Summer 1998): 235.

20. John D. Graham, Bei-Hung Chang, and John S. Evans, "Poorer Is Riskier," *Risk Analysis* 12, no. 3 (September 1992): 333–35; Frank B. Cross, "When Environmental Regulations Kill: The Role of Health/Health Analysis," *Ecology Law Quarterly* 22, no. 4 (1995): 729; Ralph L. Keeney, "Mortality Risks Induced by the Costs of Regulations," *Journal of Risk and Uncertainty* 8, no. 1 (January 1994): 95; Aaron B. Wildavsky, "Richer Is Safer," *Public Interest* 60 (Summer 1980): 23; Aaron B. Wildavsky, *Searching for Safety* (New Brunswick, NJ: Transaction Books, 1988), 59–75.
21. The fact that nuclear power and applying pesticides produce benefits as well as risks may not register on the lay view screen, and this may help produce a high-risk judgment. See Alhakami and Slovic, "Psychological Study," 1085, 1088.
22. See Howard Margolis, *Dealing with Risk: Why the Public and the Experts Disagree on Environmental Issues* (Chicago: University of Chicago Press, 1997), for a detailed discussion of how this point bears on the different risk judgments of experts and laypeople.
23. See Richard H. Thaler, "The Psychology of Choice and the Assumptions of Economics," in *Quasi Rational Economics*, ed. Richard H. Thaler (New York: Russell Sage Foundation, 1994), 137, 143 (arguing that "losses loom larger than gains"); Daniel Kahneman, Jack L. Knetsch, and Richard H. Thaler, "Experimental Tests of the Endowment Effect and the Coase Theorem," *Journal of Political Economy* 98, no. 6 (December 1990): 1325, 1328; Colin Camerer, "Individual Decision Making," in *The Handbook of Experimental Economics*, eds. John H. Kagel and Alvin E. Roth (Princeton, NJ: Princeton University Press, 1995), 665–70.
24. See Roland G. Fryer Jr. et al., "Enhancing the Efficacy of Teacher Incentives Through Loss Aversion: A Field Experiment" (working paper 18237, National Bureau of Economic Research, Cambridge, MA, 2012), www.nber.org/papers/w18237.pdf.
25. Ibid.
26. For a valuable discussion of loss aversion and its importance, see Tatiana A. Homonoff, "Can Small Incentives Have Large Effects? The Impact of Taxes Versus Bonuses on Disposable Bag Use" (job market paper, Department of Economics, Princeton University, Industrial Relations Section, Firestone Library, Princeton, NJ, March 27, 2013), www.princeton.edu/~ho

monoff/THomonoff_JobMarketPaper. Homonoff shows that a five-cent tax on grocery bags in the District of Columbia has had a significant effect in reducing grocery bag use—but that a five-cent bonus for using reusable bags had essentially no effect.

27. See Cass R. Sunstein, *Worst-Case Scenarios* (Cambridge, MA: Harvard University Press, 2007).

CHAPTER 4: THE LAWS OF HAPPINESS

1. Daniel Kahneman, Edward Diener, and Norbert Schwarz, eds., *Well-Being: The Foundations of Hedonic Psychology* (New York: Russell Sage Foundation, 2003).
2. Daniel Kahneman and Alan Krueger, "Developments in the Measurement of Subjective Well-Being," *Journal of Economic Perspectives* 20, no. 1 (Winter 2006): 3–24.
3. Daniel Kahneman et al., "A Survey Method for Characterizing Daily Life Experience: The Day Reconstruction Method," *Science* 306, no. 5702 (December 3, 2004): 1776–80.
4. Peter A. Ubel and George Loewenstein. "Pain and Suffering Awards: They Shouldn't (Just) Be About Pain and Suffering," *Journal of Legal Studies* 37 (June 2008).
5. Bruno S. Frey and Alois Stutzer, *Happiness and Economics: How the Economy and Institutions Affect Human Well-Being* (Princeton, NJ: Princeton University Press, 2010).
6. Andrew E. Clark et al., "Lags and Leads in Life Satisfaction: A Test of the Baseline Hypothesis," *Economic Journal* 118, no. 529 (June 2008): F222–43; Richard Easterlin, "Building a Better Theory of Well-Being" (IZA discussion paper 742, Bonn, Germany, 2003).
7. Kahneman and Krueger, "Developments," 3–24.
8. Ubel and Loewenstein, "Pain and Suffering Awards."
9. Andrew Oswald and Nattavudh Powdthavee, "Does Happiness Adapt? A Longitudinal Study of Disability with Implications for Economists and Judges," *Journal of Public Economics* 92, nos. 5 and 6 (June 2008): 1061–77.
10. Ibid.

11. Dylan M. Smith et al., "Misremembering Colostomies? Former Patients Give Lower Utility Ratings Than Do Current Patients," *Health Psychology* 25, no. 6 (2006): 688–95.
12. Ubel and Loewenstein, "Pain and Suffering Awards."
13. Ibid.
14. Ibid.
15. Daniel T. Gilbert and Timothy D. Wilson, "Miswanting: Some Problems in the Forecasting of Future Affective States," in *Feeling and Thinking: The Role of Affect in Social Cognition*, ed. Joseph P. Forgas (New York: Cambridge University Press, 2001), 186.
16. Ibid.
17. Ibid.
18. Shane Frederick and George Loewenstein, "Hedonic Adaptation," in *Well-Being: The Foundations of Hedonic Psychology*, eds. Daniel Kahneman, Edward Diener, and Norbert Schwarz (New York: Russell Sage Foundation, 1999), 302–11.
19. Neil D. Weinstein, "Community Noise Problems: Evidence Against Adaptation," *Journal of Environmental Psychology* 2, no. 2 (June 1982): 87–97.
20. Frederick and Loewenstein, "Hedonic Adaptation," 302–11.
21. Ibid.
22. Peter A. Ubel, George Loewenstein, and Christopher Jepson, "Whose Quality of Life? A Commentary Exploring Discrepancies Between Health State Evaluations of Patients and the General Public," *Quality of Life Research* 12, no. 6 (September 2003): 599–607.
23. Frederick and Loewenstein, "Hedonic Adaptation," 302–11.
24. Richard Layard, *Happiness: Lessons from a New Science* (New York: Penguin Press, 2011).
25. Clark et al., "Lags and Leads."
26. Daniel Gilbert et al., "Immune Neglect: A Source of Durability Bias in Affective Forecasting," *Journal of Personality and Social Psychology* 75, no. 3 (1998): 617–38.
27. Ibid.
28. Ibid.

29. Peter A. Ubel, George Loewenstein, and Christopher Jepson, "Disability and Sunshine: Can Hedonic Predictions Be Improved by Drawing Attention to Focusing Illusions or Emotional Adaptation?" *Journal of Experimental Psychology: Applied* 11, no. 2 (June 2005): 111–23.

30. Frederick and Loewenstein, "Hedonic Adaptation," 303–11.

31. Daniel Kahneman and Robert Sugden, "Experienced Utility as a Standard of Policy Evaluation," *Environmental and Resource Economics* 32, no. 1 (September 2005): 161–81.

32. Daniel Kahneman and Richard Thaler, "Anomalies: Utility Maximization and Expected Utility," *Journal of Economic Perspectives* 20, no. 1 (Winter 2006): 221–34.

33. David Schkade and Daniel Kahneman, "Does Living in California Make People Happy? A Focusing Illusion in Judgments of Life Satisfaction," *Psychological Science* 9, no. 5 (September 1998): 340–46.

34. Admittedly, this is true for plaintiffs as well as for juries. Those who bring suit are likely to focus on their injury—more so than those who do not bring suit. On purely hedonic grounds, it might well make sense to discourage (some) plaintiffs from bringing suit, because litigation will prevent hedonic adaptation. To the extent that the suit focuses the plaintiff on the relevant condition, the problem I am describing—exaggerated damage awards—is reduced.

35. Ubel and Loewenstein, "Pain and Suffering Awards."

36. See, for example, *Levy v. Bayou Indus. Maint. Serv.*, 855 So. 2d 968, 980 (La. Ct. App. 2003), awarding $50,000 for post-concussion syndrome, including vertigo and migraine headaches.

37. *Hatcher v. Ramada Plaza Hotel & Conf. Ctr.*, 2003 Conn. Super. LEXIS 255 (Conn. Super. Ct. 2003).

38. *Frankel v. Todd*, 260 F. Supp. 772 (E.D. Pa. 1966).

39. *Ledesma v. Long Island R.R.*, 1997 WL 33346870 (E.D.N.Y. 1997).

40. *Russo v. Jordan*, 2001 N.Y. Slip Op. 20062U, 9 (N.Y. Misc. 2001).

41. Amartya Sen, *Commodities and Capabilities* (New York: Elsevier Science, 1985); Amartya Sen, *Development as Freedom* (New York: Alfred A. Knopf, 1999).

42. George Loewenstein and Peter Ubel. "Hedonic Adaptation and the Role of Decision and Experience Utility in Public Policy," *Journal of Public Economics* 92, nos. 8 and 9 (August 2008): 1795–1810.

43. Ibid.

44. Peter A. Ubel et al., "Do Nonpatients Underestimate the Quality of Life Associated with Chronic Health Conditions Because of a Focusing Illusion?" *Medical Decision Making* 21, no. 3 (May–June 2001): 190–99.

45. For evidence that some debiasing strategies help and others do not, see Ubel, Loewenstein, and Jepson, "Disability and Sunshine," 111–23.

46. See *Day v. Ouachita Parish School Bd.*, 823 So. 2d 1039, 1044; Allen v. Wal-Mart Stores, Inc., 241 F. 1293, 1297.

47. See *Daugherty v. Erie R.R. Co.*, 169 A. 2d 549 (Pa. Sup. Ct. 1961).

48. See *Pierce v. N.Y. Cent. R.R. Co.*, 409 F.2d 1392 (6th Cir. 1969); *Matos v. Clarendon Nat. Ins. Co.*, 808 So. 2d 841, 849 (La. Ct. App. 2002).

49. See *Varnell v. Louisiana Tech University*, 709 So. 2d 890, 896 (La. Ct. App. 1998).

50. John Stuart Mill, *Utilitarianism* (London: Parker, Son, and Bourn, 1863).

51. Ibid.

52. Kahneman and Sugden, "Experienced Utility," 161–81.

53. See Betsey Stephenson and Justin Wolfers, "Economic Growth and Subjective Well-Being: Reassessing the Easterlin Paradox," *Brookings Papers on Economic Activity* 39 (Spring 2008); Daniel W. Sacks, Betsey Stephenson, and Justin Wolfers, "The New Stylized Facts About Income and Subjective Well-Being," *Emotion* 12, no. 6 (December 2012): 1181–87.

54. See Betsey Stephenson and Justin Wolfers, "Subjective Well-Being and Income: Is There Any Evidence of Satiation?" *American Economic Review: Papers and Proceedings* 103, no. 3 (May 2013): 598–604.

CHAPTER 5: THE RIGHTS OF ANIMALS

1. Immanuel Kant, *Lectures on Ethics*, trans. Louis Infield (Indianapolis: Hackett Publishing, 1963), 240.
2. See Jeremy Bentham, chap. 17, sec. 4 in *The Principles of Morals and Legislation* (Amherst, NY: Prometheus Books, 1988 [1781]), 310–11.
3. See John Stuart Mill, "Whewell on Moral Philosophy," in John Stuart Mill and Jeremy Bentham, *Utilitarianism and Other Essays*, ed. Alan Ryan (New York: Penguin Classics, 1987), 228, 252.
4. John Hooper, "German Parliament Votes to Give Animals Constitutional Rights," *Guardian* (London), May 18, 2002, *Guardian* Home Pages, www.guardian.co.uk/world/2002/may/18/animal welfare.uk.
5. See David Wolfson and Mariann Sullivan, "Animals, Agribusiness and the Law: A Modern American Fable," in *Animal Rights: Law and Policy*, eds. Cass R. Sunstein and Martha C. Nussbaum (New York: Oxford University Press, 2004).
6. Under its common agricultural policy, the European Union adopted the European Convention for the Protection of Animals Kept for Farming Purposes on November 17, 1978. European Convention for the Protection of Animals Kept for Farming Purposes, 1978 O.J. (L 323)12. The Convention applies to the "keeping, care and housing of animals, and in particular to animals in modern intensive stock-farming systems." In Articles 3 to 7, the Convention provides detailed principles of animal welfare. The Convention was amended and strengthened on December 31, 1992. Protocol of Amendment to the European Convention for the Protection of Animals Kept for Farming Purposes, 1992 O.J. (L 395) 22. Under the Convention, the EU has established specific regulations for such activities as the keeping of laying hens. Council Directive 1999/74/EC Laying Down Minimum Standards for the Protection of Laying Hens, O.J. (L 203) 53. Members of the European Union have enacted implementing legislation. The United Kingdom Department for Environment, Food and Rural Affairs (DEFRA) has been active. See www.defra.gov.uk.
7. See Peter Singer, *Animal Liberation*, rev. ed. (New York: Ecco, 2002).

CHAPTER 6: MARRIAGE

1. 388 US 1 (1967).
2. Friedrich Nietzsche, *Twilight of the Idols*, in *The Portable Nietzsche*, trans. and ed. Walter Kaufmann (New York: Viking Penguin, 1954), 544.
3. See, for example, *Zablocki v. Redhail*, 434 US 374 (1978).
4. *Maynard v. Hill*, 125 US 190, 205 (1888).
5. 262 US 390 (1923).
6. 316 US 535 (1942).
7. 381 US 479 (1965).
8. 388 US 1 (1967).
9. 434 US 374 (1978).
10. 482 US 78 (1987).
11. I draw here on Anita Bernstein, "For and Against Marriage: A Revision," *Michigan Law Review* 102, no. 2 (November 2003): 129; and David L. Chambers, "What If? The Legal Consequences of Marriage and the Legal Needs of Lesbian and Gay Male Couples," *Michigan Law Review* 95, no. 2 (November 1996): 447.
12. See Edmund Burke, *Reflections on the Revolution in France, and on the Proceedings in Certain Societies in London Relative to That Event* (London: J. Dodsley, 1790).

CHAPTER 7: CLIMATE CHANGE JUSTICE

1. See William D. Nordhaus and Joseph Boyer, *Warming the World: Economic Models of Global Warming* (Cambridge, MA: MIT Press, 2003), 91.
2. See, for example, William Nordhaus, "The Challenge of Global Warming: Economic Models and Environmental Policy" (unpublished manuscript, Yale University, New Haven, CT, July 24, 2007), http://nordhaus.econ.yale.edu/dice_mss_072407_all.pdf.
3. See "Frequently Asked Question 10.3: 'If Emissions of Greenhouse Gases Are Reduced, How Quickly Do Their Concentrations in the Atmosphere Decrease?'" in IPCC, *Climate Change 2007: The Physical Science Basis. Contribution of Working Group I to the Fourth Assessment Report of the Intergovernmental Panel on*

Climate Change, eds. Susan D. Solomon et al. (New York: Cambridge University Press, 2007), 125–26.

4. Nicholas Stern, *The Economics of Climate Change: The Stern Review* (Cambridge, UK: Cambridge University Press, 2007), 139; Richard Tol, "Estimates of the Damage Costs of Climate Change: Part 2, Dynamic Estimates," *Environmental and Resource Economics* 21, no. 2 (February 2002): 157.
5. Stern, *Economics of Climate Change*, 139.
6. Nordhaus and Boyer, *Warming the World*, 81.
7. Ibid.
8. Ibid.
9. Ibid., 91.
10. See Martin Weitzman, "Structural Uncertainty and the Value of a Statistical Life in the Economics of Catastrophic Climate Change" (working paper 13490, National Bureau of Economic Research, Cambridge, MA, October 2007), www.nber.org/papers/w13490.
11. Compare Jules Coleman, "Tort Law and the Demands of Corrective Justice," *Indiana Law Journal* 67, no. 2 (Winter 1992): 349 (arguing that corrective justice requires a remedy even when the infringing conduct was innocent); Ernest Weinrib, "Corrective Justice," *Iowa Law Review* 77 (1992): 403 (taking the contrary view); Bernard Williams, *Moral Luck* (Cambridge, UK: Cambridge University Press, 1981) (pointing out that moral blame can be attached to people who could have avoided harm even if they were not at fault). For a helpful discussion, see Stephen R. Perry, "Loss, Agency, and Responsibility for Outcomes: Three Conceptions of Corrective Justice," in *Tort Theory*, eds. Ken Cooper-Stephenson and Elaine Gibson (North York, Ontario: Captus Press, 1993), 24.
12. One commentator suggests 1990 as a date for when emitting activities could have become negligent. See Jiahua Pan, "Common but Differentiated Commitments: A Practical Approach to Engaging Large Developing Emitters Under L20," (2004): 3–7, www.l20.org/publications/6_5c_climate_pan1.
13. In 2010, the number was lower. See *Technical Support Document: Social Cost of Carbon for Regulatory Impact Analysis Under Execu-*

tive Order 12866 (Interagency Working Group on Social Cost of Carbon, United States Government, February 2010), www.epa.gov/oms/climate/regulations/scc-tsd.pdf. For the 2013 update, see *Technical Support Document: Technical Update of the Social Cost of Carbon for Regulatory Impact Analysis* (May 2013). See also Michael Greenstone, Elizabeth Kopits, and Maryann Wolverton, "Estimating the Social Cost of Carbon for Use in U.S. Federal Rulemakings: A Summary and Interpretation" (working paper 11-04, Massachusetts Institute of Technology Department of Economics, Cambridge, MA, March 23, 2011), http://papers.ssrn.com/sol3/papers.cfm?abstract_id=1793366. For assessments, see William Nordhaus, "Estimates of the Social Cost of Carbon: Background and Results from the Rice-2011 Model" (discussion paper 1826, Cowles Foundation for Research in Economics, Yale University, New Haven, CT, October 2011), http://dido.econ.yale.edu/P/cd/d18a/d1826.pdf; Jonathan Masur and Eric Posner, "Climate Change and the Limits of Cost-Benefit Analysis," *California Law Review* 99, no. 6 (December 2011): 1557.

14. See National Development and Reform Commission, People's Republic of China, *China's National Climate Change Programme* (June 2007), 58, www.ccchina.gov.cn/WebSite/CCChina/UpFile/File188.pdf.
15. See Ying Chen and Jiahua Pan, *Equity Concerns over Climate Change Mitigation*, Chinese Academy of Social Sciences, Global Change and Economic Development Program, Beijing (2003), www.fiacc.net/data/Justice-Y.%20Chen%20%20J.%20Pan.doc.
16. Ibid., 58.
17. Liu Jiang, vice-chairman, National Development and Reform Commission of China, "The Challenge of Climate Change and China's Response Strategy" (keynote speech at the roundtable meeting of energy and environment ministers from twenty nations, 2005, http://en.ccchina.gov.cn/Detail.aspx?newsId=38497&TId=98).
18. Ibid.
19. Ibid.
20. See *China's National Climate Change Programme*, 60–61.
21. Ibid., 2.
22. See Chen and Pan, *Equity Concerns*, 5–6.

CHAPTER 8: SEX EQUALITY VERSUS RELIGIOUS FREEDOM?

1. American law makes the basic prohibitions on employment discrimination inapplicable where religion, sex, or national origin is "a bona fide occupational qualification reasonably necessary to the normal operation of that particular business or enterprise" (42 U.S.C. 2000e-2[e]). The prohibition is generally inapplicable "to a religious corporation, association, educational institution, or society with respect to the employment of individuals of a particular religion to perform work connected with the carrying on by such corporation, association, educational institution, or society of its activities" (42 U.S.C. 2000e-1).
2. See *EEOC v. Catholic University of America*, 856 F. Supp. 1 (D.D.C. 1994), affirmed, 83 F.3d 455 (D.C. Cir. 1996).
3. See, for example, *Young v. Northern Illinois Conference of United Methodist Church*, 21 F.3d 184 (7th Cir. 1994).
4. *EEOC v. Catholic University*, 83 F.3d 455 (D.C. Cir. 1996), citing *Rayburn v. General Conference of Seventh-Day Adventists*, 772 F.2d 1164, 1169 (4th Cir. 1985).
5. *Employment Division, Department of Human Resources of Oregon v. Smith*, 494 U.S. 872 (1990). Technically, *Smith* holds that a facially neutral law will be upheld so long as it has a "rational basis," unless it is discriminatorily motivated. The Court did not overrule *Sherbert v. Verner*, 374 U.S. 398 (1963) (holding that a state may not deny unemployment benefits to a Seventh-Day Adventist who was fired because she would not work on Saturday) or *Wisconsin v. Yoder*, 406 U.S. 205 (1972) (allowing Amish teenagers to be exempted from a requirement of school attendance until the age of sixteen), but it did read those cases extremely narrowly. The *Smith* decision was surprising as well as controversial, and it remains an object of continuing debate not only in political and academic circles but also within the Supreme Court itself.
6. In *EEOC v. Catholic University*, 83 F.3d 455 (D.C. Cir. 1994), the court held, without much explanation, that *Smith* did not undermine previous holdings that there was an exception for ministers from the general sex discrimination law.

CHAPTER 9: A NEW PROGRESSIVISM

1. Dietrich Dörner, *The Logic of Failure: Recognizing and Avoiding Error in Complex Situations* (Cambridge, MA: Perseus Books, 1996).
2. See Amartya Sen, *Development as Freedom* (New York: Random House, 2011); Martha C. Nussbaum, *Women and Human Development: The Capabilities Approach* (Cambridge, UK: Cambridge University Press, 2001); Anthony Giddens, *The Third Way and Its Critics* (Cambridge, UK: Polity Press, 2008).
3. Jean Drèze and Amartya Sen, *India: Development and Participation* (New York: Oxford University Press, 2002), 52.
4. Ibid., 312.
5. I should acknowledge that it is controversial to suggest that the right of free speech runs against the private sector; some people believe that it applies only to government (as it does under American constitutional law).
6. For a detailed discussion, see Stephen Holmes and Cass R. Sunstein, *The Cost of Rights: Why Liberty Depends on Taxes* (New York: W. W. Norton & Company, 2000).
7. See Uri Gneezy and Aldo Rustichini, "A Fine Is a Price," *Journal of Legal Studies* 29, no. 1 (January 2000).
8. See Richard Thaler and Cass R. Sunstein, *Nudge: Improving Decisions About Health, Wealth, and Happiness* (New Haven, CT: Yale University Press, 2008).
9. See Harold H. Gardner, Nathan L. Kleinman, and Richard J. Butler, "Workers' Compensation and Family and Medical Leave Act Claim Contagion," *Journal of Risk and Uncertainty* 20, no. 1 (January 2000): 89, 101–10.
10. See, for example, George A. Akerlof, Janet L. Yellen, and Michael L. Katz, "An Analysis of Out-of-Wedlock Childbearing in the United States," *Quarterly Journal of Economics* 111, no. 2 (May 1996): 277.
11. See Robert Cialdini et al., "A Focus Theory of Normative Conduct: Recycling the Concept of Norms to Reduce Littering in Public Places," *Journal of Personality and Social Psychology* 58, no. 6 (June 1990): 1015.

12. See Edward L. Glaeser, Bruce Sacerdote, and José A. Scheinkman, "Crime and Social Interactions," *Quarterly Journal of Economics* 111, no. 2 (May 1996): 507–48.
13. See Marianne Bertrand, Erzo F. P. Luttmer, and Sendhil Millainathan, "Network Effects and Welfare Cultures," *Quarterly Journal of Economics* 115, no. 3 (August 2000): 1019–55.
14. See Thaler and Sunstein, *Nudge*.
15. See Ardith Spence, "Wants for Waste: The Economics of Social Norms and Household Recycling Habits" (unpublished PhD dissertation, University of Chicago, 1999).
16. See Stephen Coleman, *The Minnesota Income Tax Compliance Experiment: State Tax Results* (Minnesota Department of Revenue, St. Paul, April 1996).
17. See H. Wesley Perkins et al., "Misperceptions of the Norms for the Frequency of Alcohol and Other Drug Use on College Campuses," *Journal of American College Health* 47, no. 6 (1999); Kuran and Sunstein, "Availability Cascades," 683, 767. A good outline of contagion effects can be found in Gardner, Kleinman, and Butler, "Workers' Compensation and Family and Medical Leave Act," 91–94.
18. See George Akerlof, "A Theory of Social Custom, of Which Unemployment May Be One Consequence," chap. 4 in *An Economic Theorist's Book of Tales* (Cambridge, UK: Cambridge University Press, 1984).
19. See Sushil Bikhchandani, David Hirshleifer, and Ivo Welch, "A Theory of Fads, Fashion, Custom, and Cultural Change as Informational Cascades," *Journal of Political Economy* 100, no. 5 (October 1992): 992–1026; Kuran and Sunstein, "Availability Cascades," 715–35.
20. See Bikhchandani, Hirschleivfer, and Welch, "A Theory of Fads," 992–1026; Robert E. Kennedy, "Strategy Fads and Competitive Convergence: An Empirical Test for Herd Behavior in Prime-Time Television Programming," *Journal of Industrial Economics* 50, no. 1 (March 2002): 57–84.
21. Several of these examples are discussed in Kuran and Sunstein, "Availability Cascades," 725–35; and in Mark Granovetter, "Threshold Models of Collective Behavior," *American Journal of Sociology* 83, no. 6 (May 1978): 1422–24.

22. See World Bank, "Efficient and Equitable Strategies for Preventing HIV/AIDS," in *Confronting AIDS: Public Priorities in a Global Epidemic* (New York: Oxford University Press, 1999).
23. See Lawrence Lessig, "The Regulation of Social Meaning," *University of Chicago Law Review* 62, no. 3 (Summer 1995): 943–1045.
24. See Daniel Shaviro, "The Minimum Wage, the Earned Income Tax Credit, and Optimal Subsidy Policy," *University of Chicago Law Review* 64, no. 2 (Spring 1997): 405, 435.
25. Anne Case and Motohiro Yogo, "Does School Quality Matter? Returns to Education and Characteristics of Schools in South Africa" (working paper 7399, National Bureau of Economic Research, Cambridge, MA, October 1999), www.nber.org/papers/w7399.
26. See Raj Chetty, John N. Friedman, and Jonah E. Rockoff, "The Long-Term Impacts of Teachers: Teacher Value-Added and Student Outcomes in Adulthood" (working paper 17699, National Bureau of Economic Research, Cambridge, MA, December 2011), www.nber.org/papers/w17699.
27. Benjamin Aldrich-Moodie, Century Foundation, *The Earned Income Tax Credit, Issue Brief No. 1* (September 1999).
28. See Sunstein, *Simpler*. On default rules and environmental protection, see Cass R. Sunstein and Lucia A. Reisch, "Automatically Green: Behavioral Economics and Environmental Protection," *Harvard Environmental Law Review* (forthcoming 2013).
29. W. Kip Viscusi, *Reforming Products Liability* (Cambridge, MA.: Harvard University Press, 1991), 178.
30. See EPA, "Emissions Trading Policy Statement: General Principles for Creation, Banking, and Use of Emission Reduction Credits," 51 Fed. Reg. 43,814 (December 4, 1986).
31. See Robert W. Hahn and Gordon L. Hester, "Marketable Permits: Lessons for Theory and Practice," *Ecology Law Quarterly* 16, no. 2 (1989): 361, 374, table 2.
32. On ozone depletion, see 53 Fed. Reg. 30,566 (August 12, 1988); on water pollution, see Robert W. Hahn and Robert N. Stavins, "Incentive-Based Environmental Regulation: A New Era from an Old Idea?" *Ecology Law Quarterly* 18, no. 1 (1991): 18–19.

33. See A. Denny Ellerman et al., *Markets for Clean Air: The U.S. Acid Rain Program* (New York: Cambridge University Press, 2000).
34. Rebecca M. Blank, "Fighting Poverty: Lessons from Recent US History," *Journal of Economic Perspectives* 14, no. 2 (Spring 2000): 3, 6.
35. See Mancur Olson, *Power and Prosperity: Outgrowing Communist and Capitalist Dictatorships* (New York: Basic Books, 2000).
36. See Nussbaum, *Women and Human Development*, 5.
37. Ibid., 78–80.
38. See Drèze and Sen, *India: Development and Participation*.

CHAPTER 10: MINIMALISM

1. Hon. John G. Roberts Jr., chief justice of the United States, commencement address at the Georgetown University Law Center (May 21, 2006).
2. 410 U.S. 113 (1973). On the refusal to overrule *Roe v. Wade*, see *Planned Parenthood v. Casey*, 505 U.S. 833 (1992).
3. Stephen Breyer, "The Federal Sentencing Guidelines and the Key Compromises upon Which They Rest," *Hofstra Law Review* 17, no. 1 (Fall 1988): 14–19.
4. For a popular treatment, see James Surowiecki, *The Wisdom of Crowds* (New York: Anchor Books, 2005); a more technical account, with reference to the Condorcet jury theorem, can be found in Cass R. Sunstein, *Infotopia: How Many Minds Produce Knowledge* (New York: Oxford University Press, 2006).
5. As quoted in the *New Republic*, June 6, 1994, 12.
6. See Samantha Power, *A Problem from Hell: America and the Age of Genocide* (New York: Basic Books, 2002).
7. See Mary Ann Glendon, *A World Made Anew: Eleanor Roosevelt and the Universal Declaration of Human Rights* (New York: Random House, 2001).
8. Ibid., 51.
9. Ibid., 77 (citing Maritain); also quoted at www.catholicculture.org/docs ./doc_view.cfm?recnum=405.
10. See Henry Sidgwick, *The Methods of Ethics*, 7th ed. (New York: Dover Publications, 1966), 96–104.

11. This is the tendency in Ronald Dworkin, *Law's Empire* (Cambridge, MA: Harvard University Press, 1985).

CHAPTER 11: TRIMMING

1. Lord Halifax, *The Character of a Trimmer* (1688), in *The Works of George Savile Marquis of Halifax*, vol. 1, ed. Mark N. Brown (New York: Oxford University Press, 1989).
2. See comments of John D. Sinclair, trans., *Dante's Inferno* (1961), 49–50.
3. Donald R. Benson, "Halifax and the Trimmers," *Huntington Library Quarterly* 27, no. 2 (February 1964): 115, 118.
4. Brown, intro. to *Works of George Savile*, vol. 1, 147.
5. H. C. Foxcroft, *A Character of the Trimmer: Being a Short Life of the First Marquis of Halifax* (Cambridge, UK: Cambridge University Press, 1946), 336.
6. Ibid., 131.
7. Tim Harris, "What's New About the Restoration?" *Albion: A Quarterly Journal Concerned with British Studies* 29, no. 2 (Summer 1997): 187, 211.
8. Ibid. (quoting *Observator*, I, 242 [November 16, 1682]).
9. Thomas C. Faulkner, "Halifax's *The Character of a Trimmer* and L'Estrange's Attack on Trimmers in *The Observator*," *Huntington Library Quarterly* 37, no. 1 (November 1973): 71, 76 (quoting *Observator*, II, 177 [December 3, 1684]).
10. Ibid. (quoting *Observator*, I, 242 [November 16, 1682]).
11. Harris, "What's New?" 212.
12. Benson, "Halifax," 116 (quoting *The Oxford English Dictionary*); see also Harris, "What's New?"
13. Benson, "Halifax," 115, 132.
14. Ibid., 134.
15. See Halifax, *Character of a Trimmer*, 243.
16. Ibid., 240.
17. Ibid., 184–98.
18. Ibid., 180.

19. Ibid., 222.
20. Ibid., 223.
21. Brown, *Works of George Savile*, 111.
22. Henry Horwitz, *Parliament, Policy, and Politics in the Reign of William III* (Manchester, UK: Manchester University Press, 1977), 35.
23. Thomas Babington Macaulay, *The History of England from the Ascension of James II*, vol. 1 (1848), 227.
24. Ibid.
25. *Grutter v. Bollinger*, 539 US 306 (2003); *Gratz v. Bollinger*, 539 US 244 (2003).
26. See Mark Kelman, Yuval Rottenstreich, and Amos Tversky, "Context-Dependence in Legal Decision Making," *Journal of Legal Studies* 25, no. 2 (June 1996): 287.
27. See Dworkin, *Freedom's Law: The Moral Reading of the American Constitution* (Cambridge, Mass.: Harvard University Press, 1996).
28. Robert Goodin, "Possessive Individualism Again," *Political Studies* 24, no. 4 (December 1976): 488, 489.

INDEX

INDEX